EAST ASIA

HISTORY, POLITICS, SOCIOLOGY, CULTURE

Edited by
Edward Beauchamp
University of Hawaii

A ROUTLEDGE SERIES

EAST ASIA: HISTORY, POLITICS, SOCIOLOGY, CULTURE

EDWARD BEAUCHAMP, *General Editor*

POSTSOCIALIST CINEMA IN POST-MAO CHINA

The Cultural Revolution after the Cultural Revolution

Chris Berry

ROUTLEDGE
NEW YORK & LONDON

Published in 2004 by
Routledge
29 West 35th Street
New York, NY 10001

Routledge is an imprint of the Taylor and Francis Group.

Library of Congress Cataloging-in-Publication Data

Berry, Chris.
Postsocialist Cinema in Post-Mao China: The Cultural Revolution after the Cultural
Revolution / by Chris Berry.
p. cm. — (East Asia, history, politics, Sociology, culture)
Filmography: p.
Includes bibliographical references and index.
ISBN: 0-415-94786-3 (hardcover: alk. paper)
1. Motion pictures—China—History.
2. Motion pictures—Political aspects—china.
I. Title.
II. Series: East Asia (New York, N.Y.)
PN1993.5.C4B47 2004
791.43'0951—dc22

2003026390

This book is for my parents

Contents

Acknowledgments

This book is derived from my UCLA doctoral dissertation. I received valuable feedback and encouragement from all the members of my committee: Janet Bergstrom, Peter Wollen, Lucie Cheng, and John Horton, and particularly from the chair, Nick Browne. Nick Browne and Janet Bergstrom were also my teachers at UCLA, and their rigorous, precise, engaged, and questioning scholarship has been an inspiring model that I have sought, however imperfectly, to live up to. I am eternally in their debt.

In China, the China Film Archive made films available for me to view, as did my employer, the China Film Corporation. My colleagues in the Film Corporation answered a lot of "stupid foreigner" questions, and I am grateful for all their help. In particular, I would like to thank Shan Dongbing, Li Jiexiu, and Lai Qiuyun. Professor Cheng Jihua's assistance was vital to the completion of my dissertation, as was Chen Mei's, and I am eternally grateful to both of them. Chen Mei also kindly answered many translation questions, as did Ding Xiaoqi. I would also like to thank Terumi Inoue and Koji Kato for their help with Japanese names. In addition to those named above, there are others who asked not to be named, but to whom I would also like signal my thanks.

Finally, the dissertation that this book is derived from was not originally designed for publication. It was my intention to use the privilege of the doctoral project to work on something I considered of scholarly importance but maybe with too limited a readership for publication. I am therefore both grateful and surprised that Routledge have proved me wrong. I thank the person or persons unknown who drew my work to their attention, and also my editor, Kimberly Guinta for her patience and help.

Chapter 1

INTRODUCTION: TOWARD A POSTSOCIALIST CINEMA?

"The overriding concern of post-Mao Chinese society and culture is not postcolonialism, but postsocialism."

— Zhang Xudong

The immediate object of this study is a group of eighty-nine relatively neglected feature films made in the People's Republic of China between 1976 and 1981, eighty-one of which have been available for viewing. All or part of each film is set during what is now known as the Cultural Revolution decade of 1966 to 1976. Although the focus of the study is on cinematic discourse, discourse is understood as a practice that participates in the constitution, maintenance, and transformation of society and culture. Both China and Chinese cinema have undergone significant change since 1976, transforming China into a postsocialist society and culture and Chinese cinema into a postsocialist cinema. Examining the themes, characters, audience address, and narrative structures of the films in comparison with the cinema of the 1949 to 1976 Maoist heyday contributes to answering some questions about that change. I argue that these films constitute the first cinematic site where postsocialist Chinese culture is constructed in a significant and sustained manner. To support this claim, I also detail the discursive features of the Maoist cinema, which functions as backdrop against which these films are distinguished. Exploring these questions also entails thinking about what distinguishes postsocialism from socialism in these films, and how the appearance of these films relates to the larger social and cultural transformation.

Further details about the films are given in the appendix. The aim was to include all films made in the wake of the Cultural Revolution that represented that period in some way. The 1981 cut-off date was clear. That was the year when the script *Bitter Love* was criticized in the first major attack on a cultural target since Mao's death, and it severely inhibited further production of films reexamining the 1966 to 1976 decade. Although the period has been represented again in movies such as Xie Jin's *Hibiscus Town* (1986), they have not appeared in such numbers or with such common themes, character types, plots, and styles as in the years prior to the criticism of *Bitter Love*.

However, the starting point was harder to define. 1966 to 1976 is commonly understood as the Cultural Revolution decade today, with its end marked by the arrest of the Gang of Four on 6 October 1976, following Mao's death on 9 September. At the time, however, things were less clear. It took a while before the entire Cultural Revolution was repudiated. This process is detailed as part of chapter three.

This gradual process was also manifested in films. Inside China, the Cultural Revolution is frequently referred to as "the decade of chaos" (*shinian dongluan*). The speed with which Chinese cinema engaged in representing this trauma is striking. Certainly, the German cinema did not deal with defeat in World War Two and Nazism so quickly,[1] nor the Soviet cinema Stalinism,[2] nor the America cinema defeat in Vietnam.[3] In China, there was no hiatus. Even before the repudiation of the whole of the Cultural Revolution as a "decade of chaos," films were being made that for the first time repudiated a shorter period of the post-1949 revolutionary past. That shorter period is defined as part of the Cultural Revolution now, but not then. To register this complexity, it was necessary to choose a starting point that would allow for the inclusion of some films made before the arrest of the Gang of Four — films made during what has retrospectively become the transition towards the repudiation of the Gang and their works as part of the Cultural Revolution — and also films made after that point. This was accomplished by considering all films made in 1976 that represented the Cultural Revolution.

While not questioning the importance of aesthetic judgment in the determination of film markets and festival screenings, this book is not concerned with aesthetics; it does not aim to restore the films to the canon of Chinese cinematic treasures. Rather, it examines their significance in regard to two interrelated histories: the history of Chinese cinema, and the history of contemporary China as a social and cultural formation.

In regard to Chinese cinema, the primary issue is the place of these films in the changes that have overtaken the Chinese cinema since the death of Mao. This is understood not in terms of aesthetics but in terms of in the material elements composing film as a discourse, including what is commonly spoken of as film style, characters, themes, narrative structures, and so forth. Films produced in the People's Republic today are very different from those produced during Mao's lifetime. Whether "art films" or genre films designed for the domestic box office, today's films bear limited relation to the unabashedly propagandistic films of the socialist heyday. Even the numerous revolutionary history movies made to flatter the Communist Party of China today mark a significant change, because the representation on screen of Communist leaders by actors was forbidden during Mao's lifetime.[4] Most writers on Chinese film agree about the existence of this qualitative shift, but exactly when it occurred, how it made itself apparent, and its significance is contested.

Many note the impact of *Yellow Earth* following its international release in 1985. For example, Tony Rayns writes,

> It's tempting to put an exact date to the birth of the "New Chinese Cinema:" 12 April 1985. That was the evening when *Yellow Earth* played to a packed house in the Hong Kong Film Festival in the presence of its two main creators, director Chen Kaige and cinematographer Zhang Yimou. The screening was received with something like collective rapture, and the post-film discussion stretched long past its time limit.[5]

Rayns is right that *Yellow Earth* and the so-called "Fifth Generation" of younger Chinese filmmakers are marked out from other filmmakers working in the mid-eighties in any number of ways.

However, in a volume on Chinese film theory since 1979, editors George S. Semsel, Xia Hong, and Hou Jianping claim, "even before the Fifth Generation began its active explorations of filmmaking, equivalent explorations had already been initiated by scholars and writers committed to the art."[6] These comments raise some important questions. How is cinema to be conceptualized and studied? Solely as a set of filmic texts? As an industry, including the means of production, distribution, and exhibition? Or as a culture, including the film criticism and theory? Also, is the cinema to be studied as an autonomous object or as a socially integrated institution?

A second set of questions concerns how history itself is conceptualized and studied. Rayns's comment suggests it may be possible to put precise dates on change. Does history really move in sharp shifts from one period of relative stability to another, or is change slower and more complex? What sort of data should be consulted to provide evidence of change? Rayns appears focused on the film itself and on its critical reception. Semsel, Xia and Hou, on the other hand, assert the importance of the theoretical discourses that surround the films, where they find changes predating those that appear later in the film Rayns nominates as marking the rebirth of the Chinese cinema.

If, as is argued below, understanding film as a discursive practice entails understanding cinema as engaged in the discursive production of the very things it is sometimes said to "represent," this leads to the second history these films are to be placed in — the history of contemporary China as a social and cultural formation. Just as most commentators would agree Chinese film has changed since the socialist heyday, the same is true of Chinese society and culture. Where commentators and scholars disagree is how to interpret these changes, and how to name the socio-cultural shift they indicate. Terms under consideration include "postmodern China," "Socialism with Chinese characteristics," "Chinese modernism," and "post-socialist China."

The remainder of this introduction will discuss these issues in more detail. But first, I would like to locate this book in relation to other works on the topic. There are no other writings that focus solely on these particular films as a group.[7] However, there is one book chapter that focuses on the post-Cultural Revolution "scar" films, which depict the horrors of that decade and also form the core of the group of films under consideration here. There are also various writings that discuss some of the films in this study, or place them in a broader context, or select one film for more focused discussion. In addition, there are three related groups of writings. One group consists of the numerous short articles on particular films or trends and written in China during the period under consideration.[8] These have informed this book and are drawn upon as and where necessary. A second group consists of writings on the literature of this period, in particular the so-called "scar" (*shanghen*) literature that treats the negative effects of the Cultural Revolution decade. The vast bulk is only concerned with themes and, to a lesser extent, character. Therefore, the findings of this work are deployed in a comparison with the cinema in the third and fourth chapters, which are also on themes and characters. Finally, there is a body of writing on Chinese film theory that covers this period. This work is detailed and discussed further in this introduction.

Writings that do cover the films under consideration here in some form almost all note that the late seventies in the cinema are a period not only of recovery after the Cultural Revolution but also of change.[9] However, none of them formulate the same hypothesis that this book seeks to demonstrate, namely that these changes constitute the first cinematic manifestation of a fundamental, unprecedented, and sustained change in the social and cultural formation as a whole — postsocialism — and that they emerge relatively autonomously, indicating that postsocialism is a disaggregated phenomenon that emerges gradually in fits and starts in different parts of the socio-cultural formation in different ways and at different times.

In contrast, the survey histories covering this period treat the cinema as a mere reflection of other changes. A common pattern emerges where the period is dealt with as part of "The New Era."[10] In most cases this follows the classic Marxist base and superstructure model, with the Leninist modification of proletarian dictatorship leading the way. A typical example is *Contemporary Chinese Cinema*, a two-volume work published in 1989 and written by a team under the leadership of Chen Huangmei, which employs a tripartite breakdown of the period found in many other works. Chapter ten, "The Revival of the Cinema," deals briefly with the years 1977 and 1978, when Hua Guofeng was in charge and before Deng Xiaoping took over. In line with the government line at the time of writing, this is discussed as an era of recovery from the traumas of the last decade but also one of continuing leftist errors delaying that recovery. The task of the chapter is to demonstrate the manifestations of this in the cinema, noted as continued lack of realism, lack of complexity of characters, and lack of diversity in themes, all spurring audience discontent.[11]

Chapter eleven, "The Historic Turning Point," examines 1979. As the title implies, this marks a rebirth when the revolution is allegedly restored to full power. It examines the cinema of this year as manifesting the successful implementation of policies delayed by Hua Guofeng's leftism. If the long-standing policy to "let a hundred flowers bloom" is understood to imply diversity, then this subtends the chapter's delineation of a wider range of films, including entry into the previously "forbidden zone" of discussing leftist error in revolutionary history prior to 1949. It also examines the year's cinematic events as reflections of Deng Xiaoping's changes. First, the Party endorsed the denunciation not only of the Gang of Four and their doings in the last years of the Cultural Revolution decade, but also the entire decade. Therefore, the chapter describes corresponding thematic changes. If Deng's policy of "reform" (*gaige*) includes releasing the energies of the people by allowing greater initiative taking, the cinematic manifestation of this is increased studio autonomy, including the right to make script investment decisions without prior approval. And finally, if the rhetoric of "opening up" (*kaifang*) implies that China is lagging and must take from overseas to implement the "Four Modernizations" (*sige xiandaihua*) to catch up, then stylistic experimentation in 1979 can be explained in these terms.[12]

The framework in chapter eleven also subtends much of the discussion of 1980 and 1981 in chapter twelve, "Boldly Opening Up and Steadily Developing," which covers the years through to 1984, where the book stops. In addition, the chapter considers the critique of *Bitter Love* within the official framework of a necessary rectification emphasizing the four cardinal principles. There is no acknowledgement that this might have had a chilling effect. Instead, the sudden end to the production of films that reexamine the post-revolutionary past is understood as a need for closure.[13]

Other book chapters and articles work within the basic historical terms of survey works like Chen Huangmei's, accepting the idea of a decisive break with the "new era," however defined. They then analyze what is distinctive about the cinema of the "new era" as a whole. Director and theorist Zheng Dongtian's 1986 article "Only Seven Years" notes the growing impact of young and middle-aged directors since 1979.[14] Zhong Chengxiang and Rao Shuguang's "Film Production of the New Era in a Time of Cultural Reflection" considers Chinese social and cultural self-examination as an important characteristic of film in this period, and sees "scar" films as part of this trend.[15] Chen Xihe's 1986 essay uses the same tripartite division as Chen Huangmei and others, but details film theory where most would detail policy. He frames the period as a turn away from seeing cinema as a political "tool" so that it can emerge in the "new era" as a language and art form with its own particular characteristics. The drive for autonomy is also one of the main features discussed in Dai Jinhua's analysis of the so-called Fourth Generation of directors who graduated from the Beijing Film Academy before the Cultural Revolution but had to wait until the late 1970's to direct films.[16] For her, 1979 marks their birth, but most of her discussion is focused on films outside the period covered by this book.[17]

Finally, there is the book chapter on "scar" films mentioned earlier as the work closest to this in its objects of study. Rao Shuguang and Pei Yali's "Scar Films: Myths of Faith and Youth and Their End" is the opening chapter of their 1997 book on the cinema of the "new era."[18] In an argument similar to that of the article Rao co-wrote with Zhong Chengxiang, these films are seen as allowing reflection on the recent trauma, coming to terms with it, and renewal of faith in a good future. However, like Chen Xihe, although Rao and Pei do not explicitly contest the dominant explanation where films follow state and Party policy, they do move in different directions. Chen's article does this by substituting film theory as the overreaching determination upon the films where others speak of overall policy shifts. Rao and Pei's chapter pushes the envelope in a manner that echoes the narratives of the films themselves: it covers themes that stretch credulity in any restoration of faith, although the chapter itself never explicitly makes such an extrapolation. For example, in their discussion of how blame is assigned for the Cultural Revolution they move from fairly simple representations that put all the blame on a small number of leftists, to representations where it is unclear who is to blame, and then to films which represent an all-pervasive culture of falsehood, lust for power, twisted heroism, and blind submission to authority that leaves no characters untouched.[19]

The remaining writings all contest or complicate the Chen Huangmei-style account of the period, which implicitly or explicitly subtends the accounts detailed so far. Where Chen assumes a unified social and cultural formation, Paul Clark considers the cinema as a site where a tripartite power relationship between the Communist Party of China, filmmakers, and the audience is negotiated.[20] He examines the period under consideration here in chapter six, entitled "Beyond Yan'an."[21] In this period, according to this framework, audience tastes and demands were paid attention to for the first time in many years, and filmmakers tried to cater to them to forge an effective alliance that would help give them greater autonomy from the Party. One of the more subtle issues also raised by Clark's book is continuity. As discussed above, many scholars working in the People's Republic refer to 1979 as a "turning point," in accord with the official line on the matter. Clark assumes a defined and fixed set of players whose relationships undergo change. In other words, he works with the idea of a certain continuity running right through the period of the People's Republic. He makes this even clearer elsewhere. In an article on the Cultural Revolution period, he counters the common understanding of it as an exceptional period by showing how similar players and issues run through from 1949 to the early eighties, when he was writing.[22] And by comparing this period with the Hundred Flowers Movement of 1956, he again implies a certain continuity underlying differences within the post-1949 period.[23]

Ma Ning has published two articles covering films from this period that also imply certain continuities, complicating the dominant rhetoric of a "new era" beginning with Deng Xiaoping's ascent. In his consideration of Xie Jin's melodramas of the late seventies and early eighties, including *The Legend of Tianyun Mountain*, he places his main emphasis on the continuity of a "traditional cultural discourse."[24] Ma's other article focuses on a number of filmmakers from the post-1976 period, including Yang Yanjin, who made two films during this period, *Troubled Laughter* and *On a Narrow Street*. Ma argues that in signifying a "new era," Yang's films are part of a continuity where films continue to be determined by policy, but that the primary technique used to signify this also undermines it within the films. In both films, subjective perceptions are rendered with flashback, dream, and fantasy sequences to mark their truthfulness as opposed to the lies of the official media. Ma argues that these very techniques suggest that truth itself is not a natural given but constructed and produced. As a result, cinematic discourse emerges as a site where a break is effected with the past, but a break that is more than just the signification of a new era as mandated by the regime.[25]

Finally, the argument for a break with the past but one that exceeds that mandated by the regime is also found in Paul Pickowicz's article on films made between 1979 and 1983. Pickowicz's article is similar to Clark's approach in his assumption of a tripartite division between audiences, filmmakers, and the Party-state apparatus, and also in his narrative approach to films. But Pickowicz goes beyond Clark's conclusions by arguing that the films of this period manifest significantly different political thoughts and hopes to those preferred by the regime. Pickowicz argues that the "serious" films of this era, which include many covered here, are a "window on popular political thought."[26] For Pickowicz, it seems they come close to constituting oppositional discourse.

CHANGING CHINA

One way this book differs from the work discussed above is its underlying conception of the Chinese cultural and social formation and cinema's place within it. Only some of the other writing considers the possibility of tension, division, and difference within China. Political considerations make such an approach impossible within the People's Republic. Furthermore, although some of the work produced outside is able to consider social and political divisions, none suggests these films are part of a fundamental shift. This may be because much of the work was written before such a shift was evident. More recent work on the post-Mao period considers it as a qualitatively different social and cultural formation, but so far it has not returned to map the beginnings of this change. Placing the films under consideration here in relation to that shift is part of the project of this book.

The different circumstances in the People's Republic and the liberal democracies that determine academic discourse include the different institutions where film scholarship is based, the different purposes toward which it is directed, and most important, the different assumptions upon which it is predicated. Until recently, most film scholarship in China was based within specialist institutions attached to the film industry and under the leadership of the Film Bureau, such as the China Film Archives (*Zhongguo*

Dianying Ziliaoguan), the China Film Association (*Zhongguo Dianyingjia Xiehui*), and so forth. In the liberal democracies where writings produced outside China originate, film scholarship is mostly based in the university system. In the People's Republic, film scholarship has had a more direct connection with film production, so that film theory and analysis is often understood to have a prescriptive dimension. In the liberal democracies, the university system has placed greater emphasis on film scholarship as knowledge production ostensibly divorced from evaluation of films.[27]

Underlying each of these enterprises are quite different assumptions. These can be understood as the result of what Foucault proposes as discursive practices. Unlike the idea of ideology, because Foucault's work rejects the idea of a totalizing principle or system, there is no need to read different interpretive frameworks as expressions of something else, be it a Marxist class struggle or a Freudian oedipal conflict or any other such transcendent principle. Also, it does not involve understanding one or other interpretive framework as more or less truthful in absolute terms. Indeed, refusing a transcendent principle, such an interpretation is impossible.[28] Instead, it becomes possible to focus on what each framework makes possible and simultaneously forecloses on for specific discursive practice practices, such as the cinema.

In the People's Republic, the basic interpretive framework of public discourse forecloses on direct consideration of some of the basic questions that this book considers. This book assumes that a variety of different opinions and ideas exists in China, including ideas that differ from those of the government and the Party. However, such difference is only conceivable there as counter-revolutionary practice that must be externalized and expunged, inhibiting any academic work from addressing such a possibility directly and explicitly. This can be explained as the legacy of the democratic centralist model, whereby democracy is combined with the dictatorship of the proletariat by designating the Communist Party as the representatives of the proletariat exercising leadership after consulting with the representatives of the masses. In other words, the Party apparatus is expected to listen, but once its decisions are announced, everyone is expected to follow.[29]

Prior to Deng Xiaoping's rise to power, the result was a command-based system, where all action — including academic research and publication — waited on orders from above. In the wake of the Cultural Revolution, this system was held to have failed, and the encouragement of greater autonomy was an aim of Deng's reform program.[30] The renewed emphasis on the policy of letting "a hundred flowers blossom and a hundred schools of thought contend" was an expression of this effort in the arts, the media, and academia. However, this should not be confused with encouragement of open dissent or questioning of policy, political line, or authority. As in the case of the original Hundred Flowers Movement in 1956, this mistake was made by many.[31] The 1978-1979 Democracy Wall Movement can be understood as an example,[32] and soon after the arrest of Democracy Wall activist Wei Jingsheng, Deng endorsed the "Four Cardinal Principles," sometimes also known as the "Four Fundamental Principles."[33] These are adherence to the leadership of the Party, to Marxism-Leninism and Mao Zedong Thought, to the socialist road, and to the people's democratic dictatorship. In many ways, this book attempts to trace this process of renegotiating democratic centralism and the extent of autonomy as it shaped and was shaped by cinematic discourse.

In these circumstances, People's Republic academic work on these films tends to examine them as determined by and in line with Party policies and frameworks. For example, the 1986 overview of "new era" cinema by Xi Shanshan opens with the following remarks: "This is the tenth year since the people of our country under the leadership of the Party smashed the Gang of Four and put an end to the decade of chaos. During this decade, film production — this essay addresses feature film production — has followed the historic changes in Party and state politics, economics and cultural life into a new era, from the recovery of 1977 and 1978 to the turning point of 1979 and into the eighties."[34] As noted above, no publications from China on the topic of this book explicitly challenge this perspective, although some can be read as implying divergence.

Although it may seem an odd analogy at first, one way to understand this is through the work of Eve Kosofsky Sedgwick on closeting and homosociality in American culture as a set of social and discursive practices that police by paradoxically constructing something as simultaneously present and absent or at least hidden, in her case "the love that dare not speak its name." In this way, the feints, ambiguities, and doubly coded signals in Chinese public discourse that can be seen as signs of difference and dissent by some and are transparent and devoid of any such meaning for others are structurally similar to the language and practices of pre-Stonewall gay subcultures.[35]

For example, in Zheng Dongtian's article, he suggests that changes in cinema and art in general over the years prior to 1987 may be attributable to a change in the worldview of those producing it, and then uses this to lead into a general discussion of the generational shift that is his main focus. Zheng does not state explicitly what the differences in worldview might be. One can only speculate that older directors are more likely to have made a conscious commitment to the revolution prior to 1949, whereas younger directors in the People's Republic as a result of their parents' decisions or an accident of birth might be less invested in the revolution and less inclined to explain away the excesses of the Cultural Revolution. However, Zheng does not allude directly to this and his remark can also be read as referring to Deng's policies of "reform" and "opening up."[36] Similarly, Zhong and Rao's "cultural reflection" can be read as suggesting autonomy from the party. If there is some similarity between "cultural reflection" and what is designated here as postsocialism, then their article may be in accord with this book.[37] Similarly, if Rao and Pei's chapter on "scar" films points to elements that exceed policy and implicitly question it, then it too may agree with this book.[38]

Chen Xihe opens his 1986 article with a quote from Bazin, whose work had been translated and published in the People's Republic of China for the first time a few years previously and been very popular.[39] Insofar as Bazin's writings underlie Chen's argument that first film theory and then in its wake film practice moved away from being a political tool, this book would concur with Nick Browne's comments that Bazin seems to have been appropriated so enthusiastically because his work could justify treating the cinema as an autonomous discourse without appearing to threaten the Party or the state.[40] However, Chen does not discuss the political and social implications of carving out such an autonomous space. Dai Jinhua's article on the Fourth Generation is more explicit about the importance of Bazin's work in the drive for artistic autonomy, although she too avoids discussion of the political implications of this drive.[41]

If People's Republic work cannot explicitly consider tension between cinematic discourse and official public discourse, almost the opposite is true of work written outside the People's Republic in the liberal democracies. The reasons for this are not explicitly discussed in the work, either. Considering the large number of emigré academics working outside China now, it may be related to the absence of such discussion within the People's Republic, functioning as a compensation or displacement. It may also be a simple case of what orientalism, where lack and failing elsewhere affirms the superiority of the West.[42] The attention to openness and diversity in public discourse in this book does affirm my interest in it, but not any putative superiority of the liberal democracies, where factors like low voter turnout and high corporate contributions to political parties are raising serious questions about those political systems.

Clark, Pickowicz, and Ma's works all assume the possibility of internal political and social difference within the People's Republic, and acknowledge this difference as more evident and tolerated in the post-Mao period than before, ranging on a scale from Ma's tendency to dismiss it as mostly the official ideology of the period itself to Pickowicz's representation of it as quasi-oppositional political discourse. However, they do not consider the possibility that this shift is a manifestation of and contribution to a fundamental and sustained qualitative change in the social and cultural formation of the People's Republic. The interpretive frameworks of Clark and Ma's work seem to preclude such a possibility. Clark's book is structured by a model of a changing relationship between three enduring social forces operating within the framework of the People's Republic, and Ma's article is subtended by a culturalist theory of deep structures. However, both of these and the other articles covering the films under consideration were written before the extent of change in the People's Republic became clear. More recent work has found it necessary to consider the possibility that qualitative change in the People's Republic during the eighties has been so extensive that a new term is needed.

Zhang Xudong's *Chinese Modernism in the Era of Reforms* focuses on the efforts of intellectuals in the pre-Tiananmen Square Massacre years of the 1980s to carve out a modernist critical role for themselves within a socio-cultural formation reluctant to accommodate it. Zhang makes the remark cited at the beginning of this chapter; "The overriding concern of post-Mao Chinese society and culture is not postcolonialism, but postsocialism."[43] But this is a passing remark. Zhang does not specify what he means by postsocialism or how it relates to what he designates as Chinese modernism. However, it appears that Zhang is using postsocialism to refer to the entire period since 1976, with modernism located within it as a specific movement and moment.

The term "postmodernism" also appears on occasion in Zhang Xudong's book, but is also not examined in detail. On the other hand, Tang Xiaobing's "The Function of New Theory: What Does It Mean to Talk about Postmodernism in China?" details the Chinese debates around the term and takes up a position in relation to them.[44] Where Zhang Xudong speaks of the 1980s as a "euphoric decade," Tang perceives the culture of this period as altogether less optimistic.[45] Understanding Chinese socialism as China's modernism, he perceives the emergent culture of the late eighties as caught in a "catch 22" situation where opposition to socialist repression only pushes it towards new and not so new forms associated with a capitalist market economy it lost faith in long ago.[46] This leads to a postmodernist culture of continuous wary irony that destabilizes all efforts to anchor meaning.[47]

The debates and publications on the topic of China's postmodernism continue.[48] More recently, postmodernism has been raised again as a term to describe the post-1989 period. For example, it is claimed that the rapid development of consumerism and engagement with global capitalism have produced this phenomenon, so that "what formerly appeared to be a singular Chinese collectivity is now an ensemble of heterogenous, discontinuous, and disjunctive elements, an entity that lacks a unified global meaning."[49] Locating the phenomenon in the 1990s places this usage at odds with Tang's.[50]

This book moves in the other historical direction to ask whether this qualitative change first manifested itself in the cinema in the films under consideration here in the late seventies. Furthermore, the term adopted here for this new social and cultural condition is "postsocialism." Not only Zhang Xudong but also Xiaobing Tang and Sheldon Hsiao-peng Lu use this term in passing as a broad general term for the contemporary Chinese social condition.[51] In Chinese Studies, Arif Dirlik coined this term with different intentions before the Tiananmen Square massacre of 1989. At a time when many believed Deng's "socialism with Chinese characteristics" was a face-saving euphemism for capitalism, Dirlik responded with this term to acknowledge the changes Deng had brought about but also to note that Deng's China was not capitalist yet.[52]

More recently, Paul Pickowicz has used "post-socialism" to characterize the ambiguous culture of Deng's China, not only as seen from within the Party hierarchy but also as experienced at street-level, in an extended discussion of the films of Huang Jianxin.[53] I have also used the term to discuss late 1980's cinema, attempting to extend Pickowicz's discussion by explicitly invoking its etymological roots in the "postmodern" and considering whether postsocialism is a specific form of postmodernism.[54] Among the common characteristics noted are Lyotard's loss of faith in grand narratives manifested in the form of antiheroes and distopic narratives and, at the same time, a continuation of the old modernist (but not critical modernist) discourses of materialism, secularism, and progress to constitute a polyvocal and eclectic culture with no single source of authority.[55] However, in the People's Republic of China, those modernist discourses were state socialist discourses operating in a centralized command structure, creating important differences in the minor narratives that Lyotard suggests characterize the postmodern and also in the environment in which they have emerged. If it is accepted that by the late eighties, it was plausible to speak of the culture of the People's Republic as "postsocialist" in this sense, this book asks whether these films produced immediately in the wake of the Cultural Revolution are the earliest cinematic manifestation of that culture. Some of the key indicators of such a condition have been listed in this paragraph. However, the pertinence should also be emphasized of ambiguity in forms analogous to those discussed earlier in this section in regard to academic discourse and film theory in China, namely the appearance of films and elements of films which can be read simultaneously as transparent manifestations of Party policy in cinema and as opening up other possibilities.

CINEMA AS A SOCIAL INSTITUTION

A second fundamental question is how cinematic discourse and its relation to the larger social and cultural formation is conceptualized. With the exception of Ma Ning's writings, all existing work on the films approaches cinematic discourse in terms of "content" and "style." Content is understood as the representational — elements that refer to the real world outside the film. This is mostly approached in terms of narrative and characters. Style, also known as "form," is understood as those elements that cannot be said to refer mimetically to a world outside the film, such as editing. This approach does not preclude political debates about style; any filmmaker operating in a Marxist-Leninist state has to avoid accusations of formalism. However, because it understands style as non-referential, this approach forecloses on thinking about style as part of a meaningful ensemble.

As a result, other writing on these films often appends a list of stylistic innovations to discussion of plot and character, without much comment. Alternatively, style is discussed as implicitly subordinated to and motivated by the elements understood as content, or as a "vehicle" for content. For example, Chen Huangmei notes a renewed interest in complex and psychological characterization in films like *Troubled Laughter* and *Reverberations of Life*, both from 1979. Chen then notes a corresponding development of forms that render subjectivity, for example through dreams, flashbacks, or through music designed to communicate a character's mood, as though these are afterthoughts and not integral to the production of complexity and psychology.[56]

Missing from all this work except Ma Ning's is any consideration of how all these elements work together as a signifying combination. This foreclosure means that consideration of emergent postsocialism within these films is limited to looking for characters or themes that, so to speak, push the envelope of what is permitted by the Party-state apparatus. Since these are precisely the elements that are most easily read and monitored by non-practitioners of the cinema and censorship authorities, they are also the most unlikely places for wary filmmakers to try out new possibilities.

The effects of this can be seen in Paul Pickowicz's article on the post-Democracy Wall films. At first sight, Pickowicz's article might seem closest to this book, for both claim these films as sites where discourse autonomous from the Party-state apparatus does emerge. But Pickowicz's adoption of the content-and-style approach leads to over-emphasis of the radical quality of certain character and plot representations and to omit other areas of the discourse entirely. Specifically, Pickowicz notes the popularity, especially amongst young city people, of what he terms "serious" films in the wake of the suppression of the Democracy Wall movement in 1979 and prior to the Anti-Spiritual Pollution Campaign of 1983. By serious films, he means those that engage with contemporary problems and issues, and they include many of the films under consideration here. However, without understanding cinematic discourse as having specific characteristics of its own, he proceeds to interpret these films as a "window on political thought" in which "statements" are made that exceed the official line approved by the Party-state apparatus. Examples include the representation of severe political errors being committed as early as the 1950s in *The Corner Forgotten by Love* and *The Legend of Tianyun Mountain*, which also hint that the end of the Cultural Revolution and the arrival of the "new era" may not mean all problems have been resolved.[57]

This book does not dispute that some character and plot representations pushed the envelope, and indeed this will be discussed in detail in chapters three and four. However, it does not understand these films as making "statements," nor does it agree with the implication that the cinema simply becomes an alternative vehicle where the suppressed discourse of the Democracy Wall Movement is continued. Indeed, the critique of Bai Hua's *Bitter Love* demonstrates that any perception that a "statement" exceeding the official line had been made could lead to suppression of films, too. Instead, this book argues that understanding the specificity of cinematic discourse is crucial to account for how difference is accommodated and how it survives in the cinema where statements of the sort found on Democracy Wall did not.

Cinematic discourse can produce ambivalence that enables readings to be made by non-conformist audiences without necessarily opening the film up to attack from the authorities. Feature films are fictions rather than direct statements about reality and do not directly address, instruct, or appeal to audiences in verbal form. Furthermore, whereas the arbitrary quality of verbal language means that it can be broken down into distinct minimal semantic units (morphemes), the motivated quality of imagery means that it cannot be broken down into minimal linguistic units.[58] As a result, discourses that deploy imagery cannot contain polysemy as surely as verbal language and also can never be the direct equivalent of a verbal statement. Interestingly, Pickowicz does approach the importance of cinematic specificity towards the end of his article, when he acknowledges that the space for emotional release allowed by adoption of the melodramatic form may have contributed to the appeal of these films.[59] However, exactly how this operates is not examined further. This book examines areas such as the use of ambiguity to argue that these films open up spaces of difference that include but cannot be reduced to referentiality and representation alone.

Film theory that enables a consideration of cinematic discourse as a signifying combination, rather than separating out "style" and "content," could be understood as what David Bordwell, borrowing from Larry Laudan, terms a "research tradition": "a broadly defined field of inquiry, an approximate agreement about the central problems of that field, and shared methods of research."[60] This book draws in particular on that aspect of the research tradition that focuses on spectatorship as the nexus through which the intersection of the film with the social may most effectively be apprehended. As Linda Williams has outlined in her introduction to an anthology on the topic, this approach initially aligned audiences with an implied spectator understood as already inscribed in the rhetoric of the film.[61] However, the basic premises underpinning this approach have come into question. Seen increasingly as an "abstraction,"[62] scholars have pointed out that it does not take into account the predispositions that historically and socially differentiated viewers bring to bear in their varied actual interpretations of films.[63] Scholars have responded to this challenge in different ways. For example, the "neo-formalist" work on the history of film style pioneered by Bordwell and his adherents is characterized by an attempt to oust those research traditions now seen from within the neo-formalist perspective as scientifically unsound, because current research demonstrates that the meaning of any text is indeterminate. Bordwell has advanced his argument against interpretation most thoroughly in *Making Meaning*.[64]

Another approach is to recast meaning as socially and historically produced and circulated rather than as immanent to or traceable within the film, and Bordwell sees a place for this type of work.[65] In other words, the scholar should not engage in interpretation but may study interpretation scientifically as a historically and socially located phenomenon. This book accepts the desirability of following scientific procedures in order to reveal the assumptions upon which knowledge is built and therefore open the work to dialogue, but it does not accept the possibility of the production of universal knowledge. All knowledge entails an interpretive dimension and academic work is socially and historically located, as indicated in the discussion above of interpretive frameworks subtending academic work.

In these circumstances, this book turns to another potential model for studying the way meaning is produced in the viewing context. This is Miriam Hansen's work on early American cinema as an alternative public sphere. Early American film has long been approached by way of comparison to Hollywood classical cinema, focused on textual properties.[66] Some of this work has already included discussion of the class composition of audiences and the circumstances of consumption.[67] However, in *Babel and Babylon*, Hansen moves the focus more decisively towards a consideration how cinema functions as a social institution with alternative potential, "rather than pinning the question [of the politics of early cinema] on the class make-up of its audiences or the thematic and representational make-up of the films" alone.[68]

Hansen's intervention is grounded in Negt and Kluge's critique of Habermas's concept of the public sphere[69] as an idealization of the bourgeois public sphere and their recasting of it to produce the alternative public sphere.[70] With this approach, Hansen implicitly rethinks the cinema. She acknowledges the centrality of texts and meaning production through spectatorship and reception for contemporary understandings of the cinema, including her own.[71] But by historically locating the cinema, it is understood as a social institution, involving patterns of distribution, modes of exhibition, socially differentiated audiences in different venues, ancillary discourses ranging from advertising to newspaper criticism, and so forth. In order to pinpoint the characteristics of the cinema she examines in this way, Hansen does not limit herself to textual properties or particular interpretations mobilized by audiences, although these certainly figure in her account. Instead, such factors are integrated into an account that considers the lifestyles of audiences, their participation in other social activities, and more. For example, in her account of gender and the early cinema in New York, she points out that the cinema often constituted one of the very few public spaces where unchaperoned immigrant women of all ages were able to gather together with men they did not know, creating various possibilities for social interaction facilitated by the films they consumed and mobilized in the process.[72]

In considering the suitability of such a model for this study, two questions arise. First, is it appropriate to apply a concept derived so specifically from the European experience to China? Second, what empirical resources are available for the research? In regard to the former, the potential applicability of the public sphere and the related idea of civil society to the Chinese context has excited much debate in recent years.[73] As Frederic Wakeman, Jr. points out, in the wake of the 1989 Tiananmen Massacre and fall of the Berlin Wall, scholars wanted to understand the differences between conditions in Eastern Europe and China and one factor to consider was whether the foundations of civil society and a public sphere, or anything resembling them, had been developed.[74]

However, the very triggers for recent scholarly interest suggest problems with transferring these concepts to the Chinese context. China under Deng remained a one-party regime that suppressed public expression of politically significant difference and calls for autonomy from the control of the Party-state apparatus, not only in 1989 but also in its first year with the suppression of the Democracy Wall movement in 1979. In these circumstances, Zhang Xudong acknowledges many Chinese intellectuals in the 1980s spoke of the emergence of a "public sphere" in China,[75] but also designates this "public sphere" a "mirage."[76] If this impossibility of the public sphere is true of the "culture fever" period of the mid-eighties when the control of the state seemed relaxed, how much more true it must be for the earlier period under consideration here.

Furthermore, it is often unclear which concepts of the "public sphere" and "civil society" are being applied. As Richard Madsen points out, "the terms have often been vaguely defined and inconsistently used... insofar as different researchers seem to use the terms in different ways, without necessarily being aware of those differences, China scholarship comes to resemble a confused conversation in which everyone talks past one another."[77] Amidst this maze of different usages, one pattern emerges. Having set up their particular definitions of the different terms, each analyst then picks the widest and loosest term to apply to the Chinese context. This is also true of the examples where work on the public sphere is applied to the consideration of the cinema in contemporary China. Stephanie Donald's *Public Secrets, Public Spaces: Cinema and Civility in China* includes extensive discussion of the idea of civil society and the public sphere in China. Arguing that civil society "as formulated at present is irrelevant to the Chinese case," Donald proceeds to a broad sense of publicness and the role of cinema in its production.[78] Ben Xu draws on Hansen's work, but places his emphasis on the recasting of Habermas's concept by Negt and Kluge to broaden its meaning. He is particularly interested in their reconceptualization of the public sphere as not necessarily institutionalized and not restricted to critical and rational debate, but instead as a "general social horizon of experience" and "context of living." On the basis of this broader sense of the public sphere and acknowledging "the absence of institutional public spheres and the weakness of civil society in China," However, Xu proceeds beyond these rather broad points to note three important features of contemporary China's public sphere. The first is an emphasis on the question of the norms rather than the institutions of public discussion. Second is the difficulty of establishing public discussion free from state intervention. And third is the indirect route public discussion often has to take in light of these conditions, so that artistic discourses and other less direct forms become particularly important sites.[79]

Xu's application of the public sphere reveals both the strengths and the weaknesses of using the term in the Chinese context. By using it, Xu specifies some of the important distinguishing characteristics of the non-state discursive realm in postsocialist China. On the other hand, the characteristics he describes are quite different from anything signified by Habermas's original concept or even Hansen's usage of the term, both of which assume a liberal capitalist context of pluralism and democracy, relatively free from state intervention. In these stretched circumstances, it is understandable that William Rowe, a proponent of terms like "civil society" and "public sphere" in the Chinese context, is willing to quote some of the criticism leveled at his own work; "It appears... that a China-centered history has returned us to the 'discovery' of a single trajectory of modernization... based on histories of the same Europe that was so important for the scholars of 'China's response to the West.'"[80] Rowe proceeds to argue that he is caught between a rock and hard place, noting that "if on the other hand we exempt China from demands to be more 'like us' politically, on grounds of historical cultural differences, we are justly suspected of orientalism: other, less 'civilized' societies cannot be expected to live up to the standards we set for ourselves."[81]

Putting aside Rowe's assumptions about the grand standards of the non-Chinese "we" he speaks for, there is a danger that the specificity of the Chinese postsocialist social and cultural formation can all too easily be elided when terms like "civil society" or "public sphere" are used. It is now almost fifteen years after the events in Tiananmen Square during 1989 generated renewed international interest in China's potential "civil society" and "public sphere," but there has been no significant structural shift in that direction yet, despite the proliferation of the market sector in the economy. Indeed, the current formation has been in place for almost a quarter of a century now. Although Chinese postsocialism may yet turn out to be an extended transitional phase between Maoist socialism and liberal capitalism, such an outcome cannot be assumed. Therefore, it is also necessary to find a way of talking about the non-state discursive realm that Xu describes without relying over-heavily on terminology that can be read as implying such a teleology.

Indeed, Xu's description of the Chinese public sphere suggests something quite distinct. First, pluralism may now be possible in ownership of property and choice of commodities, but it does not extend far in public discourse. As discussed, the limit point concerns oppositionality: anything can be spoken about provided it does not imply an alternative political system or express opposition. In Xu's account this is what makes artistic discourse particularly important, for as a realm of ambiguity and imagination it is more open to hint at non-conformist significations. Again, this special focus on ambiguity and indirect signification is quite distinctive and quite different from the idea of the "public sphere" as it is generally understood.

In an effort to grasp the specific character of this discursive formation, I would suggest that cinema in postsocialist China can be understood as a social institution in the manner proposed by Hansen, but that the term "alternative public sphere" may be inappropriate. It either assumes conditions of liberal capitalist pluralism that do not exist, or sets them up as a telos towards which China is headed or as a standard against which China is measured. Instead, given the particular characteristics of the cinema as a social institution in postsocialist China, it may be more appropriate to think of it as a rhizome. In the opening chapter of *A Thousand Plateaus*, Deleuze and Guattari contrast the rhizome to the arborescent or tree-like assemblage in order to give the reader some sense of the book they have written. As they say, "In a book, as in all things, there are lines of articulation or segmentarity, strata or territories; but also lines of flight, movements of deterritorialization and destratification."[82] In other words, there are systems of order and there are areas or zones that work against the repressive structures of an order to open up difference and heterogeneity. The metaphor of the rhizome is mobilized to signify the latter.

In contemporary Western capitalist formations, with their appearance of complete pluralism, Deleuze and Guattari seem most interested in "black holes" and "bodies without organs" which open up towards asignifying practices that refuse to be made present and objectified. The Chinese postsocialist system, for all its opening up and reform, rarely allows even the appearance of political difference. In these circumstances, a rhizome or a space that opens up lines of flight within that formation does not necessarily lead towards asignification but towards the possibility of conceiving of and discursively articulating difference. This book concurs with Xu that it is this that makes the ambiguity of artistic practice so compelling. It is a place that can conform and dissent at once. And, as mentioned earlier, the inherent polysemy of motivated signs in the cinema adds to this quality. When we add to our considerations an urban middle-class audience of filmgoers and a body of filmmakers drawn from the social sectors most alienated from socialism by the experiences of the Cultural Revolution, the cinema becomes a social institution ripe for mobilization as a rhizome enabling lines of flight within Chinese postsocialism.

FILM AND HISTORY

A final question that requires consideration is how historical change is understood. Does postsocialism emerge in one sudden rupture, as many of the efforts to assign a date to it suggest? Or is the social formation to be understood as composed of relatively autonomous components, so that postsocialist characteristics might appear in the cinema of the period under consideration, but then later in the economy? A historian who held the classic Marxist belief that art was part of a superstructure directly determined by the economic base would see this as placing the cart before the horse, but I am arguing here that the evidence suggests just that.

In contrast and as noted, the dominant scheme in much of the existing writing on these works puts politics in command. Following a Leninist intervention in Marxism, it considers 1976 and the arrest of the Gang of Four as a turning point when the dominant policies of the Cultural Revolution are terminated and new possibilities open up, and 1979 as an even more crucial turning point in which change is consolidated and the foundations are laid for the period ahead. This accords with the official line during the Deng Xiaoping era. Given the highly centralized political structure of the People's Republic during the period, it is reasonable to assume that no decisive shift in film could occur without some similar shift at the political level. Therefore, the importance of 1976 and 1979 seem beyond doubt. But it is also true that, however strong the control of the Party-state apparatus, films are made by particular groups of people distinct from those setting policy at the political level and using a discourse distinct from the verbal discourses in which policy decisions are expressed. Therefore, there is a separation that at a minimum requires a process of translation before the effects of political policy can appear in film production and that could also allow for a certain slippage. This book examines the films to see not only how and when they translate relevant political discourse into filmic discourse, but also where changes in filmic discourse precede or exceed those of political discourse.

This raises the question of evidence. What sort of evidence is available for the writing of history, what its status is within the discourse, and what determinations this has on the type of history that can be written with credibility are all questions central to the revival of English-language film historiography over the past two decades. According to Jeffrey Klenotic's overview of the growth of the "new film history," also often known as "revisionist film history," academic professionalization of cinema studies and the corresponding desire for legitimacy and recognition within academia helped to motivate a concern for rigor and the provision of appropriate evidence, which had been lacking.[83]

However, much of the existing work on the films under consideration here was produced outside English-language scholarship and operates according to its own protocols. In the case of the Chen Huangmei and Shu Xiaoming books, they are written not as arguments supported by evidence but as statements. In accordance with the democratic centralist mode, they do not position themselves as arguing for a particular account among various possibilities. This tendency to write in statements of fact rather than argue has changed in leading Chinese film journals such as *Contemporary Cinema* (*Dangdai Dianying*) and *Film Art* (*Dianying Yishu*) over the last dozen years or so. However, very little of this work has been directed towards the films under consideration here, and almost none of it steps outside the framework that forecloses on explicit consideration of the possibility that cinematic discourse might depart in any way from the official line.

In English-language scholarship, Klenotic rightly nominates Allen and Gomery's 1985 text, *Film History*, as a high point in the return to and revision of film historiography, and he cites their observation about much previous work in the field: "Survey texts contributed to the problem by remaining silent as to the process by which historical questions are posed, research conducted, evidence analyzed, and generalizations drawn."[84] In response, Allen and Gomery outline current debates in historiography. They note the fundamental divide between empiricism, with its insistence on material evidence as objective, and conventionalism, which maintains that evidence remains within discourse and that what evidence is considered acceptable is itself determined by conventions of knowledge formation. They conclude by advocating a "realist" model of scientific reasoning as both addressing the shortcomings of prior film history and providing a method which combines the best of both empiricism, by insisting on evidence, and conventionalism, by acknowledging that the production of history is discursive and subject to debate.[85]

Allen and Gomery's remark about "survey texts" could be cited in regard to much of the existing literature on the films under consideration here. Certainly, there has been no attempt at a close and verifiable description of the material discursive characteristics of these films so far, and at a minimum, this book attempts that. It also attempts to gather as much evidence as is available regarding the cinema as an industry and a social institution, as well as the critical discourses that are part of it and surround it. However, like Klenotic, I share a concern that Allen and Gomery's "realist" model can slide back into simple empiricism.[86] Klenotic identifies this at two points in Allen and Gomery's account of the realist model. The first is their recommendation that in deciding what sort of evidence is most reliable, one should rely on the "least mediated" evidence. By this yardstick, low box office receipts would have to triumph over a distributor's interview statement that a film suffered from release during the Olympics to indicate that the public did not like the film. Not only is "least mediated" evidence not necessarily the best, but also the invocation of this idea indicates a belief that objectivity might exist after all. The second point is their advocacy of the principle of "non-contradiction" to resolve arguments. However, because six people say one thing, and a seventh disagrees, it does not necessarily mean the seventh person is wrong. And again, there is the apparent faith that there is a correct and universal truth that can be determined.[87]

Although this book therefore insists on acknowledging the existence of interpretive frameworks, doing so is in no way tantamount to dismissing empirical evidence in surrender to a total relativism in which anything goes, as Bottomore alleges.[88] This would only be so if interpretive frameworks were fixed and monolithic, rather than themselves capable of being challenged, changed, dropped, and transformed, and very often due to the discovery of evidence that prompts new interpretations and the development of new interpretive frameworks.[89]

The interpretive frameworks that have been deployed consciously and deliberately in this book have been discussed above. But what kind of evidence is available to support the arguments and lines of enquiry enabled by those frameworks? Here, the problem is one of searching for public difference and disagreement in a system that is founded upon the denial of its existence. Indeed, as discussed, the cinema only emerges as a rhizomatic social institution where audiences interpret filmic texts to produce lines of flight from the monolithic logic of that system because of such a denial. In other words, were it possible to express differences directly in public discourse, there would be no special hermeneutic investment of this sort in the arts in general and the cinema in particular. In these circumstances, no amount of audience interviews and surveys, no amount of oral history work, and no amount of investigation of ancillary critical and press discourses will produce direct empirical evidence that these films were read in the way this book argues they may have been.

Therefore, this book focuses mainly upon the films themselves. However, this does not constitute a return to the pure textual analysis that claimed to find a single, fixed, and true meaning immanent to the text. Rather, this is one reading among many potential readings, but not a random or purely subjective reading. Instead, it is a reading directed by an understanding of the place of the cinema as a social institution within postsocialist China, an understanding itself produced by an interpretation of what could be called the contextual or circumstantial evidence. In this, the book is again guided by Hansen's example in the face of her own problems with empirical evidence on an era too far in the past to allow for interviews. She states, "To recall Negt and Kluge, even if there were no empirical traces of autonomous public formations, they could be inferred from the force of negation, from hegemonic efforts to suppress or assimilate any conditions that might allow for an alternative (self-regulated, locally, and socially specific) organization of that experience."[90] From this perspective, the campaign against Bai Hua's *Bitter Love* in 1981 is itself adequate evidence that viewing these films had developed into a site of difference that could not be tolerated within the logic of postsocialism once *Bitter Love* had made the possibility of such a non-conformist or even dissident reading of many of these films explicit.

If this premise that the suppression of these films is itself evidence of their function as lines of flight for their audiences, then this book uses the available evidence to understand how they could function in this way. To that end, chapter two attempts to construct the "particular social horizon of reception," as Hansen puts it, against which they must be set.[91] It examines the Chinese cinema of the 1949 to 1979 period as a classical and pedagogical cinema whose textual patterns, conditions of exhibition and production, and guided reception were designed to construct audiences securely sutured into the socialist modernity of Mao's China. The four chapters that follow examine the films in the cycle under consideration here by focusing on divergences from the classical Chinese model that can be understood as sites where audiences could mobilize difference and non-conformity exceeding what is permitted in direct signification in postsocialist China. Chapter three examines narrative structures. Chapter four looks at character types. Chapter five examines the return of the long forbidden romance narrative and the structures it constructs for audience involvement and positioning. And chapter six takes the problematic conclusion of *Bitter Love*, one of the main reasons for its banning, to investigate the ambiguities and interpretive potential of the ending in this cycle of films. In a brief afterword, I return to consider the implications of this research in the politics of East–West scholarship.

Chapter 2

WRITING ON BLANK PAPER: PEDAGOGICAL CINEMA 1949-1976

We are like a blank sheet of paper, which is good for writing on.

— Mao Zedong

This chapter considers the feature film industry of the People's Republic of China between 1949 and 1976. It argues this cinema constitutes a paradigm against which changes traced in following chapters may be cast and details its institutional and textual characteristics. It also argues that although such variations as occurred between 1949 and 1976 are significant, they are not extensive enough to invalidate the description of this cinema as a paradigm. Rather, these variations operate as a set of tensions subordinated to an over-determining didactic principle.

The state-owned and controlled cinema of the People's Republic between 1949 and 1976 may be called a classical cinema, just as Hollywood during the studio era has been designated a classical cinema. This claim rests on factors that extend beyond the usual formal definitions of the term to include institutional characteristics also found in the Hollywood classical cinema. First, it was highly stable: the same basic institutional and discursive paradigm held for almost thirty years. It was set up immediately after the establishment of the Communist regime in 1949 and lasted at least until the fall of the Gang of Four in 1976, when the changes traced in this study gradually began to undermine the stability of its discursive system. However, just as many elements of the classical Hollywood discursive paradigm have persisted, features of the mainland Chinese classical paradigm remain common.[1]

Second, the cinema of the People's Republic between 1949 and 1976 can also claim to be classical because it was dominant. There were no competing feature filmmaking activities within China at this time, and distribution of foreign features, although varying in source and extent, was also limited.[2]

Third, as will be argued later in this chapter, it can be understood as a variation on the classical cinematic mode particularly associated with Hollywood during the studio era. The concept of Hollywood cinema as a classical one has been elaborated in Western film theory over the last thirty years or so, and most notably in the work of David Bordwell, Janet Staiger, and Kristin Thompson.[3]

Bordwell, Staiger, and Thompson's description of this cinema as classical has been critiqued by Rick Altman. Altman argues that they overemphasize the unified qualities of Hollywood cinema and consign features and elements that do not fit to the category of "excess." Where Bordwell, Staiger, and Thompson operate with the Russian formalist concept of the dominant, Altman seeks to modify this by introducing the idea of overdetermination. This allows an understanding of classicism, both in the cinema and in its nineteenth century novelistic and dramatic antecedents, as structured in a relation of tension with other subordinated elements, most notably those associated with popular forms such as melodrama.[4]

This insight has been incorporated into Ma Ning's work on the Chinese film melodrama in two ways. First, it provides him with a means of conceptualizing the incorporation of many features of Chinese culture before its extensive nineteenth century contact with the West into the melodramatic films of the Chinese cinema in relations both of coherence and tension with the features of the Western melodramatic film. Second, it provides him with a means of understanding those older patterns of Chinese culture as themselves driven by internal contradictions and tensions and held together by overdetermining structures.[5]

Although the following discussion continues to draw heavily on Bordwell, Staiger, and Thompson, it has attempted to incorporate these insights in its delineation of some of the variations and tensions within the paradigm. Furthermore, as will be seen in later chapters, these tensions provide the seeds for the disruptions manifested in the late seventies and early eighties films that form the main focus of this work. However, this chapter focuses more on common points holding the classical Chinese cinema together, as these stand out strongly in contrast to the 1976-1981 films examined in detail here. This should not be taken to mean that there is no variety within classical Chinese cinema, anymore than that is the case for classical

Hollywood cinema. My hope is that my remarks in the chapter will help to encourage further work on the variations between subject matter categories in classical Chinese cinema and also historical change.

More recent work on Hollywood cinema has also continued to undermine claims about dominance of realism in the classical Hollywood cinema by underlining the widespread presence of the melodramatic mode.[6] However, although melodrama and realism are usually conceived as oppositional modes, it may be more useful to consider whether or not they complement each other. Certainly, both codes of melodrama and realism exist in the classical Chinese cinema. Indeed, the emotional engagement associated with melodrama does not run counter to the pedagogical principle, provided it is ultimately subordinated to it. An example of work that has made a substantial contribution to tracing the impact of the melodramatic and the emotional on Chinese classical cinema is Ban Wang's *The Sublime Figure of History*.[7] Wang's observations of powerfully emotional identification with individual heroes and heroines in many films and works of literature during the revolutionary heyday are correct. However, this should not be constructed in opposition to the pedagogical effect or the ultimate emphasis in nearly all films of the submersion of the individual into the revolutionary collective, for emotion, entertainment, identification and other pleasures are actively pursued in Chinese classical cinema, but only in order to enhance the pedagogical structures examined below.

INDUSTRY & SOCIAL INSTITUTION

The Chinese and Hollywood classical cinemas are organized according to very different overdetermining principles. Hollywood is primarily a profit-motivated enterprise operating in a market economy. This is not to deny that Hollywood has ideological effects or that the profit motive operated in tension with other motives (most notably those bracketed as "art"). However, the production of ideological effects and the demands of "art" do not form explicit, recognized, and overdetermining principles informing industry structure, social institution, and textual product in the same way that profit maximization does.

The Chinese classical cinema shares some institutional features with Hollywood, mostly inherited from the pre-Communist industry, which took Hollywood as its main model. Like their American counterparts, the Chinese film-going public also bought tickets to see films throughout the 1949 to 1976 period. Like Hollywood films, Chinese films were produced in studios, the larger of which operated on production-line principles. However, to have subscribed to profit maximization would have been to invite condemnation. Instead, the overdetermining principle behind the Chinese cinema was didactic. All other goals were subordinated to the educational or "propaganda" needs of the state and the Chinese Communist Party operating through a command economy.[8] One overview of forty years of Chinese film distribution and exhibition puts it like this:

> Although the film distribution and exhibition industry in China was a form of enterprise that had sole responsibility for its profits or losses... netting profits was not its sole, nor even its chief, function. From its inception, the film distribution and exhibition industry of New China has been entrusted by the Party and Government with a lofty political mission — to serve as an effective medium of socialist ideological education reaching the broad masses of the population.... [9]

The Chinese cinema shared didacticism with all the other arts and media in the People's Republic before 1976. As such, these discourses can be compared to two other discourses. One is the European tradition of what Susan Rubin Suleiman terms "authoritarian fictions" in her study of what are also known as *romans a these*.[10] Although Suleiman's work focuses on late nineteenth and early twentieth century French novels, the basic drive towards an exemplary mode of narration designed to demonstrate an argument could also be applied to many other works in the Western tradition, including, as she notes, the biblical parable. In the cinema, the most proximate discourse would be the Soviet socialist realist cinema associated with the Stalin era.

A second discourse to compare the Chinese classical cinema to is composed of its Chinese antecedents. Just as Ma Ning has demonstrated the deep historical Chinese cultural sources of Chinese film melodramas, (many of which are part of the Chinese classical cinema), the roots of the didactic paradigm might be traced back a long way. Donald Munro argues that the assumption of natural equality was common to all the major early Chinese schools of thought and unique to China at the time. This is the concept that all human beings are born equal, and that therefore education, upbringing, and experience are crucial. Mao's famous comment that the people are a blank sheet of paper indicates he was in agreement.[11] An emphasis on education is a logical extension of this repudiation of predestination or biological privilege, and it is manifested both in the Taoist relationship between master and apprentice and the Confucian stress on self-improvement and broader social education.[12] Andrew Plaks's observation that early Chinese narrative did not maintain a clear division between historiography and fiction, but instead emphasized the didactic transmission of facts and information over entertainment accords with this attitude.[13] Ma Ning notes this concern with didacticism also characterizes popular fictional forms less directly under the control of social elites than those discussed by Plaks.[14]

In addition to this deep cultural foundation, Mao Zedong's *Talks on Literature and Art at the Yan'an Forum* provide a more immediate explanation of didacticism in post-1949 cinema. Produced in 1942, these strategic prescriptions were rapidly elevated to the status of dogma.[15] Mao asserts there is no separation between art and politics and that art must obey the demands of the revolution:

> In the world today, all culture or literature and art belongs to a definite class and party, and has a definite political line. Art for arts sake, art that stands above class and party, and fellow-traveling or politically independent art do not exist in reality. In a society composed of classes and parties, art obeys both class and party and it must naturally obey the political demands of its class and party, and the revolutionary task of a given revolutionary age; any deviation is a deviation from the masses' basic needs.[16]

After the Communists came to power in 1949, Mao's insistence on subordinating the cinema and the other arts to the Party translated into state control. A series of moves integrated the film industry into the socialist command-based economy. The Party's Film Bureau became the state's Film Bureau under the Ministry of Culture in late 1949.[17] This body signaled immediately that its role would be proactive, rather than reactive, by calling a national conference in November of the same year at which a plan was drawn up for production in 1950.[18] Similar annual production conferences continued to be held throughout the classical period.

Leadership by a state body was reinforced by state ownership. Both private and state-owned components of the film industry were represented at the November 1949 conference mentioned above. In 1950, distribution was organized through a network of regional film management companies, which in 1951 became a state monopoly that owned and operated all commercial movie theaters in China.[19] On the production side, by 1953, the last remnants of the commercial Shanghai film industry had been nationalized.[20]

The censorship system constitutes the third major agent of centralized control. Little information about the constitution and operations of the censorship committee is available, but it was set up in 1950, is based in the Film Bureau, and all films have to be approved by it before they can be screened publicly in China.[21] It made its presence felt within months of its establishment when the private studio production, *The Life of Wu Xun*, was banned in 1951.[22]

Having harnessed the cinema securely to the Party-controlled state, a second major feature of the didactic paradigm was to ensure maximum reach. In the *Yan'an Talks* this appears mostly in exhortations to produce texts that audiences and readers will like, but institutional change also played a role.[23] In the film industry, production targets were steadily increased and new studios were set up around the country to help fulfill them, although the swings of Chinese politics led to wild year-to-year variations in output.[24]

In distribution and exhibition, a major movie theater construction program was embarked upon in the cities and, in the countryside, where film was largely unknown in 1949, mobile projection teams were introduced to bring films to the villages. As a result, total film projection units increased from 648 in 1949 to 9,965 in 1957, and 115,946 in 1978.[25] Ticket prices were frozen at a low level by the state, especially in the countryside,[26] and attendance was also encouraged by distributing tickets free to filmgoers through their work units, or by holding free screenings within the work units themselves. Movie-going increased as a result. In 1949, there were 47 million film attendances. By 1954, this was already up to 822 million and, by 1958, it had increased to 2.8 billion.[27]

SAMPLE FILMS

The textual product delivered to this ever-growing audience, the instrument that was to write on the supposedly blank paper, was also appropriate to the didactic paradigm. The discussion that follows is based on the viewing of many films from the 1949 to 1976 period over many years, and the close analysis of six films. This constitutes a very small sample[28] of the 645 features produced between 1949 and 1966,[29] when feature film production ceased for seven years.[30] However, it is historically wide-ranging and diverse in origin, style, and subject matter, encompassing many of the alternatives available to filmmakers at different times during this period.

Bridge was the first film completed after the founding of the People's Republic in 1949. It was produced at the Northeast Film Studio, which the Communists had taken over in 1946.[31] To chart the vicissitudes of the Chinese film industry, Paul Clark constructs a spectrum with Yan'an at one end and Shanghai at the other. Yan'an is an inland city associated with those filmmakers who spent the war years being molded in the mountain heartland of the Communist base area. Shanghai, on the other hand, is associated with more cosmopolitan filmmakers who never had the benefit of this experience, but instead rode out the war in KMT (*Guomindang*) or Japanese-controlled areas.[32] The differences incorporated in this Yan'an-

Shanghai spectrum may also be understood as the elements animating the tensions held under the didactic overdetermining principle of the Chinese classical cinema. In these terms, *Bridge* (and everything else produced at the Northeast Film Studio) is very much part of the Yan'an tradition, and both director Wang Bin and screenwriter Yu Min spent the war years in Yan'an.[33]

The Unfailing Beam can also be seen as part of this Yan'an tradition. It was produced at the Army-controlled August First Studio, which was also staffed heavily with Yan'an veterans.[34] However, it was made nine years after *Bridge*, in 1958. By this time, shortages of film stock, funds and equipment were less pronounced and filmmakers were more experienced. Therefore, its characteristics cannot be put down to these factors, as opposed to, say, didactic aims.[35]

Perhaps appropriately for a film made at the August First Studio, *The Unfailing Beam* concerns espionage and the army in the "old society" before 1949, whereas *Bridge* is about the efforts of factory workers to help construct the eponymous bridge, vital to the war effort in 1947. With the addition of the third film, *Li Shuangshuang*, the sample includes one film from each of the trio of "worker, peasant, soldier" themes explicitly mandated in the *Yan'an Talks* themselves.[36] However, although *Li Shuangshuang* is about overcoming problems in the implementation of rural communication, it was produced at a Shanghai Studio in 1962. Furthermore, although neither director Lu Ren nor screenwriter Li Zhun had close connections with the liberal cosmopolitan society of Shanghai in the thirties, neither had a Yan'an wartime pedigree, either.[37] As a result, this film cannot be placed at either end of Clark's spectrum.

The three other films tend more towards the Shanghai end of the spectrum. Neither *Woman Basketball Player No.5*, nor *Early Spring in February*, nor *Stage Sisters* has "worker, peasant, soldier" themes.[38] *Woman Basketball Player No.5* takes place in the Shanghai sports world, *Early Spring in February* centers on the patriotic middle classes in the 1920's, and *Stage Sisters* is set in Shanghai opera circles.

The director and screenwriter of *Early Spring in February* was Xie Tieli. Although Xie joined the Communist Party in 1942 and was an active member of the New Fourth Army, he did not spend time in Yan'an. Furthermore, he came from a middle-class background close to Shanghai, and the film was adapted from a cosmopolitan May Fourth Movement novel of the sort associated with the Shanghai tendency in the film industry.[39]

Both *Woman Basketball Player No.5* and *Stage Sisters* were written and directed by Xie Jin, (although two other writers also worked on *Stage Sisters*). Xie comes from a well-off Shanghai family and grew up watching

Shanghai films and imported Hollywood product in the thirties. He spent the war years in Hong Kong and was involved in patriotic drama troupe activities in KMT-controlled Chongqing, a typical biographical profile for the Shanghai end of Clark's spectrum.[40]

Woman Basketball Player No.5 was produced in 1957 and was not subjected to extensive criticism from Maoists. However, in events which prefigured the Cultural Revolution itself, *Early Spring in February* was criticized almost immediately after its release in 1964 and *Stage Sisters* was one of the last films produced before the outbreak of the Cultural Revolution in 1966, after which it too was banned and criticized.[41] This places both these films as firmly at the Shanghai end of Clark's spectrum as *Bridge* appears at the Yan'an end.

Bridge, The Unfailing Beam, Li Shuangshuang, Early Spring in February, Woman Basketball Player No.5 and *Stage Sisters* span both the entire history of the mainland feature film cinema before the Cultural Revolution and Clark's Shanghai-Yan'an spectrum. However, they all share the basic features of the didactic paradigm. Like the Soviet socialist realist cinema that Godard dubbed "Hollywood-Mosfilm," they draw heavily upon the Hollywood classical cinema.[42] However, they also diverge from it in significant ways. The character of the didactic paradigm will be analyzed below by tracing this pattern of overlap and divergence. No value judgments are intended.

CHARACTERS

David Bordwell argues that the dominant in the Hollywood classical cinema is a specific type of narrative causality, and that the construction of time and space are subordinated to this overdetermining drive. The agents of this causality are mostly characters, motivated by goals defined by their traits. Unmotivated coincidence is avoided because it is seen as diluting realism, but impersonal events may appear as unmotivated givens, especially in the construction of the initial premises of the narrative.[43]

The six mainland Chinese classical films under consideration also take character-borne narrative causality as their dominant. In *Bridge*, for example, the 1946-9 civil war between the Communists and the KMT government is an initial given, as is the damaged bridge and its crucial role in the Communist effort. However, whether or not the bridge will be repaired, and a host of subordinate problems, are dependent upon the actions of the characters in the steel plant where the parts for the bridge repair are to be manufactured.[44] Events such as the May Fourth Movement and the military campaigns of the 1920's also form a backdrop of unmotivated premises for

Early Spring in February. But again the narrative itself develops out of the actions of the various characters, starting with student Xiao Jianqiu and widow Wensao fleeing these larger historical events and going to Hibiscus Town on the same boat, although they are unacquainted at this time.[45]

However, although character actions drive narrative in both Hollywood and Chinese classical cinemas, they differ in attribution of these actions. Bordwell points out that in Hollywood the traits that compose the characters are psychological and signaled by dialogue, clothing, motifs and other outward signs.[46] Character traits in the Chinese classical cinema are signaled in similar ways, but these traits are more social than psychological, in accordance with the Marxist class-based worldview favored by the Chinese Communist Party. However, it extends beyond class to include gender, job, age, and other distinctions based on social relations. Therefore, it is also cognate with the common pre-Communist, Confucian-derived definition of self in terms of social relations rather than individual psychology.[47]

In *The Unfailing Beam*, political loyalties related to class overdetermine character, and relationships between characters defined in this way signify the political struggle driving the narrative. The initial scenes oscillate between the world of the Communist Party in the late thirties and their enemies at this time, the collaborators with the Japanese and the Nationalists. The Communists are shown in Yan'an and their enemies in Shanghai, environments whose connotations have already been discussed. With the exception of a patriotic psychiatrist who works underground for the Party, all the Communists are spartan, ordinary folk. Their enemies are westernized, fond of luxury, and sophisticated. In most cases, the only other distinguishing traits are age and gender.

Heroes and villains are distinguished from the crowd not only by cinematic techniques such as close-ups, but also by degree of "Yan'an-ness" or "Shanghai-ness." Li Xia, the main protagonist of *The Unfailing Beam*, is shown to be especially brave and selfless in his first appearance; he resists being sent to do underground radio transmitting work in Shanghai, because he believes it is a soft option compared with going to the front. As the script of the film points out,

> People can see at first glance that this twenty-seven year old young man is a veteran red army man experienced on the battlefield. His eyebrows are soldierly and his eyes are deep-set and wise. He is wearing an Eighth Route Army uniform, and the red army cap on his head has a bullet hole in it. Although the five-pointed star has been lost long ago, its impression remains deep on the cap.[48]

Figure 2.1 Li Xia's first appearance in *The Unfailing Beam*.

The identity of the hero's uniform would be readily apparent to a Chinese viewer in the fifties, as would the connotations of its battle-scarred condition. (See Figure 2.1)

Where Li Xia is an extreme example of the plain-living, self-sacrificing Yan'an type, his main enemies carry Shanghai connotations to the opposite extreme. Liu Nina, who appears immediately after Li Xia is given the mission that determines the shape of the film's narrative, has a Western given name. She is sitting in the back of a car, wearing heavy make-up and flashy, expensive Western clothes; a wide-brimmed hat with flowers and fruit, prominent earrings, a fitted white suit that clings to her body, and a dark cape. She discusses the importance of concealing the traitorous negotiations between the Japanese and the Nationalists from the Communists with a Japanese man, indicating that she is a collaborator (See Figure 2.2). Male collaborators wear aloha-style shirts patterned with palm trees, wide ties and white, double-breasted Western suits. Liu Nina's Japanese superior is middle-aged, has an ashen face, a little moustache, and wears a western suit. They are chauffeured to a large hotel, where a flunky in a uniform opens the

Figure 2.2 Liu Nina's first appearance in *The Unfailing Beam.*

car door for them. These features redundantly signify the decadence, treachery, and class enmity associated with these characters throughout the film.

At no point is there any discussion of the characters' family backgrounds, childhood experiences, or any other psychologically significant formative experiences. They have few individualized, psychological patterns marking them out beyond their social identities. However, *The Unfailing Beam* is a spy movie, a genre not noted for subtle characterization. *Woman Basketball Player No.5* is a melodrama full of romance, flashbacks, and misadventures, and its major characters are distinguished from lesser characters by individualized traits and motifs. Furthermore, it is set in the sports world, where the class or political divisions that define character in many other films are at least one step removed. At first sight, it may appear to use psychological rather than social and relational characterization.

The premise of the film is the arrival of a new male coach for the Chinese national women's team. A hermeneutic is defined when it is discovered that despite his advanced age, he is unmarried. That this is troubling and unusual is signified redundantly in the opening scenes. In the first scene after the credits, coach Tian Zhenhua arrives and meets Lao Meng, an old friend he has not seen for many years. Almost the first thing Meng asks is if Tian has come alone and, then, just to make sure he is interpreting this correctly, if he is still a bachelor.[49] The young women in the team also discover Tian's situation early on when they find him scrubbing his own clothes, which they point out would normally be done by a man's wife in China at this time. Tian is distinguished by another individualized motif in addition to his washboard; an orchid plant he conspicuously carries when he first arrives at the school and is frequently shown tending afterwards. One of the players, Lin Xiaojie, remarks that her mother, Lin Jie, also has a fondness for orchids. Gradually, through flashbacks, Tian's original relationship with her mother is revealed. As the film traces the misunderstandings between Tian and Lin Jie, it also traces the tensions in Lin Xiaojie's own relationship with her boyfriend, Tao Kai.

However, all this apparent psychologization and individualization is subordinated to the social and relational. The flashbacks do not reveal psychological wounds blocking Lin Jie and Tian Zhenhua's relationship. Rather, they split up because Lin Jie's father, a capitalist team owner first seen wearing a Western coat with a fur collar and smoking a cigar, tricked each of them separately into believing the one had abandoned the other. Her father is also a traitor, because he takes a bribe from a foreign team to let them win. Tian's patriotic refusal to cooperate explains why her father wants to break the relationship up. Similarly, Tao Kai's objection to Lin Xiaojie's decision to be a basketball player is traced to his class background. His family is composed of middle-class intellectuals. Tao himself wears glasses and has a reedy physique. He is prejudiced against physical labor, believes higher education is the road to success, and is slow to understand that Lin Xiaojie can contribute to the country through sports.

Woman Basketball Player No.5 confirms the importance of social relations in defining character in the classical Chinese cinema, but it also indicates that there may be variation in the degree to which this attribution is foregrounded. The sample films indicate that this variation occurs along Clark's Yan'an-Shanghai spectrum. *Bridge*, *The Unfailing Beam*, and *Li Shuangshuang* are all set in environments where class is immediately apparent. *Bridge* takes place in a factory, where the hierarchy of management and worker positions is immediately evident. *The Unfailing Beam* has already been discussed, and in the case of *Li Shuangshuang*, class distinctions between types of peasants create an immediately evident and determining social, political, and moral hierarchy. In contrast, *Woman Basketball Player*

No.5, *Early Spring in February*, and *Stage Sisters*, take place in the sports world, among May Fourth Movement students, and among opera singers respectively. Each of these milieus stands in an ambiguous relation to class, and characters have to be traced back a step further to uncover this important determination.

A second level of variation occurs around character ambiguity. Andrew Plaks finds inconsistency among characters in pre-modern Chinese narratives and that this inconsistency often emerges as a positive trait, a mark of the ability to adapt. In the Chinese classical cinema, the function of character change is a little different. As a didactic cinema, the mainland Chinese classical cinema requires characters that are ambiguous, not so much as a mark of their adaptability as of their need for guidance. Susan Rubin Suleiman has noted that the apprenticeship structure is a common feature of Western authoritarian fictions.[50] David Bordwell also uses this term in his discussion of the early Soviet films he calls "historical-materialist," thus tracing a precedent for the Soviet socialist realist cinema.[51]

All six sample films have such "apprentice" characters. In *The Unfailing Beam*, almost everybody is clearly defined as either a villain or a good Communist but the ordinary factory worker who has to pose as hero Li Xia's wife is an apprentice character. She knows nothing about underground work, but as the narrative progresses, she learns how to pretend to be a bourgeois woman and how to help Li operate the radio transmitter.

In the other films, there are many more apprentice characters. In *Li Shuangshuang*, for example, her husband Xiwang is the most prominent character who is educated, and mostly through his wife's example. However, he is not alone. The young man Erchun is opposed to women taking part in work outside the home at first, and has to learn the error of his ways. Neighbor Sun You's wife is selfish and tries to use the commune's facilities to her family's advantage. She also opposes her daughter Guiying marrying Erchun, and tries to arrange a marriage for her with a truck driver from the city, who presumably has a higher standard of living and a coveted urban residence permit. Sun You himself is equally selfish, and gets Xiwang involved in illegal sideline activities rather than working for the common good. Both Sun You and his wife see how wrong they have been, and like Xiwang, largely because of the example Shuangshuang sets.[52]

However, although there are many apprentice characters in *Li Shuangshuang* and the other four sample films, what differentiates them is prominence. It is only at the Shanghai end of the spectrum that the main character is ever such a character. This is true to some degree of Chunhua in *Stage Sisters*. There is never any question about her correct political instincts, which can be predicted from her status as a poor peasant girl fleeing an arranged marriage. However, this same status makes it impossible for her to know about revolution and communism, and she has to be educated by a leftist reporter called Jiang Bo, who suggests she sees various plays and films and takes her round an exhibition devoted to author Lu Xun. This in turn leads Chunhua to stage an opera based on Lu Xun's short story, "New Year's Sacrifice" (*Zhufu*).[53]

However, among the six sample films, the much-debated *Early Spring in February* is the clearest example of ambiguous or, as they are called in China, "middle" characters being used as main characters.[54] There are no evident Communist heroes in the whole film, and the main character, Xiao Jianqiu, is a middle-class student whose inability to decide where his duty lies is the basic premise of the narrative. Only at the very end is he finally clear that he must leave the little backwater of Hibiscus Town, presumably to join the Communist cause. When Tao Lan, who is in love with him, races after him, this may be a decision to do the same thing. However, she has oscillated between concern for the poor and selfishness, egoism, and romanticism, and the revolutionary purity of her action is not clear. These characters are far more ambiguous than Chunhua in *Stage Sisters*.

Critics operating within a cinema concerned with psychological realism might praise such characters as "rounded."[55] However, critics of the Chinese classical cinema assessed characters in terms of their ability to serve as exemplary models for emulation on the part of audiences. As Munro points out, this formation of models for emulation occurred not only in fiction, but in all walks of life and at all levels in Communist China, and can also be traced back to Confucian ideas on self-improvement.[56] Articles extolling film characters as models for emulation are very common. Li Xia, the hero of *The Unfailing Beam*, was based on a real person, and therefore upheld as a revolutionary forerunner for everyone to learn from.[57] The eponymous Li Shuangshuang was also the focus of a major campaign.[58] In these circumstances, muddy class and political loyalties resolved late in the narrative caused anxiety among critics and their masters. During the Cultural Revolution period itself, Jiang Qing's notorious theory of the three prominences (*san tuchu*) swung far away from "middle" characters: give prominence to the positive among all the characters; give prominence to the heroes among the positive; and give prominence to the major heroes among the heroes.[59]

NARRATIVE

Whether "middle characters" or "major heroes," the characters in the Chinese classical film are the agents of narrative causality, which, as in Hollywood, can be seen as what David Bordwell terms "the dominant" or Rick Altman terms an "overdetermination" in that system. Studies of Hollywood show this causality is temporally organized along a trajectory of disturbance, struggle, and resolution. The struggle that takes up most of the film is composed of a series of logically connected events in which each element introduced into the film is used up in the cause-effect chain of the logical progression. Elements are often introduced first and then given narrative significance later as one of the conventions of Hollywood realism that avoids the appearance of coincidence.[60] The logical progression is itself broken down into a series of sequences, most of which are scenes defined by unity of time, space, and action. The scenes are organized according to the chronological order of the events they purport to represent, with gaps between scenes marked as ellipsis. The causal logic of disturbance and struggle is also played out within each scene, leaving an unresolved element to motivate the move on to the following scene.[61]

Although the attribution of character behavior in Chinese classical cinema may be different from the Hollywood variant, the domination of the same narrative logic is found in the Chinese classical film sample. The openings of *Bridge* and *Woman Basketball Player No.5* have been outlined briefly above, but more detailed consideration demonstrates their organization according to this logic.

In *Bridge*, after the opening credits, the narrative proper begins with a shot of people milling about in the foreground, and a broken railway bridge in the background. Superimposed is the title, "Early Spring 1947." Conventions of logical narrative infer that the following shots depict events occurring at this time, known to all Chinese viewers as the civil war between the Communists and the KMT that followed the end of the War of Resistance Against Japan (1937-45). Long shots, similar winter clothes worn by all characters, and similar outdoor winter settings make it difficult to discern any continuity between these shots, but also make it difficult to definitely exclude continuities, indicating that this is a montage sequence. Events depicted include: movements of infantry and supply columns through a snowy landscape; the taking of a small hill, hoisting the red flag, and taking prisoners; carrying two injured men down what appears to be the same hill; and two men on horseback galloping across a plain.

According the logic of narrative causality, the unfinished actions in this montage motivate the move to the next scene, and show connections between the elements of the montage. The next scene takes place at one head of the broken bridge shown in the opening shot. Here, the stretcher-bearers, the supply column, and the horseback riders reappear, and in that order. One of the injured men asks when he will be put on a train, but is told the railway bridge is out. A driver on the supply column also complains about the hold-up caused by the broken bridge, and then one of the men on horseback enters to ask him for directions to the North Bank Station.

This final element motivates a cut to the North Bank Station, where we follow the horseman into the station to find the officer there surrounded by men complaining about problems caused by the broken bridge. In a final example of redundant signification, he explains to the horseman that the broken bridge is disrupting supplies to the front and the transportation of the injured away from the front. (Susan Rubin Suleiman also notes redundancy as one of the main features of authoritarian fictions.[62])

The horseman promises to report the problem, motivating a cut to a shot of a telegraph message being sent. Conventions of narrative logic lead the viewer to presume it is a follow-up to the previous scene. The film then cuts to someone walking out of a building with a sign indicating it is the head office of the railways and getting into a car. Conventions of narrative causality dictate this must be a response to the message. In the scene following, the same car arrives at a railway factory, where the man proceeds to the factory director's office, outlines the problem at the bridge to the director, and explains the vital role the factory can play in solving it. The next ellipsis jumps to engineers in the plant discussing the problem, and the scene after that follows the logic of the drive towards resolution by moving down to the floor, where the effort to produce the steel and parts needed for the repairs must take place.

The opening of *Woman Basketball Player No. 5* follows an equally clear cause and effect logic. However, in this film at the Shanghai end of Clark's spectrum, not only are the ellipses between scenes implied to be much shorter, but the causal links are connected with the personal and psychological in a way that does not apply to *Bridge* at all.

The narrative begins with a long shot of traffic on what would be recognizable to Chinese viewers as a typical Shanghai street, followed by a cut to a car moving up a driveway. Conventions of narrative causality indicate the cut covers an ellipsis and, possibly, that the same car was in the traffic seen earlier. A man carrying luggage, including a prominently displayed orchid plant and washboard, gets out of the car, looks around, and notices a sign in the background. The next shot follows logical progression by showing the same sign in a close-up. It directs those taking part in the selections for national sports teams to a nearby building.

The next scene starts in a room where people are being measured and weighed. Conventions of narrative causality encourage the viewer to read this as the destination pointed out in the sign, and also that this is where the man from the car is headed. Sure enough, he enters in the next shot, and meets an old friend. Tian Zhenhua and his friend, Lao Meng, chat briefly, and, among other things, Lao Meng asks if he is still single.

The next scene shows Lao Meng and Tian on a flight of stairs. Presumably, an ellipsis has taken place, but not a large one, because Tian is still carrying the orchid and the washboard he has had in his hands since getting out of the car. Some girls who were in the room being measured earlier rush by, giggling, and casting curious glances at Tian. In the next scene, the same girls rush into a dormitory building and announce to their roommates that they think they have seen their new coach.

The next scene shows Tian and Lao Meng in another room somewhere else in the building. Narrative logic leads us to read this as occurring soon after the last scene. Again, Tian's single status is discussed, and Lao Meng suggests he should do something about it or it will affect his work as a coach. Tian is caring for his orchid plant, the full significance of which will only be revealed much later in the narrative. The girls mentioned as a trigger for potential problems appear on the balcony outside. Lao Meng sends them to gather on the basketball court, and the film cuts to the court. In this manner, the film rapidly introduces the main character and sets up a problematic around both his personal life and his new assignment, implying from the beginning that successful resolution of both situations is linked. Although cause and effect logic dominates both films, the "Shanghai" film is concerned with both psychology and social goals, whereas the "Yan'an" film is only concerned with the latter.

Generally speaking, the narrative in both Hollywood and Chinese classical cinema moves forward according to the chronological order of events and mimetic conventions. There are only two regular exceptions: moments in which the movement of the cause-effect chain is suspended; and the flashback, usually motivated by character memory.

So-called "dead" time when the narrative is suspended is considered undesirable in Hollywood classical cinema. A whole battery of devices, such as cutting on action or always talking and walking at the same time, are designed to ensure that no screen time is "wasted."[63] Such consistent and conventionalized deployments of narrative suspension as exist are linked to genre. For example, certain gag sequences in the comedy or song and dance sequences in the musical may hold up narrative progression but fulfill the requirements of the genre.[64] In her famous article, Laura Mulvey also links the suspension of narrative in Hollywood classical cinema to the deployment of spectacle, a response to castration anxiety in the form of disavowal and fetishization.[65]

Suspension of narrative development also occurs in the Chinese classical cinema. However, it does not correlate to genre, nor is it motivated by a libidinal economy. It can be found in most films regardless of genre, functioning as metatext and as part of the dominant didactic organization of the Chinese classical cinema. Suspension is a site for analysis, commentary, and judgement that directs the reading of the film. This is command of a very different sort from that discussed by Mulvey; it places epistemological command above libidinal command.

Ma Ning has also noted this metatextual tendency in the Chinese film melodramas he examines, arguing that these texts are structured in a tension between a "micro-narrative" and "macro-narrative," with the latter functioning as the metatextual level. He also notes deep historical cultural antecedents for this. First, he draws on the work of Andrew Plaks to draw literary parallels, and, second, he cites Richard Vinograd's work on Chinese landscape painting, where it was not unusual for a written commentary in the form of a poem to appear on the scroll itself.[66]

In the six sample films narrative suspension is sometimes strongly marked by the intervention of commentary from outside the diegesis. For example, in between the credits and before the opening montage sequence in *Bridge*, there is an intertitle, read out by an authoritative male voice. This intertitle not only encapsulates the entire plot of the film, removing any element of suspense and directing the viewer towards analysis, but also directs the analysis in terms of class relations and national effort.

In *Stage Sisters*, elliptical montage sequences are accompanied by choral extra-diegetic singing that comments on the narrative. For example, after Chunhua has joined the opera troupe and their wanderings are being depicted in a montage, the chorus sings of hard work, suffering, and homelessness. Over a montage that depicts their move to Shanghai after the death of Yuehong's father, the chorus sings of how their shared suffering makes the stage sisters bond like two vine stems that twist together as they grow.[67]

This singing is not entirely unconnected to the diegesis, as the film follows an opera troupe whose performances have related themes. Similarly, in *Early Spring in February*, just as the main character, Xiao Jianqiu, plays classical Western music on the piano, so important moments are underlined by emotional Western classical music welling up on the soundtrack. This could also be seen as a kind of commentary.

However, in most cases, suspension and commentary occurs within the diegesis and is not absolute. Rather, suspension occurs as relatively brief moments embedded within the narrative. Examples can be found in the opening scenes of *Bridge* and *Woman Basketball Player No.5* discussed above. At the North Bank Station in *Bridge*, when the officer presents his analysis of the situation at the broken bridge to the horseman, he is positioned centrally and frontally, surrounded by attentive listeners as he delivers his analysis. Movement by characters is minimal relative to all the action that has preceded this moment. In this way, the formal features of this shot connote a temporary suspension, or a cutting out from the narrative.

Moments like these are commonly found across all six sample films. Less frequent but more significant and also found in all six films are larger, more clearly marked examples of suspension that delay narrative progression for an entire scene or montage sequence. In their most obvious form, these noticeably static scenes are positioned at crucial moments when the narrative progression is deadlocked. In the didactic paradigm, violence is not the answer to problems and the engine of narrative progression, as is often the case in many genres of Hollywood classical cinema, but rather the force of reason and persuasion, albeit sometimes backed by implicit threat.

For example, about half way through *Stage Sisters*, Chunhua meets leftist journalist Jiang Bo after a fight with Yuehong and the suicide of an older opera singer, whom their manager had abandoned for Yuehong. Chunhua pours out her confusion about why everyone else envies Yuehong and congratulates her although she has clearly erred. Jiang Bo speaks of the importance of distinguishing right from wrong, linking together, and overthrowing oppressors. As they are shown deep in thought and looking out of the window into the middle distance, a chorus wells up again, this time speaking of enlightenment and the need to "sing a new opera." The visit to the Lu Xun exhibition follows, and Chunhua tells Jiang Bo she has seen the plays and films Jiang recommended and hopes to emulate them.

This scene is echoed when Chunhua turns to Jiang Bo again after the authorities have closed down her stage version of Lu Xun's short story, *New Year's Sacrifice*. Jiang Bo further educates her apprentice about the need for revolution. In the courtroom scene where the manager is trying to shift the blame for the acid attack on Chunhua onto Yuehong, Chunhua graduates to the role of analyst and commentator, in a sort of didactic relay effect, demonstrating her stage sister's innocence in a long monologue.

Similar, large set-piece scenes where a character with political authority analyzes and comments to break deadlock occur at crucial points in the other sample films, too. In *Bridge*, the factory director tends to take on the role of the educator, holding meetings whenever difficulties are encountered. These meetings often occur in his office, where he is depicted surrounded by attentive listeners, and speaking underneath a portrait of Chairman Mao on the wall. In some cases, small group meetings to analyze specific applications of the principles worked out in the large meeting follow. These are organized as a small version of the large meeting scenes, with a reliable secondary figure taking on the factory director's educative role and central position.

The other three sample films inflect this model of the meeting scene. *Li Shuangshuang* does have scenes where Li turns to Party authority figures for advice at moments of crisis. For example, she goes to the commune headquarters for advice from Secretary Liu, and the old Party secretary who lives in the village comes to advise her when her husband, Xiwang, leaves after another fight. However, these are not big public meetings but private, one-on-one sessions between Li and authority figures; the Communist Chinese equivalent of a trip to the therapist or priest, perhaps. Furthermore, they are not crucial turning points like Chunhua's meetings with Jiang Bo in *Stage Sisters*, possibly because Li is not really an apprentice figure. She already has a good grasp of right and wrong and a powerful analytical ability, and her rhymes and comments embedded within the various scenes in the village constitute didactic moments of suspension embedded within the narrative.

Similarly, in *The Unfailing Beam*, most of the characters know right from wrong, and blockage occurs not because of the errors of apprentice characters but in the struggle with an irredeemable enemy. A rare exception is the initial discomfort of the factory girl, He Lanfang, when obliged to play the bourgeois wife and provide Li Xia with cover. Here, he acts as educator and explains their vital mission to her. However, for the most part, moments and scenes of suspension are given over to analysis of the military situation.

Finally, *Early Spring in February* has no reliable Party-related authority figures to carry a didactic role. Suspension does occur when Xiao Jianqiu tries to analyze his situation, in conversations with Tao Lan or silent nighttime reflection accompanied by expressive music on the soundtrack. Although analysis rather than spectacle motivates suspension here as elsewhere in the mainland Chinese classical cinema, without a Party representative in the film, these scenes do not have the same didactic potential as in the other sample films.

The other main disruption of narrative progression in the Hollywood classical cinema is the flashback, itself a form of suspension that introduces anterior narrative. Bordwell notes these devices usually have an expository purpose within the logic of narrative causality. They are rarely designed to enhance a sense of subjectivity (as occurs more frequently in the European art cinema), and may often include information unknown to the character whose memory has motivated the flashback itself. Bordwell also finds flashbacks in less than 10 per cent of the films in his 1939 to 1953 sample, a period when flashbacks were relatively in vogue.[68]

The form, uses and frequency of the flashback in the Chinese classical cinema are similar to Hollywood. They are marked by the dissolve and usually a close-up of a character's face. When extended, they often contain material unknown to the character. For example, there are the two lengthy flashbacks in *Woman Basketball Player No.5*. In one, Coach Tian remembers his experiences in pre-revolutionary Shanghai and the events that led to the break-up of his relationship with Lin Jie. Included are two scenes after Lin Jie's father's henchmen have attacked him, in which Lin discovers the severity of his injury then tries to raise money for his medical expenses. He is present in neither scene and could have no memory of them. Furthermore, the shots in the scenes in this flashback where Tian himself is present do not suggest a subjective point of view. For example, a basketball match scene where he is playing in a Chinese team against some foreigners who have bribed his team's manager (who is also Lin Jie's father) is played out in a shot and reverse shot alternation between events on and off court, positioning the film spectator to apprehend all these emotions and points of view, and not just Tian's memory of them.

The deployment of the flashback is as rare in the Chinese classical cinema as in Hollywood classical cinema. *Bridge* and *Li Shuangshuang*, both towards the Yan'an end of Clark's spectrum, have no flashbacks at all. *Stage Sisters* and *The Unfailing Beam* have very limited uses of flashback (a superimposed memory of a face, and two aural memories of a line of dialogue respectively), and only *Woman Basketball Player No.5* and *Early Spring in February* have multi-shot, extended flashbacks. As well as Tian's flashback in *Woman Basketball Player No.5*, Lin Jie has a flashback soon after that recounts the events that led to their separation from her point of view. In *Early Spring in February*, Tao Lan remembers seeing Xiao Jianqiu before, and how she thought he was going to commit suicide by jumping into a lake when in fact he was only deep in thought. Beyond these extended flashbacks, there are only a few very brief flashbacks. When Lin comes to Beijing at the end of *Woman Basketball Player No.5* and is reunited with Tian, her

Figure 2.3 Chunhua remembers Little Chunhua at the Lu Xun exhibition in *Stage Sisters*.

memories of the past flash by again, superimposed over her face. In *Early Spring in February*, when Xiao Jianqiu is returning after proposing marriage to Wensao, whom he feels obliged to help, a shot of his memory of her suffering face is superimposed. In *Stage Sisters*, when Jiang Bo takes Chunhua round the Lu Xun exhibition, there is a similar superimposition when Chunhua looks at a woodcut representing the suffering woman from the "New Year's Sacrifice" story. She also remembers the unfortunate girl, also called Chunhua, whom she met once in a village, and her face is superimposed over the picture of Xianglin Sao. (Figure 2.3).

The only other connotations of anteriority are the title that occurs at the beginning of *Bridge*, discussed earlier, and the opening of *Stage Sisters*. The title at the beginning of *Bridge* assumes that the film audience is in a present and moves them back to a past time situated in a history they shared with the characters in the film. Similarly, at the beginning of the credits sequence in *Stage Sisters*, the first shot is of a contemporary, post-revolutionary urban theater. This then dissolves to an old, open-air stage of the type used by itinerant opera troupes in the pre-revolutionary society, again moving the audience back into the space of shared collective memory.

Although these are not flashbacks in the usual sense, they shed light on the particular deployment of the flashback in the Chinese classical cinema. Under the overdetermining didactic principle, flashback is less about making sense of psychologized motivations than about learning. When these opening devices in *Bridge* and *Stage Sisters* position the space of the narrative as shared with the audience, they do so as part of a pedagogical practice. Similarly, Tian and Lin's flashbacks not only explain their misunderstandings but also show the cause to be Lin Jie's father's deception and anger because Tian will not behave in accordance with the bribe and lose the match against the foreigners. Therefore, they link personal betrayal to national and collective betrayal.

In these circumstances, the flashback is largely subsumed under the category of remembering past bitterness, or "speaking bitterness," as it is sometimes referred to. In this trope, memory is not just personal, but part of a collective process of learning from experience. From the earliest days of the Land Reform in post-revolutionary China, political movements were introduced and conducted using this technique. The movement is introduced at village or work unit meetings, before which wrongdoers are paraded to be attacked. Their accusers are encouraged to remember past bitterness blamed on the wrongdoer in order to mobilize the community. Xie Jin's 1986 film, *Hibiscus Town*, represents this in the fifties and after. William Hinton's *Fanshen* details instances during Land Reform in Long Bow village.[69]

Tian's seemingly private flashback in *Woman Basketball Player No.5* is embedded within the after-match post-mortem meeting, discussed above as a primary example of full-scene narrative suspension for the purposes of analysis and education. The explicit point of the flashback is to illustrate the consequences of failure to subordinate selfish desires to the national and collective good. Interestingly, Lin Jie's flashback that follows is exceptional in this regard. It is initially private, and the whole sequence is narrated by her voice-over and addressed to Tian Zhenhua as "you." The questions that she raises about why he left are later addressed directly to him when they are reunited. This is not part of a collective learning process, but rather illustrates how, in this unusual instance, private and collective grief run parallel.

In *Early Spring in February*, although Tao Lan's flashback of Xiao Jianqiu by the lake is not shared with a larger group, it is also linked to larger, collective issues rather than private ones. Tao Lan made the romantic error of thinking Xiao was on the point of committing suicide (presumably because of a failed love affair), when in fact he was deep in thought about how to save China from its predicament. This latter theme dominates the discussion around the flashback, which in itself is yet another example of narrative suspension for analysis and commentary.

Even most of the minor flashbacks listed above function in this didactic way. Finally, the presence of remembering past bitterness in situations where no actual flashback occurs must be mentioned. In some large analytical scenes, remembering past bitterness is deployed as part of the lesson-learning process. In *Bridge*, an old worker called Lao Hou is sometimes called upon to speak at meetings. He may be framed in close-up, as though a flashback is about to begin, but although he recounts his memories of the bad old days to moblilize his listeners, there is no actual flashback. In these circumstances, although the actual flashback may be rare in Chinese classical cinema, it is part of a larger pattern of using memory for didactic ends.

MISE-EN-SCENE AND SPECTATOR POSITIONING

The individual characteristics of the mise-en-scene, framing, lighting, sound and other elements that combine to construct diegesis and a relation to it on the part of the spectator in Chinese classical cinema are similar to those of Hollywood classical cinema. They also share a broadly realist deployment. However, the Chinese classical cinema combines these elements to encourage a quite different relationship between the spectator and the diegetic world of the film. Where the Hollywood classical cinema has been analyzed as encouraging libidinal relations, the Chinese classical cinema subordinates these elements to the construction of an almost self-conscious pupil-spectator placed to observe and learn clearly laid-out lessons. However much spectators may be encouraged to recognize themselves in the main characters of mainland Chinese classical films — worker-peasant-soldier themes were encouraged for worker-peasant-soldier audiences — identification is subordinated to analysis and education.

In his discussion of space in the Hollywood classical cinema, Bordwell stresses that its realism is based on post-Renaissance classical painting traditions. Extreme long-shots draw on the landscape painting tradition and place emphasis on the lower half of the frame, whereas other shots emphasize a T-shaped zone comprising the upper horizontal third and central vertical third of the screen. Almost all shots are centered and balanced but not excessively symmetrical. Frontality is emphasized, even if this means characters at a dinner table leave one seat free so that the camera is not confronted with the back of a head, and lighting is used to emphasize depth and those parts of the frame towards which a spectator's attention should be directed.

Within the diegesis, a principle of object economy is preferred, so that only settings and props that contribute to the narrative in some form are used.[70] Many of these elements contribute to an "illusionism" that draws spectator attention away from the constructed quality of the filmic image towards the seemingly real diegesis, away from the enunciation and towards the enunciated. For example, centered framing downplays the existence of the frame itself, and cutting on action downplays the cut itself.[71]

Broadly speaking, the mainland Chinese classical cinema is composed of similar elements and follows similar principles in regard to mise-en-scene, camerawork, and editing. For example, the orchid plant and washboard that coach Tian Zhenhua is shown carrying from the car at the beginning of *Woman Basketball Player No.5* are excellent examples of economy and a certain convention of realism in the use of objects. Initially, their significance may appear obscure, but they are given meaning as a symbol of Tian and Lin Jie's love in Tian's flashback and a symbol of Tian's bachelorhood respectively. Thus they are not clutter, but have a use in the narrative and, because they have been there from the beginning of the film, they do not pop up as "unrealistic coincidences."

However, when spectator positioning is considered, a picture emerges that is significantly different from Hollywood classical cinema. Analysis of spectator positioning in Hollywood classical cinema has emphasized the construction and maintenance of a range of libidinal subject positions, often based on aligning the spectator with the desiring gaze of one "relay" character upon another.[72] However, in the Chinese classical cinema the didactic overdetermination manifests itself in patterns of cinematic tropes that are demonstrative. They combine to encourage the spectator to perceive a certain understanding of the events and characters that make up the narrative that correlates to the Party line on the issues the films refer to. Although individual tropes may be quite similar to those in the Hollywood classical cinema, if the Hollywood tropes combine to construct and maintain a sense of libidinal command, the patterns of the mainland Chinese classical cinema could be said to construct and maintain a sense of epistemological command.[73] For example, where Mulvey notes the role of reverse shot structures in Hollywood libidinality, this trope is often used in the Chinese classical cinema is to signify disorder and fragmentation of relational harmony among characters in the process of demonstrating a political point, placing the spectator in a "position of privileged perception."[74]

While this argument still holds, the analysis that follows indicates two additional points. First, the reverse shot is only one of many devices common to both Hollywood and Chinese classical cinema but deployed to construct the pupil-spectator in Chinese classical cinema. Second, the use of the reverse shot structure to signify fragmentation is only one of the most common significations it may carry within this didactic overdetermination, and other devices, tropes, and patterns may also carry a range of significations within the didactic overdetermination. What is the range of such devices, tropes and patterns and what is the range of their deployment?

A. Relays

First, as noted, all the sample films employ apprentice characters. These play a prominent role in the construction of the pupil-spectator, functioning as relays, not of the libidinal gaze but of the pupil-spectator's attention. The pupil-spectator is encouraged into this relation by both how the narrative follows these characters as they learn and also the camerawork and editing tropes deployed. For example, aligning the spectator with a series of characters operates in this fashion in the opening scenes of *Bridge* discussed above. Each character finds out about the nature of the problem at the bridge itself and then passes this on to another character. First, the staff officer who has been sent to the bridge to find out what is going on is shown doing just that. Then he passes on what he has discovered to the man at the ministry, who passes this information to the head of the factory, who then passes it to the various people working in the plant, and so on. The narrative carries the spectator along this exchange of knowledge with the characters as they perform learning and then educating functions.

Early Spring in February also provides an example. As a new arrival in Hibiscus Town, Xiao Jianqiu has the relay function in the opening scenes of the film. Indeed, he is the main apprentice character and relay in the entire film. In the first scene, where he is traveling on the same boat as widow Wensao, he is shown overhearing her conversation, and the camera follows the logic of alternation between Xiao Jianqiu and what he is observing. A similar pattern occurs in the following scenes where he is guided through the town by the local headmaster, who is Tao Lan's elder brother. However, although Xiao is the main relay, he is not the only one. In the following scene, Xiao and three other men are shown talking in a room in the Tao family house. Here, Tao Lan enters and takes on both the apprentice function and the relay role, listening intently and looking upon Xiao Jianqiu as someone interesting and whom she wants to know more about. The camerawork articulates this again in an alternation between Tao and the scene that excites her interest.

Later in the same film, even the negative rival for Tao's affections, Qian Zhengxing, has the apprentice function and acts as a relay in a scene that takes place in the school staff room. After Qian's initial attempt to ingratiate himself with Tao Lan by offering her candies is rebuffed, Xiao Jianqiu enters with Wensao's little daughter. Tao Lan is delighted with the girl, and, at the end of the scene, she, Xiao Jianqiu and the little girl exit, the little girl between them, holding their hands. The entire scene is constructed using Qian as a relay of the spectator's curious attention. Initially, an establishing shot shows Tao Lan seated facing front. The camera pans right from Tao to reveal another teacher looking at her, and then on to Qian when he makes a noise and the other teacher turns right to look at him. His gaze then motivates camera movement leftwards, back to Tao. The next shot is positioned behind Qian and moves with him when he approaches Tao with candies. Following the rebuff, a close-up shows us Qian's reaction. This cutaway is repeated twice to show Qian's reaction to Tao's enchantment with the child, and then his reaction to the quasi-family tableau of Xiao Jianqiu, Tao Lan, and Wensao's daughter exiting. In this way, the audience both observes what he observes and observes him observing.

In some cases, the function of being a relay for the pupil-spectator is carried not by a single character or a series of single characters, as in the examples just given, but by a whole crowd. In the early scene at the bridgehead in *Bridge* discussed above, when the staff officer enters the office, he joins a crowd of people surrounding the officer behind the desk and demanding explanations from him. Shots alternating between sections of the crowd and him as the object of their attention are embedded in shots that take an objective perspective on the whole scene. However, the function of the group or crowd as relay of curious attention is more evident in *Stage Sisters*, where the various audiences for stage performances often have this function. In an echo of the opening song's comment that off-stage there is another stage, many of the stage scenes with audiences are complemented by backstage scenes that also feature crowds of actors and others as onlookers functioning as relays. The crowd of villagers that witnesses Chunhua's public punishment for resisting Yuehong's arrest after she has rejected Lord Ni's advances, and the crowd of people in the courtroom in the big scene towards the end of the film where Yuehong is accused of having attacked Chunhua, also function in this way. These scenes make up the bulk of this particular film.

In *Bridge*, the crowd in the scene just discussed is part of the action, whereas, in *Stage Sisters*, the crowd is in an objective position, looking on at the action. As the examples have also indicated, a character may be both the relay of the pupil-spectator and an object of attention from whom, or about which, something is to be learned. This suggests that the identification with relay figures is not fixed, but contingent. Rather than being encouraged to identify powerfully with any one character or type of character and to maintain that identification, the pupil-spectator is placed in a number of positions, giving a privileged perspective and understanding that exceeds that of any single character. This contingent quality is further developed in the use of a series of techniques that shift the pupil-spectator back and forth between the perspectives of characters engaged in action (itself often a quest for knowledge) and a position of contemplation and consideration.

For example, it was noted that the scene in the office at the bridgehead in *Bridge* began with the staff officer entering, with establishing shots of him doing so, followed by shots from his point of view of what is happening around the desk. Here, a relative distance from the action is observed. When he joins the crowd around the desk, a more engaged position is taken. Of course, this basic movement from establishing shots to closer shots is the paradigm for scene organization in the Hollywood classical cinema, too, but the didactic overdetermination in Chinese cinema gives it a more particular function.

This tendency to embed moments of engagement within distanciation is common to all six films in the sample, and does not always involve relay characters for both positions. The embedded reverse shot structure, whether or not involving direct point-of-view, is a commonly used instance. An example of this logic at work in the organization of shots within a scene can be found in the opening section of *Woman Basketball Player No.5*, which is given over to mutual curiosity between the new coach and his team. In the first scene on a basketball court, the team lines up to report to their new coach and to listen to him. Parts of this scene are organized as a point-of-view, shot and reverse shot exchange between the team and the coach. The coach is usually isolated in the shot that takes the point-of-view of the team, and shot from below, a standard convention for glorifying a character found in many cinemas, and a signifier of their respect and attention. Shots of the team members from the coach's point-of-view, on the other hand, usually show groups of three members, and sometimes take the form of a pan along the row, as though inspecting them. This differentiated exchange shifts the audience between two different types of enquiring, curious position. To this, occasional shots are added that break out of the shot and reverse shot exchange and are taken from an objective perspective, further shifting the pupil-spectator between engagement with the characters and a more distanced position.

Ma Ning has also noted this tendency to embed or bracket shot/reverse-shot exchanges in his discussion of the backstage scene that follows the first performance scene that opens *Stage Sisters*. Although he uses this formal structure as part of his particular interpretation of a specific scene, the interpretation of the more generalized function of this pattern offered here also applies to this scene.[75]

B. Mirroring

Another common shot that promotes contemplation of what has just occurred is the close-up on the face of a character deep in thought. In *Stage Sisters*, Chunhua, the main apprentice character in the film, is sometimes shown deep in thought in a close-up at the end of a scene as she attempts to comprehend something that has just happened. Examples include Chunhua's scene alone in the dormitory after she and Yuehong have had a disagreement in Shanghai. After looking at a picture of the two of them in harmony in the past, the camera cuts to her sighing and deep in thought.

However, just as a number of different characters act as relays for the pupil-spectator's curiosity in most films, so a number of them are shown deep in thought. In *Stage Sisters*, for example, a backstage scene following the scene just discussed and involving the older opera star Chunhua and Yuehong have displaced, ends with that older opera star deep in thought in close-up, as, presumably, she contemplates her predicament. Such shots can be found in all of the films in the sample, but the tendency is most pronounced in *Early Spring in February*, where the majority of scenes end with such a close-up of a thoughtful face. The absence of Party figures in this film may account for this, as the options for signifying contemplation and analysis are reduced without Party representatives to call meetings, reflect on what is happening, and guide the characters.

This use of the close-up can be understood as a formally different type of play of identification and distanciation from that deployed with relay characters. With relay characters, the effect depends upon identification with the position of the camera on the part of the pupil-spectator. With the full-face close-up of a character deep in thought, the effect depends upon projection for identification at the same time as the pupil-spectator is observing the face.[76] The scene of Chunhua remembering her own past suffering and that of Little Chunhua in *Stage Sisters* is a powerful and unusual moment when this effect itself is represented directly (Figure 2.3). Before the superimpositions, Chunhua is shown in close-up and deep in thought (Figure 2.4). This small moment signifying memory and projective identification with others who are simultaneously observed is embedded within Jiang Bo's didactic, demonstrative discourse.

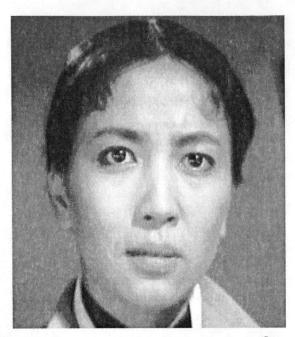

Figure 2.4 Chunhua gazes at the woodcut of Xianglin Sao in *Stage Sisters*.

The close-up of the thoughtful face at the end of a scene is not the only example of a device that simultaneously promotes identification via projection and distanced observation. Other such devices also depend upon a kind of mirror effect. Camera movement varies considerably, but it is mostly character-motivated. In these instances, a mirroring relationship is constructed between the pupil-spectator and those characters motivating camera movement. Another very common device found across all the films in the sample that also facilitates this effect is constructed by the position of the camera in a mirror relation to a particular character in a static shot. As has been noted already, the most common organization of a shot places the characters we are to attend to in the middle of the screen and with their faces fully visible. These conventions are so common as to make the mirror effect achieved by placing the camera on the same level as these main characters and perpendicular to them difficult to notice.

Finally, there is another mirroring device that promotes simultaneous projective identification and observation on the part of the pupil-spectator. This is what Ma Ning terms the "epiphanic shot." According to him, these shots signify a moment of equilibrium in the film.[77] These "epiphanic shots" consist of tableaux of characters whose movement is frozen or minimized for a moment, usually, but not always, at the end of a scene. The shot is usually frontal, creating a kind of mirror effect. Because it is also frozen, attention is drawn to it, making time for extended consideration on the part of the pupil-spectator.

All the films in the sample could be used to provide examples of the epiphanic shot. They are rare in *Early Spring in February*, where the use of the close-up on a thoughtful face at the end of almost every scene precludes or substitutes for the epiphanic shot. One of the most striking examples in the sample is in *The Unfailing Beam*. Near the beginning, when Li Xia sets out on his mission, a number of epiphanic moments within a single scene combine to redundantly signify his heroic status and the importance of both the mission and the act of leaving his comrades-in-arms. After an establishing shot, he is shot from below, silhouetted against the sky (Figure 2.5). This framing is held for an epiphanic moment, before the camera pulls out to reveal two colleagues by his side, but they themselves then form a heroic triumvirate with Li Xia in the center (Figure 2.6). When Li Xia mounts his horse to leave, he is shot from below again, and there is a pause before he actually departs, again creating a tableau effect (Figure 2.7).

However, examples such as this are relatively rare, and the most common use of the epiphanic shot or moment is to end a scene, and to end a film. Only *Early Spring in February*, which ends with Tao Lan running after Xiao Jianqiu and then a pan up to empty sky, cannot really be said to end with an epiphanic shot. In *The Unfailing Beam* and *Bridge*, the endings are excessively epiphanic. In the former, Li Xia is eventually arrested and taken off to be executed. However, in the final shot of the film, he is shown signaling, facing the camera, and with a confident expression on his face. This shot is superimposed over others of the Communist armed forces on the move in such a way that Li Xia appears to be hovering in the clouds, and a heavenly chorus accompanies this. *Bridge* ends when the first train crosses the bridge after the repairs are completed, amidst much celebration. Following the gaze of one of the participants, the camera cuts to and holds a close-up of the red flag fluttering in the breeze (Figure 2.8).

Both *Bridge* and *The Unfailing Beam* are at the Yan'an end of Clark's Shanghai-Yan'an spectrum, and in both cases the triumphant endings are associated purely with socialist success. In *Li Shuangshuang*, *Woman Basketball Player No.5* and *Stage Sisters*, a slightly more complex situation prevails. Ma Ning has noted that the ending of *Stage Sisters* features two epiphanic shots, when Yuehong and Chunhua are reunited after the triumph of the Communists in 1949, and resolve to transform themselves and sing revolutionary opera henceforth.

Figures 2.5-2.7 Li Xia leaves Yan'an in *The Unfailing Beam*.

Figures 2.5-2.7 (Continued)

Associations connected with the restoration of interpersonal harmony also underlie epiphanic shots in the endings of *Woman Basketball Player No.5* and *Li Shuangshuang*. At the close of *Woman Basketball Player No.5*, everyone gathers at the airport to see the team off as they depart for a match overseas. After the aircraft has taken off, the camera does not cut to a close-up of the red flag fluttering in the breeze, as at the end of *Bridge*, but to a close-up of Lin Xiaojie's mother's face, gazing damp-eyed into the middle-distance (Figure 2.9). Lin Jie has been the last of the main characters to be brought back into the communal folds of the team and family, and she provides the link between the two spaces through her relationship with both coach Tian and Lin Xiaojie, signifying a harmonious relationship and integration of family and broader social concerns. The closing title is then superimposed over the plane, showing us what she sees.

The problem of harmonizing the personal and the social is one of the main themes of *Li Shuangshuang*, as her loyalty to the new commune system lead to conflict with her more conservative husband, Xiwang. By the end of the film, Xiwang has seen the error of his ways, and the film ends with an epiphanic close-up that tracks with the two of them as they walk along together, before cutting to an equally epiphanic static long shot of a bucolic

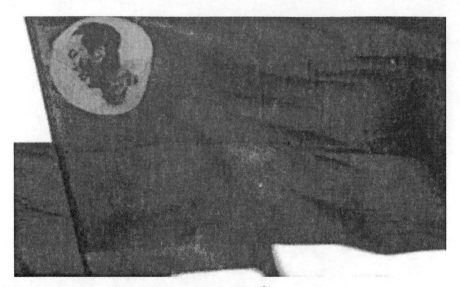

Figure 2.8 The red flag flies at the end of *Bridge*.

Figure 2.9 Lin Jie sees the team off at the end of *Woman Basketball Player No. 5*.

scene that is the final shot in the film. However, an additional element of ambiguity in this ending occurs when Xiwang walks ahead of his wife, exiting the penultimate shot before the cut to the bucolic scene. On the one hand, the fact that the camera stays on Shuangshuang's face could simply be a confirmation of her more important role. On the other hand, his action could also indicate that he is reasserting his traditional peasant patriarchal role as the household head with his wife following behind. However, Xiwang's restoration to this status depends upon yielding to his wife and recognizing the correctness of her values, so that he can be proud of her again. This and the comic mode of the entire film make for an ironic reading of Xiwang's reassertion of his status, but it does tend to confirm Judith Stacey's understanding of gender politics in China at this time as heavily linked to the Party's desire to maintain good relations with the traditional peasant patriarchy.[78]

The usage of epiphanic shots described so far has been positive and celebratory. This is the most common deployment, but on occasion an epiphanic shot may freeze a moment of irony or negativity for the pupil-spectator's consideration. In an earlier scene of *Li Shuangshuang* when Shuangshuang and Xiwang are getting along reasonably well, they disagree about who originated the idea of distribution according to labor. Was it Ma Kesi (the Chinese rendering of "Marx") or Lie Ning (the Chinese rendering of "Lenin")? The audience's superior knowledge allows it to appreciate Xiwang's bumpkin ignorance when he insists that it is the one whose family name is Ma (*"shi xing Ma"*), and the scene ends holding a close-up of their two faces deep in puzzled thought to create an ironic tableau effect. On the other hand, scenes of conflict may end with a tableau effect where the two of them are sulking and refusing to acknowledge each other.

C. Heightened Engagement

Through the operation of the patterns detailed above, the play of engagement and distanciation guiding the pupil-spectator through the films spreads throughout the sample. However, additional devices heighten engagement at certain points, giving a tempo and rhythm to the play. They simultaneously enhance identification with character emotions and thoughts and, by virtue of their very heightening quality, draw attention to themselves and so promote conscious reflection on the part of the pupil-spectator.

Instances of this heightened engagement include the close-up on the thoughtful face and the epiphanic shot at the end of a scene, and, in the case of the latter, particularly at the end of the film. The shot and reverse shot sequence is a third instance. The emphatic effect securing heightened engagement is often cinematically cued by the reduced distance between spectator and diegesis in the first of these three tropes, freezing of action or character in the frame in the second, and a combination of reduced distance between spectator and diegesis and increased tempo of cutting in the third.

These cinematic cues are also widely used in the Hollywood classical cinema, but in the Chinese classical cinema the primary effect is to heighten the didactic engagement of the pupil-spectator's attention.

The close-up on the thoughtful face and the epiphanic shot have already been discussed, but the uses of the reverse shot are many and need to be considered further. It has already been noted that one of the main functions of the shot and reverse shot sequence in *Li Shuangshuang* is to signify fragmentation and collapse of harmony within the world of the film. This occurs within an overall aesthetic where maintenance of characters within the same frame signifies bonds and harmony between them, and where they threaten to breach the frame as a sign of growing tension. Within this aesthetic, moving to a shot and reverse shot sequence, especially a direct point-of-view exchange, not only draws the pupil-spectator into identification with the characters involved, but signifies a heightening of the effect by exaggeration of the cinematic aesthetic itself. This overall pattern is confirmed by the corresponding avoidance of shot and reverse shot sequences in dialogue exchanges between people in a harmonious relationship in favor of medium shots or even long shots maintaining the characters within the frame. For example, when Shuangshuang and her female friends get together in the evening and decide to take part in the hydraulic construction work the next day, the camera cuts around them as they move around the room, maintaining the speakers in the same frame rather than opting for reverse shots.

The same overall pattern found in *Li Shuangshuang* seems to apply in all of the sample films. However, the films at the Yan'an end of Clark's spectrum, *Bridge* and *The Unfailing Beam*, use more full shots, longer takes, and make only very sparing use of cutting between characters or reverse shots in comparison to those at the Shanghai end of the scale, *Woman Basketball Player No.5*, *Li Shuangshuang*, and *Early Spring in February*. As a result, the latter films achieve a heightened pace and sense of drama throughout.

Instances of shot and reverse shot used for conflict and social disharmony are numerous in the other five sample films. Examples might include a scene in *Bridge* where one of the workers confesses that his slipshod work caused the furnace failure and he is then attacked by one of the other workers. After a shot and reverse shot exchange, the scene returns to full shots when others present intervene to resolve the dispute. In *The Unfailing Beam*, Li Xia and He Lanfang do not see eye to eye about the value of their work. This disagreement is also rendered as a shot and reverse shot sequence, reverting to full shots when he talks her round.

However, two ways of using the shot and reverse shot pattern with positive connotations also need to be noted. The first complements the conflict situation by drawing the pupil-spectator into heightened engagement with a situation just before reconciliation or reunion. In *The Unfailing Beam*, for example, He Lanfang goes to the jail to meet Li Xia on his release after his first arrest. As they see each other across the crowded room, this is rendered in a shot and reverse shot sequence ending with extreme close-ups of their faces before they are joined together in the one shot. In the logic of this formal operation, the face of one substitutes for the other in the frame with the cut, signifying both their bond and a powerful mutual emotional projection to the pupil-spectator. *Li Shuangshuang* features similar scenes when Shuangshuang and Xiwang make up and get back together. Perhaps unsurprisingly, the best example of this deployment in *Woman Basketball Player No.5* occurs when, after their many years of separation, Lin Jie and Tian Zhenhua meet again at the hospital where Lin Xiaojie is being treated for a knee injury.

The pattern with positive connotations heightens engagement in directly didactic exchanges. This trope takes two forms, depending on whether the exchange is between the authority figure or representative of the Party and one other person, or between the authority figure or representative of the Party and a group. In the former case, a simple shot and reverse shot sequence signifies the privileged moment and the precious exchange. However, unlike the other two instances, direct point-of-view is often eschewed in this pattern in favor of acute angles very close to the positions of the participants. Furthermore, where the other two instances involve balanced exchanges, this third pattern is more hierarchical. Longer takes in medium close-up are used for the one who transmits the lesson, but extreme close-ups of the awe-struck face of the enlightened one are often used to further emphasize the impact of this special moment. This pattern is used when Li Shuangshuang seeks advice from Party Secretary Liu in the commune office (Figures 2.10 and 2.11), and in many of the exchanges between Jiang Bo and Chunhua in *Stage Sisters*. In *The Unfailing Beam*, another scene in which He Lanfang doubts the task ends with a similar exchange when Li Xia educates He about the value of their work together.

This pattern is largely absent from the other three films in the sample. In *Early Spring in February*, the absence of a Party representative makes such scenes impossible. However, when Tao Lan casts Xiao Jianqiu as a wise man and seeks to learn from him, their exchanges are sometimes shot in this manner. In these cases, the close-up on the thoughtful face that ends the majority of scenes in this film is also a close-up on the face of someone enlightened as a result of the didactic experience.

Figures 2.10 - 2.11 Li Shuangshuang consults the Party Secretary

In *Woman Basketball Player No.5* and *Bridge*, however, the relative absence of this trope is because the Party representative who educates is dealing with a group of apprentice characters, rather than just one. In the former film, this is usually the team, and in the latter, all or some of the factory staff. Such group scenes are very common in all the films in the sample, with the possible exception of *Early Spring in February*, where the total absence of the Party precludes them. They have been discussed above in reference to the deployment of relays, and can best be termed meeting scenes. *Kaihui*, or holding a meeting, is one of the established patterns of life in the workplace and in all public organizations in the People's Republic of China. In filmic scenes of this activity, the shot and reverse shot exchange is rendered as an exchange between the one performing the didactic function and various members of the group addressed. Periodic establishing shots are used to provide orientation to the overall situation. The educator is usually positioned centrally in such establishing full shots, surrounded by an eagerly listening group, producing what has been termed a "Chinese chorus" effect in reference to Cultural Revolution films.[79] The shots of the listeners may be taken from a position from within the circle of people surrounding the educator, or outside.

In *Woman Basketball Player No.5*, the most pronounced instances are the various coaching sessions between Tian Zhenhua and the team, including the post-mortem session in Tian's office after a match has been lost. Lin Xiaojie is under pressure. She was on the reserve list, decided to attend a birthday party, but left a note saying where she could be contacted if she was needed. However, another player maliciously hid the note. The meeting begins with everyone arranged in a circle around Tian's desk. (Figure 2.12). At first, the camera cuts back and forth between Lin Xiaojie and the other players as they accuse her, in what is a group variation on the use of shot and reverse shot for conflict and fragmentation.

After he has let them have their say, Tian Zhenhua takes over. He speaks of his memories of national humiliation before the establishment of the People's Republic in 1949 and the importance of the cause, emphasizing that it was the nation and the people who were insulted before, not him as an individual. Here, the shot and reverse shot exchange between him and the players is of the didactic type. By the end of the exchange, most of the players have moved forward to surround Tian at his desk (Figure 2.13). Lin Xiaojie is isolated within the mise-en-scene, and becomes the sole object of the shot and reverse shot exchange. Although she is mortified rather than awe-struck, close-ups underline the impact of the meeting on her (Figure 2.14).

Figure 2.12 The team analyzes what went wrong in *Woman Basketball Player No. 5*. Lin Xiaojie is in the foreground with her back to the camera.

By the next morning, she is up before all the other players and training hard on the court, having learnt her lesson.

Bridge also has a multitude of large meeting scenes. Most are pep talks by the factory head with key members of his staff, followed by smaller group meeting scenes. A long sequence of this type occurs fairly early in the film when the factory staff members are attempting to decide how to tackle their problems. For most of the large meeting scene, the factory head takes on the didactic function, but as discussed above in the section on flashbacks, part of this scene is also given over to the memories of Lao Hou, the old worker. Whichever man performs the didactic function, the mise-en-scene and the camerawork follow the basic modified shot and reverse shot principles for the meeting scene. After cutaways to discussions elsewhere and the completion of this scene, the film moves on to three smaller meetings held on the shop floor. In these, although the transmitter of information is positioned centrally within the group and within the frame, the tendency is to avoid shot and reverse shot and keep the scenes brief.

Figure 2.13 Coach Tian remembers past bitterness in *Woman Basketball Player No. 5.*

Figure 2.14 Lin Xiaojie listens from a distance.

So widespread are the didactic meeting scene and the didactic one-on-one exchange that it could be argued a double rhythm operates in these films. One, as discussed, alternates between heightened engagement through shot and reverse-shot and other techniques and relatively less emphasized scenes. The other shifts between scenes of heightened engagement involving analysis, such as the didactic scenes just discussed, and those that are more action-oriented, such as the reunion and conflict scenes discussed. Overall, this double rhythm gives the films a dialectical movement between action and analysis within the didactic overdetermination of the Chinese classical cinema, noted by Ma Ning in many of the melodramatic films under his consideration as an aspect of the "macro- and micro-narrative" structure.[80]

D. Epistemological Command

The elements discussed so far help to explain the construction and maintenance of the pupil-spectator. A variety of additional devices encourage the assumption of a privileged position of epistemological command. First, the pupil-spectator often knows more than the characters in the diegesis. This special knowledge can include large plot elements or can occur on a much smaller scale within individual scenes. As an example of the latter, it has already been noted that Tian Zhenhua's flashback in *Woman Basketball Player No.5* contains many scenes that he himself could not have witnessed. These scenes show that Lin Jie had no responsibility for their separation. At the end of the flashback, the film returns to Tian in his office, wondering in voice-over why Lin Jie returned the medal he had given to her as a keepsake. The scenes in the flashback have already given the pupil-spectator this knowledge. Similarly, when it is later revealed that Lin Jie does not understand why Tian has returned her ring, his flashback has already given the pupil-spectator the answer. In regard to the plot connected to the team, the pupil-spectator sees Lin Xiaojie's enemy hide the note she left, and so is aware that there are circumstances mitigating her selfishness. In these circumstances, much of the hermeneutic engagement of the film is produced around enabling the characters to overcome misunderstanding by gaining the knowledge the film has given the pupil-spectator in advance.

This deployment of greater spectator knowledge is a classic melodrama device, building the pupil-spectator's engagement with issues of innocence and justice. But in the classical Chinese cinema it is further harnessed and subordinated to the pedagogical principle. For example, in *Early Spring in February*, the pupil spectator sees that the village is gossiping about his relationships with widow Wensao and Tao Lan well before Xiao Jianqiu himself realizes this. The didactic goal of the film includes demonstrating that individual acts of charity are inadequate and that full-scale social change is necessary. Therefore, prior knowledge is important in placing the pupil-spectator in an epistemological position close to the political position of the text. Prior knowledge also invokes a sense of moral and political command; when Xiao Jianqiu sees the light, he is doing what the spectator already knew was correct. That spectators may be less aware that the film has guided them towards that position enhances the sense of epistemological command.

On a smaller scale, numerous scenes are organized to give the pupil-spectator a sense of special insight. In *Stage Sisters*, a brief scene between Manager Tang and the woman who wishes to become the actresses' patroness reveals that he is plotting to separate the two sisters and has no selfless romantic interest in Yuehong. Yuehong does not know this. So, she cannot be blamed for falling for Tang, which is important for her later moral recuperation. Chunhua doesn't know it either, but she does not trust Tang, and therefore this scene not only transmits a sense of superior knowledge to the pupil-spectator, but simultaneously guides her or him as to which of the two sisters has the most trustworthy judgment.

This leads to a more general point regarding epistemological command. Camerawork is organized to give the pupil-spectator the "best" overall point of view of the action in a scene. In his work on the Chinese melodrama, Ma Ning has discussed this editing quality in relation to older painting and stage aesthetics. He notes that an individual painting may combine *zheng*, or orthodox frontal perspective on a scene, with *pian*, or unorthodox side views, to give the spectator a multi-dimensional perspective on a scene. In the theater, the Chinese outdoor stage has spectators seated on three sides, but the upper classes take the front-on positions equivalent to the *zheng* perspective, whereas the ordinary people would be seated around the sides. Ma goes on to use the terms *zheng* and *pian* to describe shots whose positions equate to these in his discussion of individual texts, including *Stage Sisters*.[81]

The sample texts indicate that the Chinese classical cinema has its own equivalent of these multi-perspectival possibilities. First, the general principle is to afford the spectator an ideal position that maximizes visibility of significant action. With the individual shot, as in the Hollywood classical cinema, camera and characters are positioned so that facial expressions are fully visible. In some films, such as *Bridge* and *The Unfailing Beam*, a perpendicular, front-on perspective is favored. In the case of other films, and *Stage Sisters* in particular, an angle to the action is more common, but not one that impedes facial expressions. This provides a certain correspondence to the *zheng* or orthodox perspective in painting.

Furthermore, the overall cutting logic within scenes of any length is often designed to take the spectator around the entire group involved in the action, so that the room, the characters and the settings are seen from all sides. This position also gives a sense of epistemological command, insofar as the spectator can receive the impression of being able to see everything there is to be seen. This pattern occurs in all the films in the sample. For example, in the scene at the beginning of *Early Spring in February* where Xiao Jianqiu is in the Tao family home, the camera begins with an establishing shot showing the table with the men arranged around it and the door through which Tao Lan is soon to enter along the left hand wall. After her entry, the characters get up and move around, and the cutting takes the camera round the room, so to speak, moving to the right of the table and round behind it, all the while giving the spectator good views of relevant facial expressions, be it a speaker or someone who is reacting, as it also gives an all-round view of the scene.

This method appears to exceed the 180-degree rule of the Hollywood classical cinema, which forbids cutting over an imaginary 180-degree line corresponding to the axis of action for fear of changes in screen direction that might confuse the viewer.[82] However, most cuts that go over the 180-degree line in the Chinese classical cinema avoid confusion, partly because the large number of characters interacting and moving about in these scenes often make it hard to establish a 180-degree axis in the first place, and partly because prior establishing shots and full shots have provided the spectator with sufficient orientation.

Most shots that go over the 180-degree line in the Chinese classical cinema are not used in any particular meaningful or systematic manner, but are subordinated to the principle of maintaining frontality and motivated by character movement. The one exception is when a large angle of cut over the 180-degree line is used to mark a sudden dramatic shift. For example, in the scene of Li Xia's departure in *The Unfailing Beam*, a frontal shot of him with one other soldier on either side of him cuts as they turn to a shot from a position directly opposite (Figure 2.15 and Figure 2.16). This marks the significance of Li Xia's leaving Yan'an, symbolically suggesting a clear line between two spaces, one now behind him. Similarly, in *Early Spring in February*, an example is connected to Tao Lan's flashback to a scene by a lake where she saw Xiao Jianqiu before. This occurs as he is playing a piano piece called, significantly in terms of the overall concerns of the film, "Hesitation." The cut over the 180-degree line marks her sudden memory and also the dramatic shift from him playing the piano to her remembering. At the beginning of the scene, Tao Lan enters and stands to the left of the piano

Figures 2.15 - 2.16 Cutting across the line in *The Unfailing Beam*.

as Xiao begins to play. The first four shots of the piano are from the right side of the piano. The fifth shot cuts over the axis to a position behind Tao on the left side of the piano. She walks across the room, and the sixth shot is a close-up of her face. The seventh shot shows us what she is looking at, namely Xiao Jianqiu playing the piano, and the eighth shot is another close-up of her face, which then dissolves into the flashback. After the flashback, the film dissolves back into a close-up of her face. She is then shown walking back over to the piano, the camera moving with her, and to the left of the piano. The camera finishes in a position similar to that of the fifth shot on the left of the piano, and so this shot is a sort of reverse of the procedure. The next shot cuts back across the axis of action to the right of the piano, the side it was on at the beginning of the scene.

The other main way in which epistemological command is evoked is the implication of widely circulated cultural knowledge and codes to guide the pupil-spectator's interpretation of the film. This knowledge and codes cover all manner of things, but two effects can be illustrated. One is the invocation of general political and ethical knowledge that the spectator is presumed to have already but which characters do not have. The second is the deployment of commonly circulated textual conventions that make the film eminently readable for the spectator, in the sense of Barthes's distinction between the readerly and the writerly.[83]

To deal with political and ethical knowledge first, although the Chinese classical cinema is didactic, it does not presume its spectators to be entirely ignorant of the lessons it seeks to teach. Rather, it is part and parcel of a wide array of Chinese didactic institutions and discourses that repeat the same lessons redundantly to reinforce their effect. For example, *Li Shuang-shuang* is not designed to introduce the idea of the commune and its benefits to the pupil-spectator for the first time. This can be observed in the opening dispute over the taking of commune firewood for private use. There are no cinematic tropes indicating that Shuangshuang's objections to this practice are correct, nor does a Party figure appear to guide correct resolution of the dispute and, by deferral, the pupil-spectator. It is simply assumed that the spectator already knows what is right and wrong. Furthermore, unless spectators are able to take up this position at the outset, they will not enjoy the comedy of Xiwang's ignorance, or derive any pleasure from Shuangshuang's triumph and the restoration of their relationship.

Other films in the sample function similarly. With those films set in the past, the pupil-spectator has the advantage of ethical hindsight, so to speak. For example, the hermeneutic of *Early Spring in February* assumes that the pupil-spectators are one up on Xiao Jianqiu and Tao Lan. By virtue of their prior knowledge that revolution is the only way to solve China's problems, the question of the film becomes whether and how Xiao and Tao will also come to this realization and act appropriately. In *Stage Sisters*, a similar relationship is set up between the pupil-spectator and the two sisters.

Knowing the correct resolution of the problem posed by each film in advance is not only a matter of prior political and ethical knowledge. It is also a textual convention. Just as the Hollywood classical cinema privileges the happy ending defined by the constitution of the heterosexual couple, so the classical Chinese cinema also privileges political happy endings. Both types of classical cinema depend upon a certain suspension of this knowledge for hermeneutic engagement. To these cinematic textual conventions might be added all the others that have been outlined in this chapter. Other instances of cinematic conventions enhancing the readability of the mainland Chinese classical text and hence the pupil-spectator's sense of epistemological command would include conventionalized punctuation devices, such as the wipe, the dissolve, the fade to black, and so forth. Generally speaking, these devices are used in ways similar to those found in the Hollywood classical cinema. A dissolve with a close-up of a face signifies a flashback, a fade to black signifies the end of a sequence, and so forth.

In addition to the specifically cinematic conventions, rhetorical conventions drawn from other discourses are also invoked. Some of these have already been noted in previous discussion of traditional sources for narrative and characterization, for example. Another specific and localized example is the borrowing of stage conventions for the shooting of journey montages. On the traditional Chinese stage, a journey was signified in an abbreviated manner by having actors move back and forth across the stage in different directions.[84] Similarly, in the two films that represent journeys, *Stage Sisters* and *Bridge*, the montage abbreviates and changes in screen direction from shot to shot are used.

The example of the journey montage is fairly specific, but other instances are more generalized. The question of right and left aesthetics as an extrapolation of *yin* and *yang* principles provides an example. Discussing the Chinese melodramatic film, Ma Ning argues that the ancient Chinese cosmological principle of interpreting the world in terms of the interrelated (rather than oppositional) binary terms known as *yin* and *yang* acts both as general cultural decoding knowledge a spectator brings to a film and overdetermining aesthetic principles for the films he examines. The various manifestations of this *yin-yang* overdetermination Ma cites are at least as numerous and various as the manifestations of the didactic overdetermination that have been detailed here.[85] *Yin* is associated with left and *yang* with right. Ma traces the manifestations of this in traditional theatrical aesthetics and argues that it also has a rigorous presence in the use of screen direction and left-hand and right-hand sides of the frame in the films he analyses.[86] For example, a pan to the right might be expected to be a pan to the positive and a pan to the left to the negative. Ma produces numerous examples to support his argument. It is plausible that the generalized significance in Chinese culture of left and right would predispose the spectator to look for codings that depend upon this significance. However, detailed examination of

the films of the mainland Chinese classical cinema, many of which fall into
the melodrama category Ma examines, suggests left-right may not be as rig-
orously and consistently manifested as Ma suggests

Examining the first backstage scene in *Stage Sisters*, Ma finds various
bipolar principles at work, including the organization of spatial relations in
a series of shots according to *yin-yang* aesthetics whereby positive characters
and actions take place on the right, and negative characters and those acted
upon are on the left.[87] In the first shot, for example, Yuehong is positioned
on the right with her father, as she pleads with him to take Chunhua, a run-
away bride at this early point in the narrative, into the troupe. The manager,
Uncle Xin, resists this idea and is to their left. When Xin takes over the action in the next shot, forcing Chunhua to leave, Ma claims he is shown
frame right. However, the situation is not simple, with much cutting and
movement from left to right of frame for all characters. The next shot further complicates matters. Here, Yuehong's father intervenes to plead Chunhua's case with Xin. Ma makes no comment about left-right aesthetics and
spatial relations in regard to this particular shot, but Yuehong's father
intervenes from the left and Xin is on the right of the frame. In this instance,
Yuehong's father is both the positive character and the one initiating action,
but he is on the left, whereas the one acted upon and negative, Xin, is on the
right. (Figure 2.17)

To complicate matters further, Teshome Gabriel has noted another type
of left-right aesthetics that is entirely contrary to Ma's *yin-yang* derived
left-right aesthetics. Discussing films made during the Cultural Revolution
period of 1966 to 1976, Gabriel argues that, in accordance with Marxist
politics where the left is the positive and the right the negative force, heroes
and heroines enter from the left and the left is privileged as the positive space
in the frame.[88] Ma acknowledges this argument briefly in his thesis, noting
that a "leftist" character may be found on the left and a "rightist" character
on the right.[89] In a more recent work, he has developed this aspect of his argument further, noting that in *Stage Sisters*, Chunhua is usually positioned
on the left-hand side of the screen. He argues that in the pre-revolutionary
part of the film, this signifies her oppressed female status, while in the
post-revolutionary section, it signifies her liberated socialist status.[90]

However, if left can be positive or negative, morally and politically, this
does seem to raise some questions about the applicability of this system.
Left-right aesthetics may not apply all the time, and the way in which they
apply may vary. However, although left-right aesthetics may not be straight-
forward, awareness of their polysemic possibilities is so generalized in Chinese culture that they may still function as an instance of the invocation of

Figure 2.17 Yuelong's father approaches Manager Xin from the left in *Stage Sisters*.

external, socially circulated, textual knowledge as part of the parcel of effects encouraging a sense of epistemological command in the spectator in the Chinese classical cinema.

Chapter 3

ENTERING FORBIDDEN ZONES AND EXPOSING WOUNDS: REWRITING SOCIALIST HISTORY

> Recently, a few works have broken into "forbidden zones," caused a sensation in cultural circles, attracted sizeable audiences, and been well-received.

— Si Ning, *Film Art*[1]

The emphasis on representation and political line in the Chinese classical cinema meant that theme was the basis of both production and critical discussion. Therefore, although the slogan "let themes take the lead" was only explicitly used during the Cultural Revolution, in fact it described the underlying logic of the Chinese classical cinema between 1949 and 1976.[2] This emphasis is clear in the different taxonomies used by the Hollywood and Chinese classical cinemas. The market-oriented Hollywood studio system regulated production through the classification system of genres, which included not only subject matter but also stylistic characteristics, settings, typical characters, and so forth. Chinese production, on the other hand, was organized according to subject matter (*ticai*) after 1949, regardless of other differences amongst films within subject matter classifications. The Chinese *Film Art Dictionary* makes this distinction quite clear in its entries for the terms "*ticai*" and "*leixing dianyinglun*" (genre theory), where it specifies the latter as a foreign system of classification.[3]

In China's planned command economy before Deng Xiaoping's reforms, film production was planned at annual meetings attended by studio heads and Film Bureau representatives.[4] Quotas of films with various types of subject matter (*ticai*) were determined according to policy needs. A studio would be told to produce so many rural films promoting the latest line on agriculture, so many films about the old society to remind audiences how lucky they are today, and so on.[5]

One of the overdetermining constants during this period was a Chinese communist myth of history, in a structuralist and structuring sense of a taken-for-granted master narrative.[6] According to this grand narrative, as Lyotard might call it, prior to 1949, life was bad, except in those liberated areas where the Communist Party already held sway. After the establishment of the People's Republic in 1949, everything was good and progressing steadily towards a communist utopia.[7] As early as the *Yan'an Talks*, Mao had stated that although works of exposure (*baolu wenxue*) were appropriate to the critique of the old society, they were not appropriate to works representing the liberated areas controlled by the Party, being neither realistic nor serving the Party's political goals.[8]

As a result, during the 1949 to 1976 period, there were no representations of any problems that could be attributed to errors by the Party. The only exceptions were the few ill-fated texts produced during the 1956 Hundred Flowers Campaign. In this campaign, Mao loosened state control but then clamped down again when his action precipitated unexpected levels of criticism.[9] All other narratives were necessarily comedies if set during or ending in the post-1949 period and necessarily tragedies if they ended before 1949 and were set outside the areas liberated before then.

The Chinese cinema underwent few structural changes after the arrest of the Gang of Four on 6 October 1976. However, discursive changes were more extensive. This chapter traces the breakdown of the Chinese communist myth of history as manifested thematically. This breakdown did not occur in one fell swoop, but rather in increments between 1976 and 1980. Initially, the image of steady progress towards socialist utopia was threatened by detailing the crimes of the Gang of Four, but great efforts were made to contain this threat. Later, these crimes extended further back, calling into question the whole of the Cultural Revolution, and eventually the whole of the revolutionary period.[10]

In trying to account for these changes, this chapter considers the close ties between the state and cultural production. It notes that film production was closely integrated into cultural production in general and cultural policy, and therefore attempts to locate changes in relation to broader cultural changes.[11] Furthermore, the chapter notes that subject matter was particularly easily translated into broader political meanings not specific to cinematic discourse. Therefore, it also attempts to locate changes in cinematic subject matter in relation to broad political changes.

THE INITIAL RESPONSE: CONTINUITY AND CONTAINMENT

A. State and Party Politics

The death of Mao on 9 September 1976 and the arrest of the Gang of Four within a month might seem such an indisputably major turning point in Chinese history that it would require an admission that things had gone seriously awry. This is indeed how it is seen now. However, such an interpretation was by no means inevitable. There were well-established rhetorical procedures to contain such ruptures and maintain continuity, and these were applied again in 1976.

Earlier shifts in Party policy and changes in leadership had occurred without disturbance to the grand narrative myth of Chinese communist history as a path of constant progress. When Mao's 1956 Hundred Flowers Campaign precipitated unexpected levels of criticism of the Party, it was followed by the 1957 Anti-Rightist crackdown. When the failure of the 1958 Great Leap Forward resulted in starvation in the early 1960s, it was rapidly abandoned. However, the disputes that preceded these shifts were relatively short-lived. They were also kept inside the Party and outside public discourse, and so there was neither public discussion nor admission of error in previous policy.

Two patterns of dealing with post-revolutionary problems helped maintain the communist myth of history. The most common was to represent problems as leftovers from the feudal past or "old society." The sample films from chapter two set in the post-revolutionary period, *The Bridge*, *Woman Basketball Player No.5* and *Li Shuangshuang*, all follow this model. In Shanghai-style films such as *Woman Basketball Player No.5*, basically sound characters have ideological problems that can be solved. In Yan'an-style films, the character embodies the ideological problem entirely, in which case the only solution is to root him or her out. This logic is also implicit in the second option, which was to represent problems after the revolution as the result of a foreign threat. Both these strategies externalize problems, by representing them either as incursions from the past (the old society) or from outside (a foreign threat). Divisions and disputes can be dealt with by branding the losers as counter-revolutionaries and/or foreign spies. Homi Bhabha has explored the similarities between the construction of the individual and the national collective. In both, threats to coherence and unity are repressed internally and, once out of view, projected onto others as part of the effort to build and maintain a coherent individual or collective self-identity with clear boundaries.[12] The model of socialism in one country made nationalism part of the Chinese communist project, enabling "othering" either on the basis of nation or class.

After the fall of the Gang of Four, the initial emphasis was on continuity. Just as before, there was no admission of error on the part of the Party or even of policy change. The arrest of the Gang was hailed as a triumph of Mao's policies. His anointed successor, Hua Guofeng, had ascended to power in early 1976 in the wake of Zhou Enlai's death. Hua's stake in policies established before the fall of the Gang led him to pronounce the "two whatevers" line less than a month after their arrest: "Whatever decisions Chairman Mao has made, those we must firmly uphold; whatever Chairman Mao has directed, that we must from beginning to end without any exceptions respect."[13] Therefore, there was neither criticism of the Cultural Revolution nor acknowledgment of any change.

In accordance with this logic, the Gang was "othered." Officially, they were arrested for attempting a coup.[14] They were branded as counter-revolutionaries, ultra-rightists, and revisionists determined to restore capitalism and exercise fascist dictatorship. Ironically, this terminology not only connoted both the foreign and the old, but it was also the same terminology that the Gang had used against their own enemies. The campaign against the Gang continued through to the Third Plenum of the Central Committee in December 1978, when it was declared successfully completed.

At first, attention to the Gang's "crimes" was largely confined to events immediately prior to Mao's death, when they had been fighting Deng Xiaoping. Condemned earlier during the Cultural Revolution, Deng had been rehabilitated in early 1975 and was pushing for the rehabilitation of many of his supporters. At the end of the year, with the help of Mao, the Gang had launched a campaign against Deng and the so-called "Right Deviationist Wind to reverse correct verdicts." After the downfall of the Gang, it was claimed that their campaign was aimed not only at Deng and his followers, but also at Premier Zhou Enlai and even Chairman Mao himself.

B. Policy and Criticism in Literature and the Arts

Operating under the dictum from Mao's *Yan'an Talks* that literature and art must serve politics, the cultural sphere was closely tied to power struggles within the Party. Indeed, cultural works were often chosen as allegorical vehicles in power struggles. For example, in 1961, the Right wing of the Party used a play set in the Ming dynasty titled *Hai Rui Dismissed From Office* to call for a turn in their direction, but this provoked Mao. Ultimately, he responded by launching the Cultural Revolution with a campaign against the play's author, Wu Han, in 1965.[15] Similarly, when fighting Deng Xiaoping's return to power in 1975, the Maoists launched a campaign against a character in the ancient novel *Water Margin*, who could be seen as an allegory for either Zhou Enlai, Deng Xiaoping, or both.[16] In 1976, one of the first indications of the fall of the Gang was a *People's Daily* article on 21 October detailing revolutionary author Lu Xun's attack on the critic Di Ke in 1936: Di Ke was the pseudonym of Gang member Zhang Chunqiao.[17]

Literature, the arts, and propaganda had been a stronghold of the Gang. Therefore, the drive to expose their crimes devoted considerable attention to literature and the arts. Details concerning Gang suppression of works believed to support Deng were released immediately. One well-known example was the film *The Pioneers*. Completed in 1974 and suspected of allegorically supporting Deng, it had been suppressed soon after its release in February 1975. After the fall of the Gang, it was revealed that Mao had told the Gang to stop "nit-picking" over this work in July 1975, making it possible to draw a line between the Gang and Mao.[18] Simultaneously, films like *Spring Shoots* (1975) and *Counterattack* (1976) that had been made in response to the Gang's call for works supporting the struggle against capitalist roaders such as Deng now suddenly changed from exemplary positive to exemplary negative films. *Counterattack* had been completed just before the Gang's fall and therefore only ever screened as a negative example.[19]

Large ongoing campaigns were constructed around these two films, but other newly negative examples were also being written about even before the end of 1976. *The Jubilant Xiaoliang River* is a typical instance. Coverage of this Shanghai Film Studio product in Shanghai's *Wenhui News* gives a sense of how its shifting representation might have appeared to the ordinary citizen. In August, following the film's release, the newspaper had carried an extensive article praising the film as an excellent exposition on capitalist roaders in positions of power within the Party and popular resistance to them. This was accompanied by a letter of praise from an amateur critics group, and a professional critic argued that no criticism of the film could be based on purely aesthetic grounds, as all criticism could ultimately be traced to class struggle.[20]

Less than four months later, after the fall of the Gang the same newspaper carried an equally thorough critique of the film attributed to its production team. This article was still concerned to identify and expose capitalist roaders. But whereas the film and the earlier articles had identified the character of veteran Party leader Vice-Director Xia as the capitalist roader, the new article defended him. Instead, it pointed an accusing finger at the young Party activist responsible for attacking Xia in the film, production brigade team leader Zhou Changlin, and the Gang of Four and their henchmen responsible for production of the film. Here, the critique claimed, were the true counter-revolutionaries and capitalist roaders.

In support of their argument, the writers detailed the secrecy shrouding production of the film; if the film had really been part of the anti-capitalist roader, anti-Deng Xiaoping campaign — still being upheld after the fall of the Gang — secrecy would have been unnecessary. They also noted Xia's exemplary class background and political record, arguing that people with such backgrounds did not fit Mao's description of capitalist roaders. Such character construction indicated the film was part of a covert attack on the Party and state leadership. Furthermore, characters like Xia are made to mouth not only Deng's words but also those of other leaders, sullying them by association with Deng. Because the film did not make Deng its explicit target, this was interpreted to mean a space was being made to extend the attack from Deng to other Party leaders including Premier Zhou and Chairman Mao. Although Deng was to be restored to some of his posts in 1977, at this point the downfall of the Gang had not precipitated an end to their campaign against him, so an attack on him was not itself an error.[21]

C. *Film Production*

The same pattern of continuity and containment is even stronger in the cinema, because the time lag incurred in film production made it slower to respond to change than less technically complex art forms. There was an initial downturn in output after the fall of the Gang, indicating maybe that filmmakers were wary of how lasting any new policy shift might be.[22] There had been a rapid increase in output after large-scale resumption in 1974. Although that year only nine features that were not recordings of stage productions were made, by 1976 twenty-six were produced. In 1977, after the fall of the Gang, the figure slumped to seventeen, just above the 1975 figure of fifteen.[23]

In terms of themes, many features made in 1977 and even as late as 1978 could equally well have been made in the last years of the Cultural Revolution. This is symptomatic of two characteristics immediately following fall of the Gang. As indicated in Hua's "Two Whatevers" slogan, the fall was positioned as an isolated event. Second, its significance was downplayed. This can be seen even in the films set in what is now referred to as the Cultural Revolution decade (1966-1976): many made in 1977 and 1978 do not acknowledge that what was later proclaimed as a major historical rupture had even occurred.

Three of the four 1977 films set in the Cultural Revolution decade could have been made during the decade. *Bear Print* is a spy film that differs from *The Unfailing Beam* only in the period of its early seventies setting and the source of the enemy spies. Just as the KMT spies in *The Unfailing Beam* were shown to have a taste for Western luxury, the same is true for the "revisionist" (i.e. Soviet bloc) spies and their henchmen in *Bear Print*. The Chinese henchmen of the "revisionists" are not implied to be in cahoots with the Gang. *Youth* is a typical Yan'an-style soldier hero story. In this case, the main character, Yamei, is a deaf mute girl whose faculties are restored by treatment during the Cultural Revolution, still portrayed as an inspiring event. *New Song of the Wei River* focuses on "Learning from Dazhai in Agriculture," a Cultural Revolution Stakhanovite campaign still being upheld.

In 1977, only one feature film and one recording of a stage production joined saturation attacks on the Gang of Four, such as the writings on *The Jubilant Xiaoliang River* discussed above, which took over the other media almost immediately after their downfall. Most recordings of stage productions are excluded from general consideration here, but *October Victory* records a variety show celebrating the Gang's downfall in songs and dances. Titles include "We Sing of Esteemed Premier Zhou," "The Sun is Reddest, Chairman Mao is Dearest," and "Resolutely Smash the 'Gang of Four'." They feature a pounding beat and easily memorized choruses, such as "The 'Gang of Four' are all bad things!" ("*sirenbang dou shi huai dongxi*"), much like the "model works" of the Cultural Revolution decade itself. The only change is in the objects of *October Victory*'s aggressive attack.

The sole 1977 anti-Gang feature film also has "October" in its title. Perhaps the emphasis on a particular month in both *October Victory* and *October Storm* is a testament to the determination to contain the potential disruption they might threaten. Indeed, in the case of *October Storm*, the entire film takes place in the few weeks between Mao's death and the arrest of the Gang, without even a single flashback to contaminate any earlier period. Released on the first anniversary of the fall of the Gang,[24] the themes of the film also stress continuity. Its heroes are two veteran cadres, factory Party Secretary He Fan and Political Commissar Xu Jian. Like Vice-Director Xia, the veteran cadre who is attacked in *The Jubilant Xiaoliang River* and rises like a phoenix in the post-downfall critiques of the film, He Fan and Xu Jian's commitment to the Party and the Revolution dates back well before the Revolution itself, and this is frequently mentioned. Loyalty to Chairman

Mao and his heirs is also redundantly stressed. The film opens with Xu Jian riding in the back of a Red Flag limousine, reading a newspaper. The camera zooms in to a close-up of headlines announcing the death of Mao and exhorting readers to follow his heir, Hua Guofeng. Arriving at a hospital where He Fan is recuperating, he finds He has left some calligraphy on his desk. Another zoom in and we see it also reminds us to be loyal to Mao and Hua. Finally, Xu discovers his own son, Xuesong is in He's room. "Xuesong" means "Learn from the pine," a tree noted in China for steadfastness, and so loyal is Xuesong that later he dies at He's side.

The second theme of the film, also found in the critiques of *The Jubilant Xiaoliang River*, is that the Gang tried to overthrow Mao's line and the Revolution under cover of apparent revolutionary premises. When He and Xu talk in the hospital grounds, Xu reminds He that after Lenin's death figures such as Trotsky threatened to derail the Soviet revolution, implying that the same could happen in China. Two henchmen of the Gang try to undermine the loyalty of He and Xu's followers, but the masses are not so easily fooled and use their knowledge of Mao's line to see through these plots.

All eleven of the 1978 films under consideration here are also either on themes that display complete continuity with pre-1976 films or confine their critique to the Gang. However, there is a shift in the ratio, with eight anti-Gang films and three thematically continuous with pre-1976 themes. The latter three are *Salimake*, *Blue Skies Defense Line* and *Thank You, Comrade*. *Salimake* is about the provision of educational opportunities for a national minority set at the beginning of the Cultural Revolution. The entire film is told from the point of view of Salimake, who remembers this period with joy. Set in the early 1970's, *Blue Skies Defense Line* is another spy drama much like *Bear Print*, but this time with the Kuomintang forces on Taiwan as the enemy. Finally, *Thank You, Comrade*, set in 1973, is an effort to extol the joys of being a sanitation worker and counter the prejudices they face. It could have been made any time after 1949.

Whereas these three films are much like their 1977 counterparts, most of the anti-Gang films made in 1978 do display some differences from *October Storm*. Only *Emergency* and *The Eventful Years* confine themselves to 1976 and focus almost entirely on loyalty to Mao's line and respect for veteran cadres. The six other anti-Gang films are set earlier, in 1974-5, and extend their critique of the effects of the Gang further, marking a change from the thematic emphasis on continuity and containment immediately after the fall of the Gang.

DENG XIAOPING'S POWER STRUGGLE: EXTENDING THE CRITIQUE

A. State and Party Politics

However, if anything, this extension of the critique in 1978 films was belated. An ongoing power struggle after the fall of the Gang of Four had appeared much earlier. Furthermore, this ongoing struggle was not between Hua Guofeng and Gang followers, but involved other forces. The political situation in seventies China was more complex than a two-line struggle.

In the two years immediately before Mao's death, most historians see a three-line factional struggle in the Party. Harry Harding calls the three factions the revolutionary Maoists, the restorationists, and the reformists. The revolutionary Maoists were headed by Mao's wife, Jiang Qing, and her three colleagues, soon to be known as the Gang of Four. They wished to uphold the radical policies of the Cultural Revolution. The restorationists, who gathered around Hua Guofeng after his 1976 rise to power, wished to see a gradual return to pre-Cultural Revolution policies. The reformists, headed by Deng Xiaoping, wished to go further, relaxing central control and introducing elements of the market economy, including opening up to foreign trade, in an effort to improve material conditions. Because this faction wished to undertake policies criticized both before and after the Cultural Revolution, they stood to gain most from public repudiation of past policies and admission of errors by the Party.

Deng Xiaoping himself had been criticized and removed from power at the beginning of the Cultural Revolution in 1966. However, in 1973, with the help of Premier Zhou Enlai, he made a comeback. By 1975, Zhou was ailing and in need of a successor. At the Fourth National People's Congress in January, he called for the Four Modernizations (of agriculture, industry, science and technology, and national defense), which emphasized material construction rather than class struggle and revolutionary politics.[25] Deng was restored to three important positions; Vice-Chairman of the Party, First Vice-Premier, and Chief of Staff of the People's Liberation Army.

In the ensuing months, a struggle broke out between Deng and the future Gang of Four. In January 1976, Zhou Enlai's death posed the question of his succession. A compromise candidate, Hua Guofeng, was made acting premier in February. In April, the *qingming* holiday to commemorate the dead became the occasion for public mourning in Tiananmen Square by Zhou Enlai's supporters. When the revolutionary Maoists attempted to suppress this activity, demonstrations broke out. The revolutionary Maoists held Deng responsible for the demonstrations, which were judged counter-revolutionary by the Party, and he was stripped of his positions. Hua Guofeng was confirmed as Premier.[26]

This brief account demonstrates that Hua was at least an indirect beneficiary of Deng's downfall and of the Cultural Revolution policies aimed against him. He did not stand to benefit from any questioning licensed by the downfall of the Gang that went back more than a few months. In contrast, Deng was a victim of the Cultural Revolution whose temporary rehabilitation was associated with the late Premier Zhou and his Four Modernizations policy. If he was to be rehabilitated again, he had to push the critique of the Gang back beyond the months immediately leading up to their arrest, in an effort to associate them with his own second downfall in early 1976.

In fact, the Cultural Revolution had deposed many powerful figures within the Party. Now that Hua was standing by the Cultural Revolution, they had to rally round someone else if they were to return to power. The groundswell of support for Deng grew within the Party during early 1977, and led to his reappointment to his three former posts at the Third Plenum of the Tenth Central Committee of the Communist Party of China in July 1977.[27] Deng's rehabilitation opened the way for the reconsideration of verdicts against many others; a process which progressed in fits and starts through the rest of the decade.[28] This was the first major public indication of the ongoing struggle between Deng and Hua.

In August 1977, Hua acknowledged the combined power of the restorationist faction that he was most directly dependent upon and Deng's reformists by declaring that the "first cultural revolution" was at an end and writing the Four Modernizations into the Party constitution at the Eleventh Party Congress. While this did not entail the admission of past errors by the Party, it was shift away from the revolutionary Maoist line.

In 1978, the reinterpretation of post-Liberation history became possible. Deng stood to gain from increased critique of past policies, whereas Hua stood to lose. Deng and his followers revived an old slogan of Mao's, "seek truth from facts." In May, it was coupled with Deng's own slogan "practice is the sole criterion of truth." These two slogans were posed against Hua's "two whatevers." Where Hua's slogans endorsed the past, Deng's opened it up for reconsideration.

Efforts were made to broaden the debate around the Gang by reconsidering their status. In May 1978, they were directly paralleled to Lin Biao, who had attempted a coup in 1971. This represented them not as an isolated aberration, but as part of an older pattern. In September, the same month Deng directly criticized the "two whatevers" for the first time, the Gang were reassessed as ultra-leftists. Hitherto, Hua and his followers had referred to them as ultra-rightists. This was significant, because Deng's past errors had been deemed rightist, whereas Hua was associated with the Cultural Revolution, which was regarded as a left-wing event.

In November 1978, the rightwards shift was affirmed by two reassessments of history. First, although the Anti-Rightist campaign of 1957 was not officially deemed an error yet, all those condemned as rightists were rehabilitated. This indicated how far Deng was prepared (or forced) to reach out to make alliances, because he himself had been a major persecutor of "rightists" in 1957. Second, the 1976 Tiananmen Square Incident was reassessed as being a revolutionary rather than counter-revolutionary event. Hua's ascent to the premiership was based on Deng's dismissal because of his association with Tiananmen. Therefore, this revision represented a major blow against Hua and presaged his eclipse by Deng.

At the same time, popular manifestations of support for Deng in the form of wall posters grew and the so-called Democracy Wall movement took off. The posters stuck on Democracy Wall called for all manner of reforms, including what Wei Jingsheng called the "Fifth Modernization," namely the introduction of political democracy.[29] Deng encouraged these activities, and in December the adoption of many of his reform policies at the Third Plenum of the Eleventh Central Committee of the Communist Party affirmed his control.[30] Early in 1979, his follower Hu Yaobang was made Secretary General of the Party and all the "whateverists" except for Hua were forced to resign from the Central Committee.

B. Policy and Criticism in Literature and the Arts

Jiang Qing's close involvement in culture from the earliest days of the Cultural Revolution licensed broad-ranging criticism of Cultural Revolution literature and arts policy very early on in the post-Mao period, at a time when other aspects of the Cultural Revolution were still being held up as achievements. For example, in May 1977, before Deng's rehabilitation had been confirmed by the Third Plenum of the Tenth Central Committee, the national daily newspapers were calling for more variety in literature and the arts and criticizing Jiang Qing's Theory of the Three Prominences, which called for emphasis to be placed on heroes.

By the end of the year, pre-Cultural Revolution works were being republished and pre-Cultural Revolution films were being selectively re-released.[31] Zhou Yang, a cultural commissar severely criticized during the Cultural Revolution, made a public reappearance, although it was another year before he was formally rehabilitated. Jiang Qing's "theory of the sinister

line," which had led to the banning of pre-Cultural Revolution literature and
arts on the grounds that they had been perverted by the activities of Liu Shaoqi and his followers, was repudiated. Even the so-called "middle characters" that were not clear heroes were endorsed again, provided they were
transformed by the end of the narrative. In 1978, various cultural figures condemned during the Cultural Revolution returned to prominence and organizations and publications that had been closed down were reopened.

Liberalization in production and criticism kept pace with and helped to
define the themes that policy changes in 1977 and 1978 were making permissible. For example, in November 1977, Liu Xinwu's short story "The
Class Teacher" created debate by pushing the boundaries.[32] Its main characters included two students whose lives and psychologies had been seriously damaged by Gang of Four policies in education. Therefore, Liu was
risking the charge of writing "exposure literature" (*baolu wenxue*) on the
post-revolutionary era. However, Liu and the short story survived the criticism that followed.[33]

Liu's survival encouraged more risk-taking in 1978, as did the now established literary policy calling for a diversity of themes and themes attacking the damage done by the Gang of Four. Liu's follow-up story, "The Place
of Love," published in September 1978 and discussed in further detail in
Chapter 5, became the first love story published since 1965.[34] Lu Xinhua's
short story, "The Scar," published in August 1978, pushed exposure of
Gang crimes and their after-effects to new heights by writing the first socialist tragedy. In this story, a girl rejects her mother while the latter is being criticized during the Cultural Revolution. Although the mother is rehabilitated
later, she dies before her repentant daughter can reach her.[35] Again, this provoked debate, and following its justification, a whole new round of works
in 1979 exposing socialist tragedies attributable to the Gang of Four. These
works became known as "scar literature."[36]

C. Film Production

The extension of the anti-Gang critique in films prior to Deng's elevation
during the Third Plenum at the end of 1978 was evidence of the ongoing
power struggle. However, compared to the rapidly expanding and often daring range of literary themes mentioned above, it was also relatively weak.
The time delays involved in film production and the relatively high degree
of state and Party control made it difficult for filmmakers to respond as
quickly as other artists. A comparison between the three 1978 films whose
themes could have been found in any pre-1976 movie and the six films that
extended the anti-Gang critique beyond the months of 1976 immediately

preceding their fall, along with consideration of their literary equivalents, is revealing.

All three films that show continuity with the Cultural Revolution period are set well before the mid-seventies and focus on themes not directly connected with Party politics or the central leadership. *Salimake* takes place around the beginning of the Cultural Revolution in the mid-sixties and concerns education and the national minorities. *Thank You, Comrade* is set in 1973 and focuses on sanitation workers. *Blue Skies Defense Line* is set in the early seventies, according to a voice-over narration at the beginning of the film, and is a spy drama.

In contrast, the six films extending the anti-Gang critique — *Lights, Hard Struggle, The Amnesiac, In the Vanguard, Blue Bay* and *Not a One-Off Story* — go back no earlier than late 1974. They also focus on issues directly related to the Fourth National People's Congress, held in January 1975, where Zhou Enlai made his call for the Four Modernizations. This shows how limited the extension of the critique was in the cinema. Literary endeavors like Liu Xinhua's "The Classroom Teacher" and Lu Xinwu's "The Scar" had already gone much further, showing the negative consequences of Gang activities and policies in the very periods and areas that 1978 films like *Salimake, Thank You, Comrade* and *Blue Skies Defense Line* were still displaying as untainted.

For example, *Blue Bay* takes place in the months before the Fourth National People's Congress. As with the films set in the months preceding the fall of the Gang like *October Storm, Emergency* and *Eventful Years*, the hero is a veteran cadre with an impeccable record. However, loyalty to Chairman Mao and Hua Guofeng is stressed in *October Storm*, but Chief Commander Ling Yong's loyalty to Premier Zhou is prioritized in *Blue Bay*. The film opens on a boat bearing Ling, Office Director Wen Minghong and an outsider back to Blue Bay. Ling Yong explains he has recently learnt that the project to build a new wharf has been personally approved by Premier Zhou. It turns out that Wen Minghong is in cahoots with Zhen Shikui, a Gang of Four follower, and attempting to sabotage the project. Like his counterpart Zhang Lin in *October Storm*, Zhen Shikui is associated with the media as the vice-editor of a newspaper, whereas Ling Yong, like his counterpart He Fan in *October Storm*, is associated with industrial production. However, whereas the news of the fall of the Gang of Four is decisive in enabling He Fan and Xu Jian to move against Zhang Lin in *October Storm*, in *Blue Bay*, the concluding scenes include Ling Yong phoning from Beijing where he has been attending the Fourth National People's Congress and has been invited to a personal audience with Premier Zhou. Empowered by his meeting with Zhou and the announcement of the Four Modernizations, Ling returns to find his followers have stopped Wen from escaping. After criticizing Wen, Ling turns to announce the Fourth National People's Congress as a great victory for Chairman Mao at which Premier Zhou gave the work report. The film then ends with a montage of shots of Blue Bay as music wells up and Premier Zhou's voice-over is heard announcing the Four Modernizations goal.[37]

The Gang of Four's interference with production in the effort to gain power as early as 1974 also appears in other 1978 films. *Lights* is set in 1974 in a navigation light factory and concerns overcoming efforts by Gang of Four followers to block new developments and production. *Hard Struggle* also has a Gang of Four sabotage theme, this time set in early 1975 in a railway safety inspection office. In *The Amnesiac*, it is experimental production of chemical equipment that is blocked in 1976, *In the Vanguard* locates the effects of the Gang in the military in 1975 and associates them with a journalist again, and *Not a One-Off Story* concerns obstacles to agricultural research in 1976.

Like *Blue Bay*, *Not a One-Off Story* and *The Amnesiac* explicitly link the production efforts that are sabotaged to the Four Modernizations. Although the 1976 setting of both films does not push back the time period, it does allow them to sanctify Zhou Enlai, who died early that year, in the same manner that *October Storm* sanctifies Mao. Zooms into black-shrouded death portraits communicate the inspirational effect of Zhou on positive characters. The shift of emphasis to Zhou implies a shift to Deng, as Zhou was widely believed responsible for Deng's 1975 rehabilitation, made public at the same Fourth National People's Congress where Zhou announced the Four Modernizations. Furthermore, given Zhou's advanced illness, Deng read out his report for him, associating him with the Four Modernizations as well as Zhou himself.

DENG CONSOLIDATES POWER: BEYOND THE CULTURAL REVOLUTION

A. State and Party Politics

At first sight, it appears difficult to explain the continued production and release between 1979 and 1981 of films whose themes move further and further away from validating politically endorsed leaders. After all, Deng's reformist policies had been adopted at the Third Plenum in late 1978. However, the political situation was not so clear-cut as this might imply.

Although his supporters had been forced to resign, Hua Guofeng himself retained his positions. This indicated that Deng was, so to speak, on probation and still needed to consolidate his position. However, having a firm grip on power already also seems to have forced him to reconsider how he should go about doing that. Instead of simply putting pressure on the incumbents, he seems to have decided to pursue a more ambivalent line, punishing some in an effort to satisfy conservatives in the Party while at the same time encouraging those who could continue to help him put pressure on the surviving beneficiaries of the Cultural Revolution decade. Specifically, direct political activity not initiated by the Party was unacceptable, whereas cultural activity that helped to consolidate his position and further weaken what was left of Hua's was to be indulged.

In March 1979, Deng suffered setbacks when the border war he launched against Vietnam did not go well. Under pressure, he criticized the democracy movement and had Wei Jingsheng arrested. However, these setbacks were temporary, and, later in the year, a speech by the elderly Marshal Ye Jianying to mark the thirtieth anniversary of the founding of the People's Republic included further reassessment of history, acknowledging not only that mistakes had been made in the ten years of the Cultural Revolution but also that they went as far back as the 1957 Anti-Rightist Campaign. Around the same time, Wei Jingsheng was tried, found guilty, and sentenced to a long jail term.

Although Ye Jianying's reassessment was in Deng's interests, it took almost two more years before this position on post-1949 history was enshrined in the Party document "On Questions of Party History" adopted at the Sixth Plenum of the Eleventh Central Committee in June of 1981. In the interim, Deng needed to keep pursuing a line that put pressure on the Party to come round to his position, while at the same time demonstrating that he would protect the Party against outside pressure. At the end of 1979, Deng had Democracy Wall closed down and clamped down on remaining dissidents. In early 1980, remaining left-wingers like Kang Sheng were criticized while right-wingers like Liu Shaoqi and Peng Dehuai were rehabilitated.

In September 1980, at the Third Plenum of the Fifth National People's Congress, Hua Guofeng was forced to step down as Premier and Deng's candidate, Zhao Ziyang, took over. At the end of the year, the trial of the Gang of Four sealed their fate.[38] And in June of 1981, Deng's power consolidation was completed at the Sixth Plenum of the Eleventh Central Committee of the Party when Hua was also forced to relinquish his Party Chairmanship to another Deng candidate, Hu Yaobang. This marked the point at which Deng's interests and those of the Party became aligned. There was no longer any reason to indulge independent voices outside the Party. Within a month, the campaign against *Bitter Love*, which had faltered in earlier months was revived and pursued with intensity.

B. Policy and Criticism in Literature and the Arts

In retrospect, Deng seems to have pursued a divide and rule policy in the three years between 1979 and 1981. However, at the time, his relative liberalism may have seemed much more genuine. Certainly, in his efforts to build support, he tried to reassure intellectuals that he would give them relative autonomy and that the Party would not pursue campaigns against them. In literature and the arts, Zhou Enlai's 1961 speech calling for relative openness and tolerance was republished in February of 1979 to legitimate the critical cultural works Deng needed at this time.[39] The republication of the 1957 works that had followed the launching of the Hundred Flowers Campaign in 1956 set an example for young writers, many of whom had been producing a wave of "scar" literature about the impact of the Gang of Four since late 1978. Whether or not "scar" literature was "exposure" literature became a point of contention again in the middle of 1979, when the conservatives attempted to attack it on these grounds.[40] Either way, it certainly exposed a wide range of problems and sufferings attributable to erroneous post-1949 Party policies for the first time since the 1956 Hundred Flowers campaign.

The relatively relaxed mood in the cultural sphere extended to the Fourth National Congress of Writers and Artists in November of 1979, even though it followed less than a month after the sentencing of Wei Jingsheng. At the Congress, the newly rehabilitated Zhou Yang had to admit to having made mistakes and been too strict before 1966, and well-known figures including Bai Hua and Xia Yan made speeches anticipating great works in the wake of the new relaxation of political control.[41] Mixed signals in 1980 made it possible for liberal artists and intellectuals to believe they were still winning a battle for greater autonomy. In late January and February, a special conference was called to criticize film scripts considered too negative about present-day society. But in July recognition of the new status of literature and the arts and their relative autonomy from the state and the Party were granted when the slogan which had governed them since the Yan'an Forum, "let literature and the arts serve politics," was amended to "let literature and the arts serve the people and socialism."

When the great film actor Zhao Dan died towards the end of the year, his last article, calling for freedom from state and Party control of the arts, was published.[42] However, as soon as the trial of the Gang of Four was over, the general political climate became chilly again. In culture, there was an attempt to launch an anti-Bai Hua campaign, directed against the writer of the screenplay *Bitter Love*. He had been particularly outspoken at the 1979 Congress. The campaign faltered until Hua Guofeng was finally removed from the Party Chairmanship half way through the year, at which point it picked up. The whole event will be discussed in greater detail in the last chapter, but the overall effect was to signal limits on criticism of past Party policy and problems in socialist society by artists and writers.

Film Production

The overall loosening of central control between late 1978 and June of 1981 gave filmmakers time to catch up with the efforts of their colleagues in the other arts to push thematic boundaries. The idea that film had lagged behind the other arts was discussed openly. Writing in the first issue of the newly republished *Film Art*, Peng Ning, soon to become notorious as a director of *Bitter Love*, and He Kongzhou, noted that, "in literature and the arts, poetry has been the pioneer and short stories and plays have been at the forefront, but film has been unable to keep pace with the times and has lagged behind," and proceeded to analyze the reasons for this delay.[43] The increased confidence that the very publication of such an article indicates was not only manifested in a general increase in film production. A large number of films also elected to represent episodes that undermined the communist myth of post-revolutionary history over a far greater range of years than just the mid-seventies and with a far greater range of themes than had been attempted hitherto.

The themes of interference by the Gang in the construction of the Four Modernizations, which had started in 1978, continued in 1979, as did films dealing with the earlier established theme of Gang of Four sabotage in late 1975 and 1976. The majority of 1979 films set in the Cultural Revolution decade still took place in its closing years.

Among the Four Modernization films, *Wedding* focuses on attempted Gang sabotage of a Four Modernizations project concerning chemical production equipment. In *Winds and Waves*, the same struggle takes place around the construction of a new fishing vessel. Some films that focused on Gang plotting in late 1975 and 1976 were also similar to those that had been made in preceding years. For example, *Roar, Yellow River!* concerns an effort by the Gang to besmirch the good name of the composer of China's national anthem, Nie Er. *Troubled Heart* concerns the persecution of a recently rehabilitated cardiologist in 1975 and 1976. Where these films do differ is in a toning down of emphasis on continuing Chairman Mao's line and quoting from Mao. And as with films focusing on the Four Modernizations, Premier Zhou is more frequently invoked in these than in earlier films.

However, one particular thematic development in films set in 1976 is more important. On November 15 of 1978, the verdict on the so-called 1976 Tiananmen Incident had been reversed as part of Deng's power struggle with Hua. Anti-Gang protesters had mourned Zhou Enlai during the *qingming* holiday, and the resultant demonstrations had been declared counter-revolutionary. Now they were declared revolutionary, a number of films set in 1976 depicted these events and the persecution of the demonstrators by the Party and the state. This is a rare positive depiction of allegedly spontaneous and autonomous political action carried out by ordinary citizens without Party and state support. (Ironically, the Cultural Revolution itself was one of the few other events represented this way.)

Films taking up this *qingming* theme in 1979 include the Four Modernizations film *Wedding*. The plot revolves around three sisters. One is engaged to a supporter of the Four Modernizations, but another is engaged to a Gang of Four follower. The Four Modernizations supporter visits Tiananmen Square during the *qingming* demonstrations and brings back a notebook with some of the commemorative poems posted and circulated at the time. The Gang supporter uses this notebook to incriminate the Four Modernizations supporter, whose fiancée marries him as a mark of her commitment while they wait for his imminent arrest.

Other films about *qingming* include *A Silent Place*, *Spring Rain*, *Reverberations of Life* and, in 1980, *Not For Love*. *A Silent Place* and *Reverberations of Life* are both quite similar to *Wedding*. *A Silent Place* also concerns a young man who becomes a fugitive because he possesses copies of poems circulated during the demonstrations, and in *Reverberations of Life* the young hero is a violinist who has composed and played a concerto commemorating Premier Zhou. In both cases, a young woman also decides to stand by these young *qingming* heroes regardless of the risk to her own safety.[44] *Spring Rain* concerns a young fugitive from the demonstrations being looked after by a nurse on a train out of Beijing. She has to persuade her policeman husband to help the fugitive escape instead of arresting him. In *Not For Love*, the arrest and apparent death of a young man because of his participation in the *qingming* demonstrations forms the premise of the film. His fiancée goes through various tribulations before getting set to marry someone else, but after the smashing of the Gang of Four, it is discovered that he is alive after all.

Although most 1979 films are still set in the last two years of the Cultural Revolution decade, this is also the first year in which films stretched the disruption of the communist myth of history back to the early days of the Cultural Revolution. *Fast As Light* has an unusual theme in this regard. However, it is also one that is hardly innovative, for it focuses on the Lin Biao episode of the early 1970's, a period discredited long ago although not dwelt on much before in fictional representations.

Other films, however, locate themes of unjust persecution and blocking material development earlier, at the beginning of the Cultural Revolution. In *Tear Stain*, a woman's madness is traced back to the death of her husband following persecution then. In *A Silent Place*, the young man facing persecution's mother was attacked then. In *Loyal Overseas Chinese Family*, this is when a man who returned to China faces attack because his foreign connections make people suspect he is a spy. And last, the class of former science students traced in *My Ten Classmates* graduated in 1957. Their fates vary, but many of them were persecuted from the early days of the Cultural Revolution.[45]

Furthermore, in each film, persecution enables persecutors to climb to positions of power, which, in many cases, they are still hanging onto in the present day, after the arrest of the Gang. In *Tear Stain*, the persecutors of the dead man are now powerful figures in the county. *A Silent Place* revolves around a visit by the persecuted woman to the old colleague who betrayed her in order to protect his own position during the Cultural Revolution. This theme clearly suited Deng's efforts to weed out Gang supporters and replace them with his own henchmen. However, the theme that the Party and state were riddled with evildoers and had been for more than a decade could hardly have done much for the old myth of infallibility.

Finally, 1979 films also deepened the critique of the post-revolutionary period by taking up the portrayal of socialist tragedy initiated in literature. In *Troubled Heart*, the cardiologist rehabilitated in 1975 is then so severely criticized by Gang followers that he dies before he can see their overthrow. Likewise, in *Fast As Light*, the hero has to sacrifice himself to stop the Lin Biao gang's machinations. In *Tear Stain*, the madwoman's husband cannot be restored to life no matter how many changes of policy occur. Not all the classmates in *My Ten Classmates* have survived the Cultural Revolution decade.

The representation of socialist tragedy and the extension of the period in which such events could be represented continued apace in 1980 and 1981. Only a few of the 1980 and 1981 films confined their focus to the 1974 to 1976 years anymore. *Loyal Heart* is about Zhou Enlai's support for scientists in the year before his death, and in the manner of the various Four Modernizations films produced since 1978.[46] However, other films even in this group with an unadventurous period setting pushed the thematic envelope. As mentioned, *Not For Love* used the *qingming* demonstrations as a backdrop. *Whom Does He Love?* uses the rapid swings in policy in 1975 and 1976 for a drama about opportunism, centering on a young man who switches fiancées according to their fathers' changing political fortunes. Instead of emphasizing the importance of the correct political line like most previous films, it implies that citizens need to be guided by a separate inner moral code, creating an alternative center of authority to the Party itself. Similarly, in *The Traitor*, the hero is a fine upstanding scientist for whom politics is not a guide in life but the source of unprovoked persecution in the final years of the Cultural Revolution. Finally, *Ghost* is a police drama in which Gang of Four henchmen take the role of wicked villains. The arrival of police dramas will be discussed in more detail in the next chapter, but again the police represent an alternative authority to the Party.

In 1981, only the two rural films *Laughter in Moon Bay* and *Xiaoyan and Dayan* are set wholly in the period at the end of the Cultural Revolution. Other films set mostly in these years, for example both versions of the other rural films *Xu Mao and His Daughters* and *The Corner Forgotten by Love*, have flashbacks to the horrors of the earlier Cultural Revolution period.[47] Although *Laughter in Moon Bay* and *Xiaoyan and Dayan* do not have flashbacks, frequent dialogue references are made to the injustices of the earlier Cultural Revolution period, which continue to effect the present. While the earlier films of 1978 set in the final years of the Cultural Revolution also confined the period of incorrect policy, injustice, and crime attributable to the Party and the state to these two or three years, both these films represent such errors and crimes as covering the whole 1966 to 1976 period.

A significant minority of 1980 and 1981 films push the historical boundaries back not only to the beginnings of the Cultural Revolution, but even further. They do this in two directions. Some represent problems before 1966. Others suggest that all had not yet been resolved post-1976, a theme already implicit in some 1979 films. Furthermore, the representation of socialist tragedy begun in 1979 became commonplace in 1980 and 1981. *The Legend of Tianyun Mountain* combines all three of these developments, and so has been remembered for its comparative thematic daring. Although it covers the Cultural Revolution decade, its focus is more on both earlier and later periods, using a complex narrative structure motivated by flashbacks from the present.[48] The present-day plot concerns the on-going investigation into the possible rehabilitation of Luo Qun, who ekes out a living as a carter on Tianyun Mountain. Song Wei is not only the Vice-Head of the local Party Committee Organization Bureau responsible for rehabilitations, but also intimately involved in Luo's case history together with her husband, Wu Yao. Through Song Wei's flashback memories, the details of this involvement and history are given, and it becomes clear that Wu Yao's ascent to his current position of power was dependent on the persecution of Luo Qun.

The Legend of Tianyun Mountain is not the only 1980 and 1981 film to suggest that justice in the present is being blocked by those who ascended to power because of injustice in the past despite the fall of the Gang in 1976. Among 1980 films, in The Child Violinist, a brother and sister audition for admission to a music conservatory in 1977 but discover that the Head of Admissions is the same man who was responsible for their father's death at the start of the Cultural Revolution. Similarly, in A Late Spring, a young man's admission to university after the fall of the Gang is blocked because of his parents' poor political background.[49] In Come Back, Swallow, young lovers discover that one of their parents had persecuted another viciously in the past, and that the persecuted mother remains unrehabilitated.

Given Deng Xiaoping's desire to sift through the entire Party and state hierarchy after his ascent in late 1978, this repeated theme of continued obstacles to justice after 1976 makes sense. However, in 1981, there is a small shift indicating that many filmmakers were alert to the slightly less open climate of that year. Themes of problems concerning authority and relations between the state and the people in the post-1976 period give way to themes of problems amongst the people in this period but caused by pre-1976 political injustices and incorrect Party policy, implicitly absolving the current Party and the state hierarchy for ongoing problems in a way that 1980 films like The Legend of Tianyun Mountain did not.

For example, The Investigator is basically a detective film in which present-day efforts to solve a case revealing problems which could be interpreted as hangovers from the Cultural Revolution. This includes the main investigator's son having become a delinquent as a result of neglect while his parents were sent down to the countryside. In May Love Be Everlasting, a would-be adoptive mother becomes resistant to her adoptee when she discovers he is the orphan of the man who killed her own first husband during the Cultural Revolution. In The Spiral, not only delays in missile design development are attributable to the disruption of the "chaotic decade," as it was often called, but also delays in the romance between the missile designer and the chief test pilot. Revival also represents a relationship blighted by the politics of the past, but is less rosy about the possibilities of completely over-coming these problems in the present.

Although this 1981 trend lays less responsibility for contemporary problems at the door of the Party and the state apparatus, in other ways it marks a further level of autonomy from the Party and state apparatus. In earlier films, especially classical Chinese films at the Yan'an end of the spec-trum discussed in Chapter Two, it is impossible to imagine any problem being handled without reference to the Party line of the day and involvement of Party and state representatives. Themes like those just discussed in the 1981 films suggest the emergence of a conceptual space autonomous from the state and the Party. This quasi-private or civil realm is represented as a place where problems can be made and decisions resolved without reference to higher authority.

One 1981 film that participates in this tendency to represent present problems as the product of the past rather than ongoing political errors is particularly interesting because of its narrative complexity. Like the charac-ter of the investigator's son in *The Investigator*, one of the young characters in *Set Sail* is represented as having been led astray by past political events. But unlike the investigator's son, Lu Yaqing regrets her past action, and the film focuses on the question of forgiveness and redemption. Furthermore, it is suggested that the roots of her delinquency go back before the Cultural Revolution. Her father died when he was caught up in the 1961 purge of Peng Dehuai and Huang Kecheng, two right-wing figures in the Party. In this way, *Set Sail* takes part in the stretching of the period in which Party and state errors occurred back before 1966.

Many of these films which stretch the period of errors and problems go back earlier to dwell on the persecution of so-called "rightists" following the Hundred Flowers Campaign of 1957. The rehabilitation of "rightists" had been declared in late 1978 at the same time as the *qingming* 1976 events had been declared revolutionary. But Deng himself had been closely involved in the Anti-Rightist Campaign, and so this may be a sign of just how far he had to go to consolidate his power. Again, the most direct representations of this period occurred in 1980 rather than 1981 films, and *The Legend of Tianyun Mountain* is an outstanding example again. Many of Song Wei's memories are taken up with the late fifties period and the Anti-Rightist campaign. She remembers how Luo Qun had led a team of young people surveying the Tianyun Mountain district in the hope of opening it up. She was part of that team, fell in love with Luo, and became engaged to him. Then Wu Yao, whom Luo had earlier replaced, was given responsibility for the implement-ing the Anti-Rightist Campaign in the district and made Luo one of his major targets. Ironically, Wu Yao himself is persecuted during the Cultural Revolution. Although no one dared to make this interpretation in print at the time, a viewer could not be blamed for noticing that the ups and down of Wu Yao's political history and their timing were similar to Deng's own.

The Legend of Tianyun Mountain is the most direct and sustained representation of the Anti-Rightist campaign to appear in the films under consideration here, but other films also trace current problems back to this period of injustice. In Come Back, Swallow, the mother has been condemned as a Rightist, as has the father in A Late Spring. In The Traitor, the snake expert has a long history of being persecuted going all the way back to the Anti-Rightist campaign. This combination of past injustice stretching back to the late fifties and continued injustice in the present undermines the communist myth of history, because it leaves very few years in which some members of the communist hierarchy are not implied to be wrongdoers.

The Legend of Tianyun Mountain also participates in the 1980 and 1981 increased representation of socialist tragedies, or injustices that can never be rectified. Although Song Wei breaks off her engagement to Luo Qun when he is accused of being a Rightist, Feng Qinglan is less easily convinced of his guilt and ends up marrying him. Not only does she die of overwork and exhaustion before Luo's case can be rectified, but also in the present of the film during the winter of 1978 to 1979. This locates socialist tragedy as still occurring well after the fall of the Gang of Four.

Unjust and premature death or permanent physical injury is also the main signifier of socialist tragedy in other films. Among those of 1980, in Sea Love, the character Nanxia dies of persecution during the Cultural Revolution, as does the violinist's father in Child Violinist, the marshal in Death of the Marshal, and various characters in Evening Rain including the poet's wife. In Maple, the young rebels kill each other during the armed struggle unleashed at the height of the Cultural Revolution, and in Ghost, Xia Zhenglan kills herself to protest her innocence. In After the Nightmare Comes the Dawn, the tragedy is accidental bigamy, when a wife thought to have been persecuted to death turns out to be alive, bringing undeserved grief to the young woman who has taken her place.

This backdrop of socialist tragedies continues unabated in 1981. Although many films focus on how to go on despite this irreparable harm, often the solution is worked out in a quasi-civil or private space autonomous from the Party and state apparatus. This is often symbolized by the formation of a new couple and often also a new family. In May Love Be Everlasting, a new couple is formed out of the widow of a man killed in the

Cultural Revolution and his friend. This new couple continues to be responsible for two other members of the household; the daughter of the widow and the dead friend, and an old man who is the surviving father of widow's first fiancé, who died in an avalanche. In both versions of *Xu Mao and His Daughters*, the fourth daughter marries the widower of one of her sisters, who has been persecuted to death during the Cultural Revolution, and takes over parenting her surviving daughter. In *Set Sail*, already discussed above, deafness is the tragedy, for Lu Yaqing became a Red Guard during the Cultural Revolution and beat up a famous singer who became deaf as a result. The solution entails a tortuous plot full of coincidences which leads Lu to fall in love with the singer's son. The singer's ability to forgive Lu at the end of the film promises the formation of a new family symbolizing the healing of these wounds. In *The Corner Forgotten by Love*, one sister has committed suicide during the Cultural Revolution, in the face of what is now characterized as "ultra-leftist" disapproval of her romance with a young man. In the present of the film, her younger sister is inhibited about forming a relationship with a man as a result of this, but overcomes that, symbolically healing the tragedy of the past. The last 1981 example in this particular pattern is *The Crystal Heart*, in which Yuan Wenping dies as a result of persecution during the Cultural Revolution, leaving a daughter. At the end of the film, her former boyfriend Lai Zhiqing has formed a relationship with another woman and is also looking after Yuan's daughter.

Socialist tragedy also occurs in other films. *On a Narrow Street* features a range of different endings for the audience to choose from, some of them more pessimistic than others. In one, the young woman in the central couple is blind. In *The Investigator*, the tragedy is not only the delinquency of his son, but ultimately the son's suicide and death. And finally, in *Spirit of the Foil*, a film about fencing, an old coach is persecuted to death, but his daughter goes on to win an international championship watched by the surviving members of his family and team.

Chapter 4

POSTSOCIALISM AND THE DECLINE OF THE HERO

Art is the reflection of life, and people are the agents of social life. Chairman Mao said, "Revolutionary literature and arts should create a variety of characters of all kinds on the basis of real life."... The majority of characters in our films have no impact on audiences, lack individual personality, and are not flesh-and-blood people. They are just illustrations of one political concept or another, glorified so-called positive characters and "heroes."

— Peng Ning and He Kongzhou

Chapter two noted the importance of characters that could both drive the narrative and provide unambiguous positive (and negative) exemplars for the audience in the classical Chinese cinema. The last chapter showed how the power struggles of the post-Mao years enabled themes that not only depicted the Party in an unprecedented negative manner but also moved beyond the direct fictional illustration of policy. This chapter sets out to investigate what happens to character in the films under consideration. It finds that, as with themes, characters remain central. However, the exemplary hero is on the wane, suggesting that the didactic paradigm of the classical cinema is further compromised.

One set of changes concerns character traits. First, many have observed a concern to produce more complex characters during this period. Within the critical discourse, this is motivated by a rhetoric of realism, but it refers concretely to political and moral complexity. Second, less discussed in the literature but also justified in terms of "realism" is a broadening out from a narrow range of lead characters with pure class backgrounds and strong Party affiliations. Insofar as realism is based on believability, both these changes indicate a crisis in credibility. Furthermore, although it is not noted in the contemporary discourse, character complexity has clear implications for the entire pedagogical project of classical Chinese cinema: the implication of the contemporary realist discourse is that the more believable a character is the less clear it will be whether they are being deployed as a negative or positive model in relation to the projects of the Party-state apparatus.

A second set of changes concerns character function, or what sort of character plays what sort of role and how they are related. This is not so frequently discussed in the contemporary discourse. This chapter argues that changes here go beyond a mere reversal of good and bad character roles to a series of more complicated changes in the types of characters present and their relationships. This transformation is marked by the increasing marginalization to the point of disappearance of characters constructed as Party representatives. Combined with increased character complexity, this points towards the decline of the hero and heroic narratives. Without characters suitable for emulation or policy-driven narratives, the pedagogical project of the classical Chinese cinema seems not only in crisis, but also possible in the process of being superceded by an emergent alternative.

COMPLEXITY

The two-part division between traits and functions above follows most English-language studies of character, and is an approach is often traced back to Aristotle.[1] However, writing in 1978, Seymour Chatman commented, "It is remarkable how little has been said about the theory of character in literary history and criticism."[2] More recently, Baruch Hochman interprets this as part of a sustained attack this century on the individualist and humanist emphases of nineteenth century Romanticism.[3] When Chatman and Hochman observe a decline in attention to character, they mean attention to character traits and in particular to the construction of the "rounded" character beloved of nineteenth-century realism.[4]

This lack of attention to traits may be true in the English-language situation, but almost the opposite is the case in mainland Chinese literature and arts criticism. There, the didactic paradigm impels attention to character in the majority of articles and books written on film. After theme, it is probably the major focus. Although it calls for a greater emphasis on the unique visual language of cinema are issued during this period, this does not result in less emphasis on character in any films produced at this time.[5] Whereas structuralist studies such as Propp's work on the Russian fairytale have encouraged greater emphasis on actions and functions than on traits in English-language discourse,[6] in the Chinese discourse the main emphasis is on traits, or "molding" (*zaoxing*) as it might more literally be translated.

The quote beginning this chapter is typical of the contemporary Chinese discourse, albeit more direct than most. Writing early in 1979 in the first issue of *Film Art* after it was restored to publication and in the wake of the Third Plenum of the Eleventh Central Committee of the Communist Party of China, the future director of *Bitter Love* and the critic He Kongzhou strategically shield themselves with a quote from Mao's *Talks at the Yan'an Forum on Literature and Art* (carefully footnoted in the original), and then proceed to lambaste what they perceive as the shortcomings of characterization in the contemporary Chinese cinema.[7] The Mao quote is chosen because it legitimates a primary concern with realism ("on the basis of real life"). Under this umbrella, they complain of a lack of realism in terms that refer directly to the political heroism favored by the "Three Prominences" policy of the Cultural Revolution era. In other words, realism is rendered to mean complexity or roundedness, further specified as lack of direct link between character traits and political policy or concept.

This pattern is found in many writings from the period and also in more recent survey histories. For example, Chen Huangmei notes that in 1977, audiences were expressing a concern that Chinese films still had a "whiff of the Gang" (*bangqi*) about them, a concern that seems to have covered both themes and characters.[8] Chen marks 1979 as the real turning point away from the Three Prominences and towards less heroic characterizations,[9] citing *The Legend of Tianyun Mountain* as a specific example of more complex characterization.[10] Many of the non-Chinese commentaries make similar comments.[11]

The films under examination here support these general observations. Therefore the move away from the Three Prominences emphasis on pure heroes with the gradual reintroduction of more complex characters, first in secondary roles and later in leading roles, will be discussed relatively briefly. However, the type of less heroic leads that came to the fore will be discussed in more detail. In fact, the type of agonized "middle character" torn between different values that is described and praised in the existing literature is relatively rare. Most non-heroic protagonists are less "rounded" or complex, but, it is argued here, they are at least as challenging to the didactic paradigm.

As mentioned in chapter three, the critique of the Three Prominences began in the middle of 1977, and "middle characters" were approved again. Although pre-1966 films with "middle characters" were re-released in 1977, in films made in 1976, 1977, and 1978, there are only pure heroes and villains. However, even in these films, there are some more complex characters, but confined to minor roles. This is true for those films made before the arrest of the Gang of Four and for those made afterwards. This demonstrates that what was at stake with the Three Prominences policy was this distribution rather than the absolute elimination of complexity. Furthermore, returning to the pre-Cultural Revolution films discussed in chapter two, while films at the Shanghai end of Clark's spectrum may have complex or so-called "middle characters" in lead roles such as Tao Lan in *Early Spring in February*, films at the more hard-line Yan'an end also have such characters, but confined to more minor "apprentice" roles in which they gradually see the error of their ways.

Examples in 1976, 1977, and 1978 films are numerous. In *Wild Goose Calls on the Lake Shore* (1976), the production brigade leader Song Changyou is a basically good character, as his poor-and-lower-middle peasant class status would indicate. However, he is duped by the class enemy Lin Daquan, who is trying to hang on to his position of power in the commune's medical station. Similarly, the eponymous heroine's adoptive father Hu Genmao in *Shanhua* (1976) is fooled by the degenerate Party Secretary Guo Shunfeng and the capitalist roader Sun Guanzong in their money-making schemes. Both these examples were made within the Cultural Revolution decade and before the death of Mao. In terms of theme, the 1978 film *Salimake* is very different. The eponymous heroine is accused by leftists of pursuing a "capitalist line in education" when she tries to set up a "horseback primary school" for students on the steppes. But the film is similar to its predecessors in that both Salimake and her accusers are purely good or evil, and only minor characters are more complex, such as her fiancé Kabu, who is temporarily taken in by her accusers. Here, the strategy of containment and damage control by minimal change noted in chapter three is extended to character traits, but the didactic paradigm is maintained.

In chapter three, it was noted that thematic change really started to be felt in 1979. Not only minor but also secondary characters start to acquire complexity in this year, and in the case of one film, *Troubled Laughter*, even the lead character exhibits this trait. To give an example of the secondary characters first, *A Silent Place* is a two-generation story in which the parents of a pair of lovers have been enemies. He Shifei has exploited the opportunity of the Cultural Revolution to write false evidence against Meilin. When this is revealed, his own wife and his daughter — who is one of the lovers — renounce him. In this sense, they are middle characters and apprentice characters who have come to see their mistakes.

However, *A Silent Place* pales in comparison to *Troubled Laughter*, where the difficulty of telling right from wrong is central to the whole film. Almost all the characters lack the moral and political certainty shared by almost all Chinese film characters up until this time. The lead is Fu Bin, a reporter recently returned to work, presumably from reform through labor, in the dying days of the Cultural Revolution. He discovers that the two people closest to him, his wife and his best friend at work, have become more concerned with survival than telling the truth. The latter has as a talisman a little figure that smiles on one side of his face and grimaces on the other. The former pleads with him to think about her and his daughter and not to write articles exposing corruption in high places. She accuses him of being willing to "sacrifice your own family and children to soothe your soul," which drives him to the very unheroic gesture of hitting her, which he almost immediately regrets. Although Fu does speak his mind in the end, he gets arrested for it and only does so after agonies of indecision. Furthermore, as Rao and Pei point out, there is nothing to indicate his wife and best friend realize that their more careful behavior is wrong.[12]

Troubled Laughter is the earliest film among those under consideration here to have a middle character that undergoes an apprenticeship in a lead role. The film is repeatedly praised for this in later histories, as are *The Legend of Tianyun Mountain* and *Evening Rain*, both released in 1980. The basic story of *The Legend of Tianyun Mountain* was introduced in chapter three. The character praised in Chen Huangmei's history as a complex one is Song Wei. She conforms to a primary classical cinema criterion for a positive character; unwavering loyalty to the Party. Yet, ironically, it is precisely this loyalty that leads her to make the error of abandoning Luo Qun when he is accused of being a Rightist in the fifties and to waver when she is challenged to rectify this error in the late seventies. Like the lead character of *Troubled Laughter*, she spends most of the film in doubt. Furthermore, unlike him she is shown to have made very major mistakes in her life that have destroyed those of other people. For this reason, she may be even more complex than him, and is unlikely to be easily deployed as either a positive or negative exemplar.

Two factors complicate this judgment of Song Wei and *The Legend of Tianyun Mountain*'s divergence from the didactic paradigm. First, is Song in fact the lead character, or just another secondary apprentice character? In the 1983 book about the film, she is not treated as the lead. The actor who plays her does get to write an essay about the experience, an indicator of the importance of the character, whom she explicitly says she saw as a "middle character."[13] But this essay only appears after an essay by the actor who plays Luo Qun.[14] Furthermore, screenwriter Lu Yanzhou discusses Luo Qun first and as the lead character in the segment of his essay on characterization.[15] Song Wei only gets discussed after both Luo Qun and Feng Qinglan, his self-sacrificing wife. Why does Lu do this? His discussion of Luo Qun indicates the continued dominance in critical discourse of the didactic paradigm and its need for heroes that can be emulated. He states that many young and even middle-aged people have lost some faith in the Party as a result of the Cultural Revolution, but that he wanted his lead to maintain his belief in the Party and the masses regardless of the wrongs done to him.[16] In other words, as the most perfect hero among the heroes — to borrow from the Three Prominences — Luo Qun must the be the lead, and as the next most perfect, Feng Qinglan must be second, as they are the two characters most worthy of emulation. However, in terms of screen time and also because her flashbacks authorize large segments of the film, Song Wei is a stronger contender for the lead, if defined discursively. Luo Qun has no flashbacks and is not a relay for the enunciation of the film.

Second, apart from Song Wei, all the other characters in *The Legend of Tianyun Mountain* are simply good or bad. Luo, Feng and the young woman Zhou Yuzhen, whose questions prompt Song Wei's memories, are all straightforwardly positive. Song Wei's husband and the persecutor of Luo Qun, Wu Yao, is straightforwardly evil. In comparison, the secondary characters in *Troubled Laughter* are more complex, even though many of the minor characters are straightforwardly evil. Both Fu's wife and his best friend are far from clearly good or bad, and the film never explicitly condemns their tendency to compromise. While *The Legend of Tianyun Mountain* stretches the historical bounds of socialist fallibility, its characters are less adventurous than those of *Troubled Laughter*. In the former, only one albeit crucial character is a "middle character" and apprentice character, whereas in the latter film the middle character and apprentice character is the most positive character in the entire film and those surrounding him are even less heroic than he is and do not undergo an apprenticeship.

Evening Rain differs from the two films just discussed in its complete absence of evil characters. Indeed, screenwriter Ye Nan was moved to defend this unusual feature of the film on the grounds of realism.[17] The story concerns an arrested poet during the Cultural Revolution being transferred under guard on a Yangtse River ferry. During the journey, we get to know his various traveling companions. The main candidate for an evil character would be the young Red Guard escort, Liu Wenying. However, when the poet dives into the river to save a young girl, she sees his goodness and helps him to escape, making her more a middle and apprentice character.

Liu Wenying does differ from Fu Bin in *Troubled Laughter* and Song Wei in *The Legend of Tianyun Mountain* because we have no access to her subjective thoughts: her moral and political agonies are not presented directly. In regard to the didactic paradigm, all these characters are less clear-sighted than the positive heroes of the past. Nonetheless, as apprentice characters, they are still amenable to the overall concerns of the didactic paradigm. Furthermore, although celebrated in the literature, this type of complex character full of doubts and indecisions is rare. Instead, another type whose traits diverge from the heroes of the classical cinema in a different way dominates in 1980 and 1981: the character that makes mistakes effecting their personal life rather than incorrect decisions concerning the Party and society. Instead of agonizing over difficult decisions, they act as a result of misunderstandings, of being duped, or of being misled. An example in 1980 might be *Maple*, an altogether darker film than *Evening Rain*, but also concerning Red Guards. The confused young leads are lovers who do not realize they are being misled until it is too late. Enthusiastic recruits to different "rebel factions" heeding Mao's call to rebel at the beginning of the Cultural Revolution, they die pointlessly in the fighting that ensues.

By 1981, this tendency towards duped and mistaken characters is completely generalized across the group of films under consideration. Almost every significant character that is not a villain is enmeshed in networks of misunderstandings that complicate their personal lives and often stem from simple lack of information. For example, *Laughter in Moon Bay* uses the policy twists and turns of the past as premises for rural family comedy. Old farmer Jiang Maofu's efforts to find a wife for his son are stymied because he has been condemned as a "capitalist roader" for growing a few fruit trees and no one wants anything to do with him. Later, the press is searching for an example of a prosperous farmer and he suddenly becomes a model. The same man who turned down Maofu's marriage suggestion changes his mind now, but this time it is Maofu who turns him down. Just when it seems these misunderstandings have been overcome, Maofu is condemned again, and his son's prospective father-in-law turns up at the wedding to drag his daughter away. There is no suggestion that either Maofu or the father of the bride is morally or politically bad; instead, they do bad things as a result of misunderstandings. Similarly, in *Dance Love*, Xiang Feng and Qumuahzhi are separated because she was attacked during the Cultural Revolution. Since then, he too has suffered in the Cultural Revolution. The film is ambiguous if Xiang Feng's failure to stand by her at the time is understandable or a lack of moral strength and courage on his part, but it is clear that he feels guilty.

In terms of a realist preference for "roundedness," complexity of psychology, moral agonizing and so forth, these characters are far less interesting than those of *Troubled Laughter*, *The Legend of Tianyun Mountain* or even *Evening Rain*, because they are blameless. However, in terms of divergence from the didactic paradigm, they are even more challenging. They are not represented as agents in the larger moral and political projects of the state-Party apparatus, and as a result they are not candidates for the role of the conventional hero for emulation, not even as apprentice characters. Mao-fu is not focused on trying to follow the correct Party line or serve the masses. His priorities are trying to look after his family and do right by his children, but he is blocked by incorrect policies. Xiang Feng and Qumuahzhi are primarily lovers, and their romance is disturbed by incorrect policies. This is even true for Lü Danfeng and Li Honggang in *Maple*, who are lovers first and foremost. To understand this kind of greater divergence from the didactic paradigm, it is necessary to examine another set of character traits: class background and Party allegiance.

CLASS BACKGROUND AND PARTY AFFILIATION

The potentially very politically sensitive issue of social background and political affiliation is not much discussed in the Chinese literature on the films under consideration here. However, sometimes writers do speak of "ordinary people" (*putongren*) as being more prevalent or preferred. For example, directors Wu Yonggang and Wu Yigong use this term when discussing *Evening Rain*. Although the poet Qiu Shi risks his life saving the girl from the Yangtze, they insist "there is nothing extraordinary about Qiu Shi; he didn't do anything us ordinary people wouldn't think of or do."[18] Liu Guiqing also claims that after 1979, the films "no longer make it possible to deduce character according to political categories, but determine their flavor with ordinary people in mind."[19]

As with moral and political complexity, change in class and political background does not come immediately. In the first three years of the period under consideration, lead characters are clearly members of the Party or representatives of the Party, and most have exemplary *gongnongbing* ("worker-peasant-soldier") backgrounds. Educated youths sent down to the countryside function as emissaries from the Party in *Wild Goose Calls on the Lake Shore*, *New People of the Mountain Villages*, and *Faith* (all 1976). Local-level Party secretaries or other Party functionaries take the lead in *Shanhua*, *Counterattack*, *Song of the New Wind*, and *Red Plum in the Mountains* (all 1976), in *New Song of the Wei River*, and *October Storm* (both 1977), and in *Salimake, Hard Struggle, The Amnesiac*, and *Thank You, Comrade* (all 1978). Commune brigade and team leaders from peasant backgrounds are the main characters in *Jewel of the Sea* and *The Jubilant Xiaoliang River* (both 1976). Children of three ethnic groups and presumably of peasant backgrounds are the leads in *The Secret of the Ahxia River* (1976). Members of the armed forces take the lead in *South Sea Storm* (1976), in *Youth* (1977), and in *In the Vanguard* and *Blue Skies Defense Line* (both 1978). Workers lead in *Emergency*, and *Eventful Years* (both 1978).

However, the insistence on close Party affiliation for lead characters and the narrow definition of politically acceptable class backgrounds was overturned by the end of 1978. To deal with class background first, on 18 March 1978, Deng Xiaoping transferred the educated classes (*zhishifenzi*) — spurned before and during the Cultural Revolution as members of the bourgeoisie — to membership of the proletariat, in line with the new emphasis on economic construction in the Four Modernizations policy.[20] Two 1978 films feature the previously despised educated professional as a positive lead character. In *Lights* and *Not a One-Off Story*, the heroes are both engineers, a profession very suited to construction for the Four Modernizations.

Thereafter, more and more educated professionals take lead roles. In 1979, there is a surgeon in *Troubled Heart*, an airplane designer in *Fast as Light*, a journalist in *Troubled Laughter*, a music composer in *Roar, Yellow River*, another engineer in *So Near, Yet So Far*, a business executive and young woman about to go to college in *Reverberations of Life*, and a professor and her various university classmates in *My Ten Classmates*. In 1980, there is a heart specialist in *Loyal Hearts*, a scientist in *Sea Love*, a family from the music world in *The Child Violinist*, a poet in *Evening Rain*, a number of doctors in *Come Back, Swallow*, a group of athletes and coaches in *Volleyball Star*, and a teacher in *After the Nightmare Comes the Dawn*. 1981's films include researchers in *May Love Be Everlasting*, engineers in *The Spiral*, a folk singer in *Whirlpool Song*, and dancers in *Dance Love*.

Although all these characters are educated professionals, not all of their professions lend themselves to plots concerning promulgation of Party policy as easily as engineering fits the Four Modernizations. This is particularly true of those involved in areas such as the arts, sports, or medicine. While their achievements may contribute to society, they seem more likely to be at least at one step removed from the Party-state apparatus in comparison with the old Party Secretaries and brigade leaders who were directly concerned with implementing and explaining Party policy and state programs.

Another development is the appearance of public security bureau officers (or policemen) in lead roles. Police officers are clearly loyal servants of the state, but they are not Party functionaries. In fact, they are strikingly rare in the classical Chinese cinema prior to 1976, and the detective film is not a genre in that cinema. Therefore, the tendency towards police films that begins in this group of films with *Bear Print* in 1977 might indicate that the Party's authority had become tainted by the twists and turns of previous years and that more neutral authority figures were more likely to inspire public confidence. Indeed, Liu Guiqing notes the popularity of *Bear Print* compared with other 1977 films about Party struggles and political issues.[21] *Bear Print* itself is actually a spy drama, in which the hero who pursues the foreign (presumably Soviet) spies is the head of the intelligence section in River City public security bureau. This plot shifts the entire focus away from struggles over Party political line and towards national issues.

As a genre, the police film became common in following years. Like *Bear Print*, some of the films in the corpus because of the times they are set in also tend away from politics and towards more commonly agreed upon values manifested in criminal law. For example, the 1980 film *Murder in 405* is a conventional murder mystery only included in the corpus because the precise time of its setting is not clear. However, another pattern is more common: police officers are called in to investigate a crime, such as a murder, and then they link the crime to Gang of Four activities. The 1979 films *Spring Rain* and *Sacred Duty* both fit this pattern, as do the 1980 films *A Handcuffed Passenger*, *The Tenth Bullet Scar*, and *Ghost*, and the 1981 film *The Investigator*.[22] For example, *The Tenth Bullet Scar* begins with the blowing up of a bridge and the discovery by recently rehabilitated public security officer Lü Hong that his own son is one of the criminals. As he investigates, he discovers that his son had been recruited into a Cultural Revolution "rebel faction" by the aunt in whose care he had been left while his parents were being persecuted during the Cultural Revolution.[23]

Also noteworthy is the fact that in many of the later films under consideration, class and political background is either unclear, quite removed from the typical traits associated with the particular class background in classical Chinese films, or not very relevant. Given that class background used to be a sure indicator of whether a character was a good model for the pupil-spectator, this is also a significant departure from the pedagogical model. For example, the leads in *Romance on Lushan Mountain* are Geng Hua, son of a Red Army general, and Zhou Yun, Chinese American daughter of a KMT general. Although they are both from soldier backgrounds, Zhou's father was on the wrong side in Chinese internal struggles. However, in the late seventies, with Deng's policy of opening up and seeking investment, reconciliation with overseas Chinese was being followed. Nonetheless, even if we disregard Zhou's father's background, neither she nor Geng are warriors hardened through fighting for the Party cause. Indeed, they have had very privileged upbringings, and are both training to be architects. In one memorably sentimental and nationalistic scene, Geng is practicing English by standing in a pine forest and shouting, "I love the morning of my motherland." However patriotic the phrase, learning English was not a proletarian pursuit at this time. Zhou Yun changes outfits with every scene, fitting the old stereotype of a vain and bourgeois American. So, are they of "reliable" or dubious class background? It isn't clear. Nor is it particularly important or relevant. To understand what is meant by "not relevant" and its relation to a move away from the pedagogical model, it is necessary to turn to a discussion not only of traits, but also of actions.

REVERSAL OR TRANSFORMATION OF ROLES?

In the classical model, heroes were mostly of worker-peasant-soldier background, clearly affiliated with the Party, and morally and politically pure and certain in their vision. Not one of the lead characters in the 1980 or 1981 films in the corpus combines all three of these characteristics, whereas the great majority of the films made between 1976 and 1978 do. Perhaps this helps to explain Paul Pickowicz's description of characterization in his article on the popular cinema of this period as effecting a reversal of "stock roles."[24]

As indicated, Pickowicz's claims are understandable if one looks at lead characters' traits alone. However, as soon as some of the other secondary characters are taken into consideration, and their narrative functions in terms of their relationships to each other are examined, a more complicated picture emerges. What emerges is not a simple reversal within an otherwise stable model but a transformation of roles that indicates a transformation of the underlying cinematic paradigm.

First, if some of the characters other than the lead are examined, two significant patterns of variation emerge. One concerns the Party affiliation and class background of the villain and the second concerns guide characters. To look at villains first, Pickowicz is correct that in the 1950s and 1960s the villains are usually "rightists" and other figures of bad class background, whereas in 1980 and 1981, the Party officials often take this role. In *Stage Sisters*, Manager Tang, the bourgeois who runs the opera troupe in Shanghai, is the main villain. In *Woman Basketball Player No.5* another bourgeois has this role — the owner of the basketball team before the revolution. Even in *Bridge*, class enemies skulk around the factory. On the other hand, in *The Legend of Tianyun Mountain* the villain is clearly Party Secretary Wu Yao who schemes to have the heroic Luo Qun condemned as a "rightist."

However, this comparison of 1980 and 1981 films with those from before the Cultural Revolution ignores the films of the late seventies. Party officials appear as villains as soon as film production recommences in the 1970s. Indeed, Party figures are the villains as early as some of the films made during the Cultural Revolution in 1976 considered here. Examples include Vice-Secretary Chen Tu in *Wild Goose Calls on the Lakeshore*; Party Secretary Guo Shunfeng in *Shanhua*; and Country Revolutionary Committee Vice-Director Wei Ruxue in *Red Plum in the Mountains*. Other villains in these films are government officials, not rightist class enemies. This is in line with the Cultural Revolution, which was directed against so-called revisionists within the Party and the state hierarchy: the Cultural Revolution marked the point when disputes became impossible to resolve within the Party and were publicly contested.

After the fall of the Gang of Four, Party members continue to appear as villains. However, whereas it was figures on the right of the Party and the state hierarchy who were villains in Cultural Revolution films, now it is leftists who are villains. In the 1977 film *October Storm*, the battle is between good veteran Party officials and the henchmen of the Gang of Four, who were also a faction in the Party leadership. In 1978, the villains include Party Vice-Secretary Huang Xuan in *Lights*; municipal Party Committee member Lin Fan; Party Vice-Secretary Hu Yichuang in *The Amnesiac*; and Party Secretary Li Mengliang in *Eventful Years*. In these circumstances, instead of the simple reversal Pickowicz suggests, we need to recognize that in regard to Party affiliation there is a series of four shifts. There are Party heroes and bad class background villains before the Cultural Revolution; left-wing Party heroes and "rightist" Party villains from 1974 to the fall of the "gang"; right-wing Party heroes and "ultraleftist" Party villains after the fall; and non-Party and educated professional heroes and Party villains after 1979.

This pattern is further complicated when another type of secondary figure is taken into account. These are the wiser (and usually older) figures guiding the main characters. In the classical Chinese cinema, these are mostly Party officials. This pattern is continued immediately following the fall of the Gang of Four. From 1976 to 1978, many heroes and especially those who are not Party functionaries themselves are supported and guided by an older, male Party figure at a higher level. In most cases, this support is signaled subtly. The senior supporter is rarely present in the main areas where the action takes place and is only turned to directly for advice or support at crucial moments.

Among the pre-Cultural Revolution films considered in chapter two, in *Li Shuangshuang*, the title character can turn to the Commune Party Secretary, who lives in another village. And in *Stage Sisters*, the Party member who recruits Chunhua, the journalist Jiang Bo, performs this function. In *Bridge* and *The Unfailing Beam*, the leads are direct representatives of the Party themselves. In the 1976-1981 films under consideration, educated youth Lan Haiying is supported by the local Party Secretary in *Wild Goose Calls on the Lake Shore*, as is educated youth Fanghua in *New People of the Mountain Villages* and educated youth and Red Guard Wang Xiaolei in *Faith*. Among the brigade and team leaders, Ling Yanzi in *Jewel of the Sea* is supported by the Commune Party Secretary Zhou. The children in *The Secret of the Ahxia River* are guided by Party Committee member Grandpa Qingshan. The railway locomotive team in *Emergency* is supported by Party Secretary Fang Lei, and in *Eventful Years*, Party Secretary Liao Pingshan supports Gong Fang.

However, what is different about the pre-Cultural Revolution films and those made between 1976 and 1978 is that there are often also negative guide figures in the later films. In the earlier films, the villains are usually class enemies with no older and wiser figure to turn to. If such a figure does appear, he or she is a socially isolated old renegade, and certainly not a Party official. But between 1976 and 1978, when internecine disputes in the Party are prominent subject matter, there is usually a guide figure on both sides. Especially in the films made after the end of the Cultural Revolution, the villain guide does not appear but is clearly implied to be a member of the Gang. For example, in the 1977 film *October Storm*, Ma Chong claims to be on a mission from "the commander," a term used to refer to Mao's wife Jiang Qing towards the end of the Cultural Revolution, and the evil journalist Zhang Lin has been sent by Wang Hongwen, one of the Gang members.

After 1979, as the lead characters become more complex and less likely to be Party members of worker-peasant-soldier background, the number of older and wiser Party officials discretely supporting and backing lead characters and villains declines. This means that even when lead characters are ordinary peasants or workers, they are positioned in a quite different relation to the Party. No longer its loyal agents on the local level, they are now autonomous from it. For example, the novel *Xu Mao and His Daughters* was adapted into a film twice in 1981. The main characters form a typical peasant family, and the narrative focuses on their vicissitudes during the final years of the Cultural Revolution decade. Unlike Li Shuangshuang in the film of the same name, neither Xu Mao nor his daughters have a local Party Secretary or other wise figure in the Party hierarchy to turn to. Jiang Maofu in *Laughter in Moon Bay*, already discussed above, may not be a poor peasant, but he is certainly not wealthy. He, too is the victim of the policy changes that sweep through the countryside, and has no Party functionary to turn to for advice or support. This is equally true for the various educated professionals who take the lead roles in so many other films.

Taking these other characters into account, what develops after 1979 is a significant break from the pre-1979 patterns, and more than just a reversal. Before 1979, it is not simply that the lead character was often a local Party official or a person of trustworthy class background. They were also always linked to the higher levels of the Party-state apparatus through these guide figures. After 1979, not only are many of the lead characters not Party officials or members of the old revolutionary classes. They are also not linked to the Party-state apparatus in any direct way. In chapter three, we have already seen the emergence in these years not only of themes that push the boundaries of when socialist errors were made and their representation in film. We have also seen that themes distant from the concerns of the Party-state apparatus become prominent, including love themes. Putting all these factors together, this suggests that by this period, the didactic paradigm has been transformed. Themes are not necessarily centered on Party policy or state programs. And lead characters are no longer connected to the Party and not even necessarily clearly good or bad. In these circumstances, it is time to examine not only how these films diverge significantly from the didactic paradigm, but also what they are instating in its place. This is the project of the next chapter.

Chapter 5

A FAMILY AFFAIR: SEPARATION AND SUBJECTIVITY

> Engels points out that emotional relationships have existed amongst human beings, and particularly between the sexes, since human beings came into existence.
>
> *— The People's Daily*[1]

This chapter adds the examination of editing patterns and spectator positioning to theme and character examined in previous chapters, and pursues the question of the break away from the didactic paradigm further to ask what, in a positive sense, emerges out of these changes. What type of engagement replaces the pupil-spectator model of the classical Chinese cinema? The answer to this lies in the appearance of romantic love in the films, for this is at the core of the new pattern that emerges here.

The appearance of romantic love as a Westernized alternative to loyalty to the Party has been noted in surveys of contemporary literature. This chapter concurs with that conclusion and some others in regard to film. However, where those studies abstract romantic love from the various texts, this chapter also notes the broader discursive context in which romantic love is narrated, encouraging patterns of engagement for the spectator. Two significant features are identified and discussed, both of which modify the usual characterization of romantic love as only a Western import.

First, more romantic love is part of a broader pattern, including increased representation of affective ties among family members and a setting in the Cultural Revolution period. These elements frequently motivate narratives structured between the poles of separation and disagreement on the one hand, and reunion and the restoration of harmony on the other. This larger context realigns the meanings of romantic love away from individualism. Second, most of these films involve complex networks of flashbacks shared among family members or between lovers. This encourages the spectator into an engagement that differs from both the construction of epistemological mastery in Chinese classical cinema and of libidinal mastery in Hollywood classical cinema. Instead, it constructs a nostalgic, affective communalism based on the peer group rather than hierarchy. This type of engagement has a long history in China as a countercultural pattern. Its emergence again here in this particular form constitutes the earliest transformation of the didactic socialist paradigm of the classical Chinese cinema into a postsocialist paradigm. It appears in this frequently despised popular form of the family-based romance well before its later and more respected appearance in the cinema of the Fifth Generation of younger Chinese directors in the mid-eighties.

THE INCIDENCE OF ROMANTIC LOVE

Love is not absent from the films of the Chinese classical cinema discussed in chapter two. In fact, they are filled with love: love for the Party; love for the nation; love for the masses; love for the People's Liberation Army; love for the workers; love for the peasants; love for the commune's new tractor; love for Chairman Mao; love for the people; sometimes love for one's family; but rarely romantic love. Even where love for family and romantic love do occur, they are subordinated to the larger didactic concerns of the film.

In *Bridge* and *Stage Sisters*, there is no romantic love. Although quasi-familial love is invoked in the separation of the "sisters" in *Stage Sisters*, it is part of a broader lesson on the dangers of being seduced by bourgeois decadence. Similarly, in *Woman Basketball Player No.5*, the separation of Lin Jie and coach Tian Zhenhua is used to communicate the evils of the old society. In the same film, the tensions that arise between the young lovers, Lin Xiaojie and Tao Kai, are due to his failure to understand the contribution of sport to the nation. Similarly, the differences that cause the friction between Shuangshuang and Xiwang in *Li Shuangshuang* are due to his failure to understand the socialist morality appropriate to the new commune system. In *Early Spring in February and The Unfailing Beam*, the lead female characters experience a growing attraction towards the hero of each film, but this is inspired by his political dedication. There are no sex scenes, no bed scenes, and no kissing scenes in any of the films. The libidinal gaze is also absent, even when love is represented, severely limiting both the signification of desire and the implication of the spectator into networks of libidinal cathexis.

In contrast, love becomes very prominent after the Cultural Revolution is over. Chapter three has detailed the gradual quality of political and cultural change in these years. Given this and the amount of time it takes to produce a film compared with other cultural works, the shift towards love manifests itself slowly during these years. Romantic love does not appear in any of the fifteen 1976 and 1977 films considered here. The earliest would have been made before the end of the Cultural Revolution period, and some others may have been based on amended versions of scripts written then. Of the eleven 1978 films, only *Salimake* and *Not a One-Off Story* feature a love story.

In 1979, after the Third Plenum of the Eleventh Central Committee of the Communist Party saw the affirmation of Deng Xiaoping's ascendancy, five of the fourteen films under consideration feature love, but in three it is a very minor element indeed. In *Tear Stain*, the cadre's wife Kong Lina and her dead husband's relationship could be considered as a tragic romance of sorts, but it never appears on screen. The relationship between the main character's daughter and her boyfriend forms a very minor subplot in *Roar, Yellow River!*, and the relationship between the singer and the girl who looks after him in *Reverberations of Life* is implied to have romantic undertones, but these are not developed.[2]

It is in 1980 and 1981 that romantic love takes over the screen in a big way. Sixteen of the twenty-three 1980 films and fifteen of the eighteen 1981 films under consideration feature romantic love.[3] The reappearance of love themes has been noted in Chinese language scholarship on the period in general,[4] as well as on individual films such as the revolutionary history film *Eager to Return*.[5] However, no scholarly work has been found on this phenomenon in the cinema.

LITERARY COMPARISONS

By contrast, the flood of love stories has been noted in English-language work on contemporary Chinese literature. Most writing on this topic attends to three factors; chronology, characteristics, and causes for and responses to the first two factors. In the most extensive analysis, Kam Louie notes that love made its first appearance in post-Cultural Revolution literature in 1978 with Liu Xinwu's "The Place of Love," and that it rapidly became a staple ingredient in fiction.[6] Given the slower pace of film production, it is not surprising that love does not appear to have become as commonplace in the cinema until 1980.

Louie breaks down the characteristics of love in Chinese literature in the late seventies and early eighties into two periods. First, in the earliest pieces, written in 1978, love is based on and subordinate to "a shared commitment to socialism."[7] This socialist love echoes the representations found in pre-Cultural Revolution films. Second, in 1979, with broader political and cultural loosening up, a greater variety of love stories appears. Complications that prevent happy endings, such as inadvertent incest or the death of a lover during the Cultural Revolution, are introduced. Also, love is represented as an autonomous feeling, rather than something stimulated by and subordinated to the demands of socialism, and fulfillment of love faces all sorts of political and social obstacles, ranging from the opposition of parents and double standards against women who are too educated or not virgins to poverty and prior entanglements.[8] This could be said to be romantic love, as opposed to the socialist love that preceded it. Despite this change, sexual desire remains taboo throughout.[9]

Similar developments can be traced in the films considered here. In the earlier examples, politics determines romance in the manner Louie finds in fiction, and socialist love predominates. If two lovers share the same correct political philosophy, their love is good; if they share the same incorrect philosophy, their love is bad; and if they do not share the same philosophy, their love is subject to tension until the partner with the incorrect philosophy sees the light. This applies to all the 1978 and 1979 films under consideration and some of the later films, too. In 1978, conflict between the eponymous heroine and her fiancé, Kabu, in *Salimake* is provoked by disagreement over her noble plans to set up a "horseback primary school." In *Not a One-Off Story*, an intellectual persecuted by the Gang and sent down to the countryside's continued commitment to technologically advanced agriculture wins him the love of the local Party vice-secretary.

Politics continues to determine love in 1979. However, how this occurs was changed by the late 1978 decision that the 1976 Tiananmen Square Incident was not counter-revolutionary but revolutionary.[10] This decision made attitudes to Zhou Enlai during the last days of the Cultural Revolution a new determinant of political correctness. The play from which *A Silent Place* was adapted was discussed as a positive example of the reassessment of the 1976 Tiananmen Square Incident.[11] In both play and film, He Yun dumps her boyfriend, Ouyang Ping, because he has been branded a counter-revolutionary after participation in the incident. By the end of the film, she has seen the light and they are reunited, firm in their stand against the Gang. In contrast, in *Roar, Yellow River!*, He Xiaoli dumps her boyfriend when he writes an essay against Premier Zhou. *Wedding* ends with one couple marrying despite facing imminent disaster as a result of their commitment to Premier Zhou, which connotes them to be good, and another celebrating raucously despite the Premier's death, which connotes them to be bad.

In 1980 and 1981, although common ideals still inspire many couples, romantic love begins to take over from socialist love. More complex situations of the sort Louie finds in literature in 1979 start to appear. In *The Legend of Tianyun Mountain* (1980), the entanglements caused by the mistaken 1957 Anti-Rightist campaign and the Cultural Revolution are inextricable.[12] Song Wei and Luo Qun were lovers united by common and correct political ideals before the Anti-Rightist campaign. When Luo is labeled a Rightist, Song Wei is persuaded to "make a clean break" with him and marries his enemy, Wu Yao. Her friend Feng Qinglan continues to admire Luo, looks after him, and becomes his wife, dieing as a result of the hardships they suffer before he is rehabilitated. Song and Wu eventually break up, but there is no way to turn back the clock.

Politics creates obstacles to romantic love in film after film. In *Not For Love* (1980), *After the Nightmare Comes the Dawn* (1980), and *Whirlpool Song* (1981), a lover thought to have died as a result of persecution is discovered to have survived. This is also significant because it hints at the taboo subjects of adultery and bigamy, mentioned as examples of vulgar and pornographic representations of love to be avoided in two November 1981 articles in the *People's Daily* on the correct handling of love in literature and the arts, both published during the conservative anti-Bai Hua campaign.[13]

The same conservative articles name incest and love between Chinese and foreigners as further negative examples. Two 1980 films hint at the latter possibility. *Not For Love* features a woman character called Wilma whose father was a foreign revolutionary martyr and whose mother was Chinese. This pedigree goes against the taboo, but is above criticism because of the exemplary political background of the parents. The man who rescues Wilma and forms an attraction to her that destroys his existing relationship insists she is really Chinese despite physical appearances, but his ex-girlfriend sees things differently. In *Romance on Lushan Mountain*, Zhang Yu plays the daughter of a Nationalist general now living in the United States. Zhou Yun is not racially foreign and so the taboo technically remains unbroken, but her overseas upbringing alludes to the possibility.

Wilma's Chinese revolutionary heritage in *Not For Love* makes it possible her love is based on shared socialist ideals regardless of racial difference. However, although Zhou Yun and the son of a Communist general she falls in love with are both ethnically Chinese, shared faith in socialism is not a possible basis for their love. Instead, she and Geng Hua share a common nationalist concern for the construction of China. When he practices his

English by calling out "I love the morning of my motherland" in the pine forest, she acts as his echo, shouting the same phrase back. However, Zhou Yun and Geng Hua's mutual attraction cannot be reduced to a politically respectable variation on the shared ideals formula. Although there is much patriotic rhetoric, the visuals do not match the verbiage. In most films where love is based on shared ideals, these ideals are demonstrated by actions as well as words. In *Not a One-Off Story*, discussed above, Li Nong is attracted to Zhang Heng because she sees him working to advance agricultural technology. In *Romance on Lushan Mountain*, neither of the main protagonists is ever seen engaged in any sort of productive activity. Instead, love blossoms amidst the consumption of pleasures and luxuries beyond the reach of the average Chinese viewer.

As an overseas Chinese, Zhou's first trip to China, before the fall of the Gang of Four, is as a tourist. She meets Geng Hua at Lushan Mountain, and almost all the scenes in the movie use famous scenic sites as backdrops. Furthermore, she has all the wealth and privileges associated with a Caucasian American. In the first scene of the film, which takes place at the beginning of her second trip to China, she is pictured being chauffeured to a guesthouse on the mountain. Most moviegoers would have been used to traveling by bicycle. The room she is allotted is luxurious beyond imagination by Chinese 1980 standards, including a prominently displayed air conditioner. She is also notably prone to self-adornment, something not encouraged in post-Liberation China until well into the 1980's.[14] In the opening scenes, she appears in a figure-hugging white pants suit. In the next scene, as she remembers her first sighting of Geng Hua, she appears in red slacks and a white top. When she witnesses him drawing a future city in the mountains, she is wearing a fuchsia-colored angora sweater and a necklace, and so on.

Zhou's American upbringing also motivates behavior that would be seen as immodest for a woman by the Chinese standards of the time. She pursues Geng, suggesting they become friends and offering to shake hands. After they are reunited during her second trip she wishes aloud that he might be a bit more forward, and when he doesn't respond, kisses him on the cheek. The setting at Lushan with all its legends prompts him to describe her as a fairy come down from the heavens. She calls him her Confucius, and when she first spots him on a famous rock, imagines him as the ancient seer her father told her once sat there reading. This would have been condemned as feudal superstition during the Cultural Revolution.

Finally, it must be noted that the cinematic representation of love in *Romance on Lushan Mountain* borrows heavily from the Chinese imagination of what love looks like overseas. When Zhou and Geng meet again after five

Figure 5.1 Reunion in *Romance on Lushan Mountain.*

years, they first spot each other from different sides of a lake. The camera cuts back and forth between them as they call out each other's names and race down to the lake, Zhou moving rightwards, and Geng leftwards. In one shot, the frame is even split into three columns, Zhou and Geng running towards each other in each of the side panels, and the lake in the central one (Figure 5.1). When they reach the lakeside, items of clothing are shown flying into the air, although the following shots reveal that they have not stripped completely. They then dive in and race to embrace in the center of the lake. Again, nation building does not appear to be at the forefront of their minds.

Romance on Lushan Mountain was one of the most successful films of 1980. Shanghai Film Studio followed up by casting the same two lead actors, Zhang Yu and Guo Kaimin, in a 1981 follow-up love story, *On a Narrow Street*. This film features a premise based on the well-known legend of Zhu Yingtai and Liang Shangbo. Instead of having to disguise herself as a boy to gain access to education, as in the original legend, the female of the couple cross-dresses to avoid the worst excesses of the Cultural Revolution. Before this is known, the two form an elder brother/little brother pair. In addition to the latent homoerotic possibilities of this scenario, the audience is also titillated by the prospect of her true identity being revealed in various scenes, including one where she falls into some water and may have to take her clothes off. Sympathy for her sufferings forms the basis of his love, but there are no common shared political ideals bonding these lovers.

In regard to causes for and responses to the above tendencies, the same reasons critics have suggested for the Party and state's reservations about romantic love in literature may also apply to film. Kam Louie notes that the widening scope and range of love stories as they moved away from the "shared commitment to socialism" of 1978 represents a trend towards individualism and liberalism.[15] Perry Link states that, "romance encourages self-indulgence, which implies obedience to inner impulses in preference to externally imposed rules."[16]

These observations echo the concerns expressed in the 1981 *People's Daily* articles discussed above. However, earlier policy changes excluded the possibility of banning the representation of romantic love. Party leader Hu Yaobang had already sanctioned "lighter subjects" in early 1980, meaning that politics did not have to be at the center of every work and that romance was permissible.[17] Also in early 1980, the venerable playwright, critic, and screenplay writer Xia Yan specifically sanctioned romantic themes in an interview.[18] Accordingly, the *People's Daily* articles and the *Beijing Review* summary of the debate all state that no one is opposed to the representation of love itself. However, apart from the representation of certain subject matters considered vulgar and pornographic listed above, it is stated that good representations of love do not show love for love's sake alone but connect it to social construction and the pursuit of lofty ideals. Westernization is singled out, with "scenes of young men chasing after their lovers, kissing and embracing" in Chinese films being noted out as prime examples of inappropriate copying from the West.[19]

ROMANTIC LOVE, THE FAMILY, AND THE PARTY

The existing critical discussions of romantic love in the literature and arts of late seventies and early eighties mainland China are plausible, so long as love is abstracted from works in which it appears and treated separately. This approach produces a binary understanding of love between characters in both film and literature. On the one hand, there is socialist love; a Communist Chinese representation in which love is born out of and subordinated to socialism and the drive for the Four Modernizations. On the other hand, there is romantic love; a Western import in which love is represented as an individualistic and autonomous force, often at odds with the demands of socialist construction.

Although both Chinese and Western discourses share this binary understanding, they understand it differently. Most of the Western scholarly discussions stem from a Chinese Studies tradition characterized by "humanist" values ascribed to the May Fourth Generation and its celebrants such as C.T. Hsia. Within this discourse, characteristics ascribed to both early twentieth-century and post-Mao romantic love such as individualism, liberalism, free choice, idealism, and even Westernization resonate with the broader "humanist" values ascribed to the May Fourth movement.[20] For the *People's Daily* columnists, dubbing romantic love as a Western import and foreclosing on local connections plays into their deployment of nationalist sentiment against threats to the authority of the Party.

The idea of romantic love as a Western import is plausible. Scenes such as the one where the lovers run Cathy-and-Heathcliff-like towards each other in *Romance on Lushan Mountain* are reminiscent of Western romantic fiction and film, even if as filtered through Taiwanese melodrama. Furthermore, there are historical reasons for this Chinese association of romantic love with the West. As Tonglin Lu points out in a comparative study of narratives of desire in China and France, *aiqing*, the very term used in China to characterize these "love films" (*aiqing pian*), is a late nineteenth century neologism, "possibly deriving from some translations of Western novels."[21] Beginning in the late nineteenth century, the right to love was espoused along with many other ideas considered Western.[22] This was then taken up as part of the May Fourth Movement, which began in 1919 and was intended to empower by appropriating from the West and overthrowing established feudalism.[23]

However, in this case, the right to pursue love was not quite the same thing as in the West. Certainly, it involved and was directly modeled on a range of experimentation and activities similar to those pursued in the West at the same time. However, its significance was overdetermined by the local context, where it stood in opposition to the power of the family over the individual in the determination of marriage and relationships, a power which was far stronger than that exercised in the West at this time.[24] The Communist Party took up these values, forbidding arranged marriages, bride-selling, concubinage, and other "feudal" practices in favor of freedom of choice and freedom of divorce, although they are considered to have faltered in implementing policies after coming to power in 1949.[25]

If freedom to love could mean something rather different in its Chinese context, maybe the same is true for romantic love. Indeed, by returning it to its discursive context, one important difference between the earlier twentieth century and the late seventies and early eighties representations can be seen immediately. Prior to the late seventies and early eighties, the Communist Party was aligned on the side of romantic love against the feudal family. However, as has been indicated, in the late seventies and early eighties, romantic love and the conservative forces in the Party are represented in opposition.

This major shift becomes even clearer if the increasing representation of romantic love in the films under consideration is correlated to two other elements. The first is the appearance of lead characters without significant romantic or family ties. Figures such as these were very common in the films of the classical Chinese cinema, especially during the Cultural Revolution period, when they were frequently exemplary Party figures. The second factor is the appearance of narratives structured in part around separation or tension among family members or between lovers.

The appearance of lead characters without significant romantic or family ties correlates inversely to the appearance of romantic love in the films. Such figures are a hallmark of the first three years of the six-year period under consideration, when romantic love is largely absent. Ten out of the eleven 1976 films, all four of the 1977 films, and nine of the eleven 1978 films feature such characters.[26] Most frequently, they are authority figures such as Party branch secretaries, revolutionary committee leaders, and so forth. Even in the 1976 films where the lead figure is a new bride as well as a Party representative, such as *Song of the New Wind* and *Jewel of the Sea*, the exogamous tradition makes these women outsiders both to the village and the family, and affective ties are de-emphasized in favor of their ability to bring new insight and leadership to their new environments.

In contrast, the last three years of the period under consideration, when romantic love becomes more common, feature few such figures. Only four of the fourteen 1979 films feature unattached lead characters.[27] For 1980 and 1981, the figures are three out of twenty-three and one out of eighteen respectively. Significantly, four of these seven figures are police officers. These are the leads in *Sacred Duty, A Handcuffed Passenger, Murder in 405,* and *Ghost.* As discussed in chapter four, while this maintains their authority, it places them at one remove from the Party. The leads in the other three films, *Fast As Light, My Ten Classmates,* and *The Side Road,* also have no significant direct connection to the Party. Therefore, even those few films of the last three years that do have unattached lead characters do not continue the classical cinema paradigm.

On the other hand, the representation of romantic love correlates to the appearance of narratives constructed around separation or differences between family members or the members of a romantic couple. Again, these are very rare between 1976 and 1979, with only one each of the eleven 1976 and eleven 1978 films and none of the 1977 films featuring such narrative structures. The exceptional films are *South Sea Storm* (1976) and *Salimake* (1978). Between 1979 and 1981, most films include such narratives. Of the fourteen films made in 1979, nine include such narrative elements; nineteen of the twenty-three 1980 films include them; and fully seventeen of the eighteen 1981 films include them.[28]

The inverse correlation between the decline of the lead character with no family or romantic ties and the rise of romantic love can be accounted for in terms of the opposition between the conservative forces in the Party and romance as a force that diminishes the authority of the Party and the state. The direct correlation between the rise of romantic love and the rise of narratives featuring separation or difference among members of the family or romantic couple, on the other hand, suggests a homology between the narrative function of the family and of romantic love in these films. This triadic relationship between elements in the films of the late seventies and early eighties indicates a major shift in the significance of love in twentieth century China. It is not merely that romantic love with its Western and rebellious connotations returns in these films, but also that its significance is quite different. Where in earlier texts the family represented feudal authority and the Party and romantic love were aligned against it, in these films the Party represents negative authority and the family and romantic love are at least implicitly aligned against it.

This new homology between romantic love and the family can be seen quite clearly in the films of 1980 and 1981. In film after film, Party policy intervenes to disrupt family and romantic ties, and the hermeneutic of the narrative is structured around whether these obstacles will be overcome. For example, as the synopses given in Appendix One reveal, lovers and/or family members taking different political lines causes separation and dissension in *They Are In Love, Death of the Marshal, Sea Love, The Legend of Tianyun Mountain, Volleyball Star, Maple, A Late Spring, Rays Penetrating the Clouds,* (all 1980), *Xu Mao and His Daughters, Laughter in Moon Bay, On a Narrow Street, May Love Be Everlasting, The Spiral, Set Sail, Revival, Whirlpool Song, Spirit of the Foil, Dance Love,* and *The Corner Forgotten by Love* (all 1981).

Two further narrative patterns reveal the full ideological force and significance of the rearrangement between the Party, romantic love and the family. First, although a few films still represent feudal attitudes as an obstacle to romantic love, where this occurs, these attitudes run with rather than against incorrect Cultural Revolution policies. Second, where parents and family still form an obstacle to romantic love and this obstacle is not represented as feudal, it is the result of political authority, usually in the form of the Party and its policies during the Cultural Revolution.

The homology between feudalism and the Party as parallel obstacles to romantic fulfillment occurs in the two versions of *Xu Mao and His Daughters* and *The Corner Forgotten by Love* (all 1981). All three films are set in the countryside, a standard setting for "backward" behavior, and in all three films parents are opposed to their daughters' love affairs and attempt to push them into arranged marriages. In each case, Party figures do not intervene to prevent these feudal practices but exacerbate the situation. For example, in *The Corner Forgotten by Love*, the discovery of a pre-marital affair during the height of the Cultural Revolution years leads to imprisonment on a charge of rape for the young man and suicide for the young woman.

The second pattern, where politics stimulates parental objections or obstacles to romantic love, is more common and more various in the forms it takes. This pattern occurs in *Romance on Lushan Mountain, Come Back, Swallow, Rays Penetrating the Clouds*, (all 1980), both versions of *Xu Mao and His Daughters, Laughter in Moon Bay, Set Sail, Whirlpool Song*, and *The Corner Forgotten by Love*. In *Come Back, Swallow*, for example, the lovers discover that their parents were on opposite sides during the Cultural Revolution, and therefore their history provides an obstacle to their romance. Similarly, in *Romance on Lushan Mountain*, Geng Hua's father was a Communist general, whereas Zhou Yun's was a Kuomintang general. In *Set Sail*, the obstacle occurs because the girlfriend discovers that her boyfriend's mother is a woman she beat up when she was a Red Guard.

Returning romantic love to its discursive context in these films enables a different understanding of its significance. First, although its characteristics may be Westernized, its socio-political functions are different, because it is aimed at a different authority than before. Second, in these texts, the experience of romantic love is not simply a foreign affectation as suggested by the *People's Daily* line, but represented as homologous to and often an integral part of the experience of the family and kinship relations in Communist China.

MEMORY, SUBJECTIVITY, AND COMMUNITY

Furthermore, the use of editing to encourage the spectator to take up certain positions also particularizes and differentiates the specific local character of romantic love in this period, as well as differentiating it from the Chinese classical cinema. This difference occurs on the level of enunciation rather than narrative, and concerns the deployment of flashback and subjective devices.

As discussed in chapter two, flashback and subjectivity are extremely rare in the classical Chinese cinema. Instead, the camera maintains a third person perspective that gives the viewer knowledge of the situation analogous to that of the Party and state authority figures in the film. The social position of these figures is connoted to be as detached and as objective as that of the camera and therefore the viewer. Also like the viewer, they are usually outsiders whom the narrative follows as they acquire knowledge. In this way, although they do not usually act as sole relays for the camera via camera position, they are connoted to be relays of enunciation. The overall effect is to give the viewer a sense of a privileged perspective beyond that of any single character that permits epistemological mastery.

So far as the films under consideration here continue to have such Party and state authority figures with no significant romantic or family ties to other figures, this enunciation is usually maintained, even when these figures are police officers autonomous from the Party. Almost all the narratives I have examined from 1980 and 1981 and many of the 1978 and 1979 ones, too, are told from a time after the political trauma that either disrupts romantic love or family relationships. Some of the 1977 and 1978 films that also follow this pattern deploy an investigative Party secretary or other authority figure to trace the past. *Tear Stain* is an example.

The premise of *Tear Stain* is the appointment of a new Party secretary, Zhu Keshi, to Jin County. This is a typical situation for a classical Chinese film, with the Party and state authority figures entering the main setting from outside, and having no family or romantic attachments to any of the other characters. Zhu's appointment takes place soon after the downfall of the Gang, and as he travels around he discovers problems that have their roots in the past ten years. These are symbolized by the presence of Kong Nina, the mad widow of former Party Secretary Cao Yi, wandering the streets. This reference to causes located during the Cultural Revolution is also typical of the post-1976 films. Zhu Keshi then proceeds to investigate. Throughout, the third person enunciation typical of the classical Chinese film is maintained. Although a number of characters relate their terrible experiences during the Cultural Revolution, there are no flashbacks and no access to their subjectivities. Rather, the enunciation is maintained as parallel to the observation of Zhu Keshi.

Even though the third person enunciation and the unattached lead character of *Tear Stain* is similar to the typical pattern found in the classical Chinese cinema, even this film differs from that model in important ways. The film does offer the epistemological mastery of the classical model, but it breaks with that model's pedagogical project. Although Zhu Keshi is a new Party secretary, he behaves more like a detective investigating a crime. And his motivation is the solving of a crime rather than the promotion of a particular policy. As noted, this model of third person enunciation and epistemological mastery is also common in films featuring police officers in the lead. Therefore, in addition to distancing themselves from the Party and its policies, these police films mark themselves out from the didactic paradigm by moving from constructing a pedagogical engagement for the spectator towards a hermeneutic, mystery-solving engagement. Here, there is a vital difference from the epistemological mastery of the didactic paradigm. Whereas the spectator tends to know more than any of the characters in the didactic paradigm, the spectator's knowledge follows that of lead characters and investigators like Zhu Keshi in these police films.

However, as has already been noted, figures such as Zhu Keshi were on the wane by 1979, and police officers are not particularly prominent in the films under consideration. How is enunciation structured in other films? How does this relate to the characterization of romantic love as a Western import? And how does this effect the relation of the spectator to the film? For the most part, films without lead characters with no romantic or family ties do not maintain objective enunciation. In contrast, these films employ a high degree of subjectivity through the use of the flashback and other subjective devices. With the possible exception of the film noir, there can be few other cycles of films that are so dependent upon complex flashback structures as these late seventies and early eighties films depicting the Cultural Revolution period.

In these films, unlike *Tear Stain*, a flashback structure told from the point of view of the characters that are victims of the trauma is most common. *Romance on Lushan Mountain* features two trips to China by Zhou Yun, one during the Cultural Revolution and one after it. She and Geng Hua are separated during the first, and the film begins with the second trip, using her flashbacks to recount what happened before. Moving back and forth with Zhou Yun's thoughts through her various experiences creates a complex narrative chronology, and the emphasis on her subjectivity is added to by the use of fantasy sequences, as for example when she imagines Geng Hua as a legendary scholar. However, this is a relatively simple example. Much more complex articulations occur more frequently, in most cases involving more than one character. It is impossible to single out any one film as typical, but detailing a few will illustrate the variety and complexity of the flashback structures.

In many films, one character may be privileged in the way that Zhou Yun is, standing as the main relay of narration. However, while this character may have a flashback that starts the narrative and sometimes encompasses the entire narrative, other characters will also have flashbacks within this frame flashback. In *The Legend of Tianyun Mountain*, Song Wei has the frame flashback and carries the main weight of the enunciation. Although her memory concerns an investigation into an appeal against a Rightist verdict, her position is quite different from that of Zhu Keshi in *Tear Stain*. Where Zhu is an outsider, she is intimately involved in the case she is investigating and morally ambiguous. After the credits, the film starts with Song's voice-over in the present as we see the beginning of the story she is telling us on the soundtrack. Within this frame flashback, she experiences a number of other lengthy flashbacks as events in 1978 cause her to remember the 1950s and what happened between her, Luo Qun, Feng Qinglan, and Wu Yao. Ellipses in these flashbacks are bridged by her voice-over narration. Further complicating Song's flashbacks within the frame flashback are other subjective effects, including further flashbacks. During the major crisis when Wu Yao tells her Luo Qun has been accused of being a Rightist and urges her to break with him, Song Wei experiences brief memories of her experiences, usually single shots, interspersed with shots of her face in shock in the present time of the lengthy flashback to the 1950s. These flashes of memory communicate her turmoil. The next day, as she tries to write a letter to Luo breaking with him, she has aural flashbacks of Wu Yao's words over further flashback images of her experiences with Luo. She also either remembers or fantasizes close-ups of the faces of people pressing her to break with him; it is impossible to tell which, because we have not seen these images before. Still within the same lengthy flashback to the fifties, at the wedding reception following her marriage to Wu Yao, she experiences a vision of a horse galloping. This is a reference to Luo, as he is associated with horse riding in the film. Finally, at the end of the film, her voice-over memories bring the frame flashback up to the present from which she is narrating and close the film.

However, unlike *Romance on Lushan Mountain*, which also has a female relay of enunciation and complex flashback and fantasy structures, Song Wei is not the only character to have memories in the film. Indeed her own memories are prompted by a story a young friend tells her about meeting Luo Qun and Feng Qinglan. This story is told in two flashbacks within the frame flashback. More interestingly, Song Wei and Feng Qinglan can be said to share a flashback. Song Wei reads a letter from Feng Qinglan relating what has happened to Feng and Luo after Song Wei broke off with Luo. As Song imagines Feng writing, she also imagines Feng remembering what she is writing about, which then leads to a lengthy flashback authorized through them both and featuring much voice-over from Feng's letter. At one particularly dramatic moment, when Feng is speaking in the voice-over of the beatings she received, the film returns to Song in 1978 and Song imagines she sees Feng in her room staring, almost accusingly, at her. The shots of

Feng are taken from Song's position, enabling the audience to share her experience of this moment.

Other films do not employ the frame flashback device, but also do not attribute flashbacks to only one character. Instead, a number of characters have them. Most frequently, this device is motivated as part of the reunion and separation narrative structure. Characters separated will miss each other and remember each other, and once reunited will tell each other what they went through while they were separated. A 1980 romance called *Dance Love* provides an example. The couple consists of a Han Chinese man and an Yi minority nationality woman. Both are professional dancers, and the film begins after the Cultural Revolution during which she is thought to have died. The initial flashbacks cover his memories of their meeting, prompted by a train journey back to her home area. Then, after she is discovered to have survived and he is searching for her, she spots him and this prompts her memories of what she perceives as his betrayal.

The differences between them are finally overcome when they exchange dances they have choreographed. In each case, the dances depict their sufferings during the Cultural Revolution, so this is a case of self-referentiality; the text within the text, itself suggesting a possible model for the spectator's relation to the film. As each looks at the written and drawn version of the dance, they imagine it being performed. In the course of the imagined performance, they also imagine segments of the other's earlier flashbacks. Their individual knowledge and suffering is shared, and thus the ground is laid for the overcoming of their individual isolation and their reconciliation.

Many other 1980 and 1981 films also combine narratives constructed around the separation and reunion of family and/or lovers with complex flashback enunciation and subjective devices including fantasy segments.[29] Despite the many different types of flashback and subjective device deployed in different films, certain generalizations can be made. First, only sympathetic characters have flashbacks or access to subjectivity, and these sympathetic characters are nearly all people who have been the objects of political authority, suffering the trauma of separation from family or loved ones as a result. This further emphasizes the shift away from the perspective of the Party and towards that of the family and/or lovers, and the homology between the family and lovers.

Second, these flashbacks and subjective devices are rarely simply private memories or instances of libidinalized fantasy. The relatively high level of libidinality in Zhou Yun's memories and fantasies in *Romance on Lushan Mountain* is unusual in this regard, and may be attributable to her Americanized upbringing. Rather, they are more usually part of a process of sharing private grief and pain and of bridging gaps in knowledge. This is clearly the case in *Dance Love*, where separation has caused misunderstandings that can only be bridged in this manner. In some cases, such as *The Legend of Tianyun Mountain*, the films are tragic, in that someone has died and so there is no way of restoring the family or the romantic couple, or ambiguous, because the restoration has not yet occurred. Nonetheless, the enunciation of these films deploys the flashback as a means of sharing experiences and implying the spectator into the network of characters who share these experiences.[30]

This mode of enunciation further indicates that post-Mao romantic love has a particular local and historical significance distinct from a generalized Western model. Although flashbacks and subjective devices are used, they rarely construct an individualized romantic subject or a libidinal relation on the part of the spectator. Rather, romantic love in these films is part of a process of sharing subjectivities, and particularly suffering, and this process is again homologous to that which characterizes family and kinship bonds.

Second, this enunciation is quite distinct from that of the Chinese classical cinema. Instead of instating a knowledge analogous to the position of the Party and connoted to be privileged, objective, outside, and beyond that of the characters caught up in the narrative, these films emphasize the experiential knowledge of the participants in the narrative, the objects of political authority. Furthermore, by sharing these flashbacks amongst the characters and with the spectator, the films also set up an intense affective bond among peers including the spectator — a sort of nostalgic, emotional community that is implied to have lost a prior shared subjectivity and to be attempting to reconstruct it.

THE PEER GROUP AND CHINESE COUNTERCULTURE

This shared subjectivity and experience is that of the peer group, as opposed to the hierarchy, and the peer group as both a resistant force and a countercultural refuge from official society has a long tradition in Chinese culture. In the leftist film canon of the 1930s, for example, peer groups of young men and women, be they students, workers, or refugees, are frequently the main protagonists. Examples include *Big Road* (*Dalu*), *Crossroads* (*Shizijietou*), and *Street Angel* (*Malu Tianshi*). Previous studies have examined the constitution of the peer group in *Big Road* and *Street Angel*, and in both these films, like *The Legend of Tianyun Mountain*, female characters play a powerful role in the construction of the shared subjectivity of the peer group through flashbacks and fantasy structures, the latter often motivated by the lyrics of songs they sing.[31]

Going back further to imperial times, martial arts legends and other tales about outlaws such as *Water Margin* also celebrate bands that constitute peer groups outside and often in conflict with the social hierarchy. On an even broader level, Robert Thaxton has argued for the existence of an "egalitarian peasant counterculture." Although this does not diminish hierarchy within the peasant household, it does promote the peasant patriarchs as a type of peer group struggling for autonomy versus the centralized social hierarchy.[32] Ma Ning has used this concept in his study of melodrama in Chinese cinema.[33]

The significance of post-Mao romantic love in the cinema cannot be understood in isolation. It is as modified from the Western form it assumes as a formal model in Chinese films of the late seventies as freedom to love was for former generations. In other words, it is a dynamic hybrid. Where freedom to love was adopted and adapted to form part of a struggle aimed at feudal authority symbolized by the family, romantic love has been co-opted into the countercultural struggle to carve out a space of autonomous experience distinct from and possibly also in opposition to that of Party. As such, while its egalitarian and voluntary form may be valued, individualism is downplayed in favor of an homology with the family, which itself is also refigured in these movies as a resistant, countercultural peer group where common status is based on having suffered as a result of the policies and programs of the Party-state apparatus.

This transformed group of films about the Cultural Revolution also breaks with the didactic paradigm of the classical Chinese cinema in a manner that constitutes it as the first sustained instance of postsocialist Chinese cinema. Its primary themes are not the socialist modernist construction of a brave new world but the threats to and the maintenance or otherwise of the affective bonds that bind its characters together. Those characters are not the agents of the Party-state apparatus and the implementers of its policies and programs but the objects of those operations, and their primary motivations are not how to learn to do what the Party-state apparatus expects of them but how to manage, deflect, dodge, and overcome the obstacles those demands constitute to the maintenance of their affective ties. And finally, the enunciatory structures of this cinema do not try to place the spectator as a pupil but as an empathizer and as a virtual member of the group. This is a cinema that breaks free of the monolithic and conformist grand narratives of modernist progress to focus on the localized, experience-based narratives of individual characters and the groups they participate in. In these circumstances, although this group of films has not won lasting praise according to the aesthetic art house standards of international festivals, it marks the beginning of China's postsocialist cinema.

Chapter 6

ENDING IT ALL: BITTER LOVE

I have seen the movie *Sun and Man*, which follows the script of *Unrequited Love*. Whatever the author's motives, the movie gives the impression that the Communist Party and the socialist system are bad. It vilifies the latter to such an extent that one wonders what has happened to the author's Party spirit. Some say the movie achieves a fairly high artistic standard, but that only makes it all the more harmful. In fact, a work of this sort has the same effect as the views of the so-called democrats.

— Deng Xiaoping

In this 17 July 1981 article entitled "Concerning Problems on the Ideological Front," Deng Xiaoping clarifies an apparent point of confusion at the end of the seventies. He is prompted to do this by the debate around the film script by Bai Hua called *Bitter Love* (also translated as *Unrequited Love*). The film that resulted, whose title literally means *The Sun and the Man*, never saw the light of day. But it was screened for Deng and other party leaders upon completion. After making the comments quoted above, Deng emphasizes that no matter how many flowers are allowed to bloom in the arts, nothing is allowed to transgress the basic rule, "the essence of the four cardinal principles," that Party leadership is to be upheld above all else.[1]

The banning of *Bitter Love* did not happen discreetly, although later accounts from within the People's Republic follow the official line of describing it as only a "rectification."[2] In fact, it was accompanied by public attacks on the film, the script, and its author. This was the first time an individual artist and an individual work had been held up as a negative example since the end of the Cultural Revolution. Officially this was not a "movement" or "campaign" (*yundong*), because the leadership had promised no more movements at the Third Plenum in 1979. But it bore all the hallmarks of a movement.[3] It effectively put an end to the cycle of films that used the Cultural Revolution years as a setting. Such films did not disappear completely. For example, Xie Jin's famous melodrama *Hibiscus Town*, was made in 1986. However, such films were sporadic and no longer part of a dominant cycle.

The twists and turns of the attacks against *Bitter Love* and Bai Hua have been recounted often and in detail.[4] Briefly, the script was published in 1979, but no attention was paid until the film was completed early in 1981.[5] After seeing it, Deng gave permission for public criticism in March because he felt the film did not uphold the four cardinal principles.[6] The *Liberation Army Daily* led the attack on Bai Hua and the film. In the spring and early summer, Hu Yaobang and other moderate leaders tried to restrain the attack. For example, Hu criticized the critics for being excessive in public remarks at a symposium in May, and this was followed by a *People's Daily* article in June. Many others rallied behind this.[7] But in June 1981, once the leftist Hua Guofeng had stepped down from his remaining posts, Deng decided it was time to crack down more on those on the right, whom he had indulged in his efforts to build his power up. This is when he made the remarks quoted at the beginning of this chapter. Attacks continued, stressing not dwelling on the mistakes of the socialist era and looking towards the bright future. In October 1981, the editors of *Literary Gazette* published a criticism of Bai and the film, as demanded by Deng.[8] This should have marked the end of the virtual campaign. However, the army press continued its attacks until Bai made and published a self-criticism.[9] At the end of the year, Hu Yaobang was able to declare the matter settled and that Bai Hua would continue to work as a writer.[10] This brought great relief to the arts world, but it also clearly defined the limits to the new artistic freedoms that had been won in the late seventies. And while Bai may have gone on working as a writer, no more films like *Bitter Love* were made.

Why were Bai Hua and *Bitter Love* selected for attack? The film itself is about a painter called Ling Chenguang. His experiences growing up in the thirties and forties turn him into an ardent socialist in Shanghai. However, he becomes an inadvertent overseas Chinese when an ocean liner he has taken refuge on sets sail. In the United States, he becomes a famous artist, but his patriotism leads him to return to China. There, his dreams are dashed during the Cultural Revolution. He takes refuge in marshlands. When people come to try and rescue him at the end of the Cultural Revolution, he mistakenly believes that they are going to persecute him more and so flees deeper into the marshes. Before they can reach him, he dies. As seen from his would-be rescuers' helicopter, his body forms the dot at the base of a big question mark he has drawn in the snow.[11]

The October 1981 *Literary Gazette* criticism is extensive and synthesizes most of the various lines of attack on the script and film made elsewhere during the year. A primary concern is that *Bitter Love* is unpatriotic in its attitude towards socialist China. "In this work, the authors confused the Gang of Four with the motherland, thus treating the motherland that was suffering under the tyranny of the Gang of Four as the object of the denunciation. This cannot but give people the impression that both the Communist Party and the socialist system are bad."[12] To support this conclusion, the *Literary Gazette* criticism cites various scenes, such as the one when his daughter asks him if his country loves him in the same way he loves it, and he is unable to reply.[13] In his careful analysis, Michael Duke points out that whereas the painter uses the broad term *zuguo*, meaning "ancestral land," his daughter uses the more specific term *guojia*, which means "nation-state," and therefore in this case the People's Republic itself.[14] In response, in his self-criticism, Bai Hua acknowledges that he failed "to define the boundaries between the Gang of Four and the socialist motherland, the party and the people."[15]

Another specific scene discussed features Ling asking a Buddhist monk why the statue of the Buddha in a temple is blackened, and being told this is because so many people have burnt incense before it. This was understood as a reference to the personality cult surrounding Mao, and was criticized for painting a completely negative picture of Mao and the Party leadership rather than presenting a proper analysis of the personality cult.[16] Again, Bai acknowledges this error, confessing that the image "constitutes a taunt and a simple negation of Comrade Mao Zedong" in which "the revolutionary leader was likened to a 'Buddha image' and a symbol of feudal superstition."[17] In other words, he failed to draw the proper line between old and new China.

Ling's overnight success after his arrival in the United States is also criticized for suggesting that, whereas he faces terrible problems in his own motherland, "[T]his capitalist world of America is a heaven for Chinese intellectuals and for artists."[18] Bai does not specifically mention this point in his self-criticism. But the failing here is to draw the proper line between capitalism and socialism.

The time lag of over a year between publication of the script and the criticisms casts doubt over whether the script alone triggered the response. The changing political circumstances of 1980 and 1981 may have only made it possible for conservative forces to take action at this particular time rather than earlier. Indeed, the brief summary of the virtual campaign against *Bitter Love* given above indicates close links to political events that would fit this account. Some commentators have also noted that Bai Hua had a long history of speaking out against conservative policies in literature and the arts, which may also have predisposed those on the left to single him out for punishment.[19]

THE IMPORTANCE OF ENDINGS

This book does not pursue the question of why Bai Hua and *Bitter Love* were singled out any further. To do so without new material evidence would be to indulge in speculation. However, in keeping with the overall question of how the films under consideration here break with classical Chinese cinema, it does use the ending of *Bitter Love* to consider the question of endings. Didactic narratives tend to privilege resolution as an important element in the effectiveness of message transmission, and to value clear and unambiguous resolution as a means to that end.

Therefore, it is not surprising that the criticisms of *Bitter Love* frequently cite the ending as a problem. For example, *Literary Gazette* mentions it as further evidence of Bai Hua's failure to draw an adequate line between the Gang of Four and the Communist Party.

> The filmscript gives Liang [sic] Chengguang a tragic ending — he dies of frostbite and despair while on the run. The authors even made him draw, by crawling on his stomach on a snow-covered field, a big question mark to show his (and the authors') immense doubt and strong condemnation of the results of this "unrequited love." In many parts of this filmscript and with the question mark, the essential difference between the [old] society and socialist society were obliterated and our socialist system was confused with the crimes of the Gang of Four.[20]

The authors refuse to interpret the question mark as ambiguous, and insist on seeing it as purely negative.

In his work devoted entirely to the analysis of endings in cinema, Richard Neupert points out that, although endings in literature have received attention, the same is not true of the cinema.[21] To develop a model for the analysis of different types of ending, Neupert follows the distinction common in literary criticism between the resolution of the story (the events told or *énoncé*) and the closure of the narrative discourse (the telling of the events or *énonciation*).[22] On this basis, he develops a four-part model.[23] The following chapters in his book examine each in turn. First, there is the closed text, in which the story is resolved and the narrative discourse closed. The classical Hollywood film is given as the standard example. Second is the open story, in which the narrative discourse is closed but the story is unresolved. Here, the art film and in particular certain early French New Wave films such as Truffaut's work and Italian neo-realist films are cited as examples where the cinematic language offers closure, but the text signifies that it is "realistic" by leaving some major action codes in the story unresolved. Third is the open discourse, a largely theoretical category in which the story is resolved but the narrative discourse is open. And fourth is the open text, in which the story is unresolved and the narrative discourse open. Godard is the example for extended analysis.

Neupert points out that the Hollywood closed text is so dominant that, when confronted with other types of texts, spectator habit tends to encourage readings which attempt to impose both narrative closure and story resolution regardless.[24] The classical Chinese cinema is also a closed text system. The major action codes composing the stories of all six films discussed in chapter two are resolved, and cinematic discourse is deployed to signify closure. Like the Hollywood film, the happy ending is almost universal. The only break with the preference for total closure and resolution is a suggestion that the resolution achieved within this story and text lays the foundation for a better tomorrow. For example, *Early Spring in February* ends with Tao Lan and Li Jianqiu leaving Hibiscus Town. In a very limited sense, this could be said to open on to a new story. However, the major action codes have all been concerned how they should contribute towards the cause for a better China. Leaving Hibiscus Town marks the resolution of this question, presumable with a decision to join the revolution.

As the criticisms of *Bitter Love* remind us, the founding principles of the People's Republic require a clear line between the "old" society and the "new." A tragic ending can be permitted in the old society, although the classical Chinese cinema prefers a gesture towards a brighter tomorrow, like the ending of *Early Spring in February*. The eponymous bridge in *Bridge* is also completed so that the struggle to establish the People's Republic may continue, and Chunhua in *Stage Sisters* is reunited with Yuehong soon after the founding of the People's Republic. In the new society, nothing less that an optimistic faith in the Party and progress towards a better society is acceptable. *Li Shuangshuang* is able to persuade everyone including her husband of the benefits of the commune and the work point system, and they march off into a bright future together at the end of the film.

However, unlike classical Hollywood cinema, this system is not maintained by the discipline of the box office, but by the Party-state apparatus through various proactive and reactive mechanisms outlined in chapter two, including an active censorship system. In these circumstances, audience habits may be different. The disaffected may be looking for moments of ambiguity and irresolution. Given the importance of a clear ending for the didactic paradigm, they may be sensitive to elements they can mobilize against the obligatory socialist happy ending.

In the remaining sections of this final chapter, those elements of both story resolution and narrative closure which might seem to diverge from the obligatory socialist happy ending will be examined with an eye towards the emergence of ambiguity. There is no argument that these moments constitute the films as truly open texts. Rather, in this manner these films not only constitute a break with the past abut also offer a different kind of gesture towards the future from the socialist happy ending.

First, and still within Neupert's closed text model, the potential problem posed for the conventional socialist happy ending by the appearance of socialist tragedy in these films will be examined. The section will argue that the majority of films with major action codes ending in socialist tragedy counter the potential for this to become part of an ending unacceptable to the authorities in various ways. This is even the case for *Bitter Love*, although this effort did not work. Second, and within Neupert's open story model, the introduction of both false and genuine open story endings will be examined in more detail with close readings of some other films.

SOCIALIST TRAGEDIES AND OBLIGATORY HAPPY ENDINGS

Socialist tragedy occurs when something bad that cannot be put right occurs after the 1949 establishment of the People's Republic and can be attributed to the policies and programs of the Party and state. The death of Ling Chenguang after persecution at the end of *Bitter Love* is a good example. Yet, it is clearly not the first film in which socialist tragedy is represented. As detailed in chapter three, socialist tragedy first appears in the corpus films in 1979, and it proliferates thereafter. Prior to that, and in line with the policy of damage control and containment immediately after the Cultural Revolution decade, socialist tragedies are absent and not only the major action codes of the stories but also the narrative closure is always positive. In this way, the fall of the Gang of Four acquires the same quality of an absolute dividing line between the bad old days of the Cultural Revolution and the good days of the new era that 1949 had already had for so long.

After 1979, the death of a good person as a result of persecution or incorrect policy is the most common form that socialist tragedy takes in the films examined. In that year, the old heart surgeon Luo Bingzhen dies of persecution before the end of the Cultural Revolution in *Troubled Heart*; the plane designer Shi Feng and various colleagues die protecting their new plane from the Gang of Four in *Fast as Light*; the madwoman Kong Nina's husband has died during the Cultural Revolution in *Tear Stain*; some of the ten classmates die during the Cultural Revolution in *My Ten Classmates*; and Wang Gongbo dies performing his sacred duty and saving Yang Qiong in *Sacred Duty*. In 1980, the marshal is persecuted to death in *Death of the Marshal*; one of the four young men whom *Sea Love* focuses on is persecuted to death by one of the others; the father of *The Child Violinist* is persecuted to death in the Cultural Revolution; the son of an elderly woman in *Evening Rain* has been killed in the armed struggles of the Cultural Revolution; the self-sacrificing wife of Luo Qun dies of exhaustion in *The Legend of Tianyun Mountain*; one of the lovers who join opposing rebel factions during the early days of the Cultural Revolution in *Maple* dies in the fighting and the other is executed as a counter-revolutionary for having caused her death; and various people die because of the machinations of the Gang of Four and their followers in the murder mystery, *Ghost*. During 1981, the title character loses his son as a result of the "gang" in *The Investigator*; the main character's friend dies during the Cultural Revolution in *May Love Be Everlasting*; the dedicated fencing coach Qiao Fang dies of persecution during the Cultural Revolution in *Spirit of the Foil*; the elder sister is so persecuted during the Cultural Revolution for an illicit relationship in the rural film *The Corner Forgotten by Love* that she commits suicide; and before Yuan Wenping herself dies in remote exile in a mountain village in *The Crystal Heart*, her mother is persecuted to death during the Cultural Revolution for having translated *The Biography of Einstein*. This is an impressive litany.

Permanent injury is another form that socialist tragedy can take. The 1981 film *Set Sail* features a singer who has gone deaf as a result of a beating during the Cultural Revolution and the male lead in *On a Narrow Street*, also made in 1981, goes blind after a beating in the Cultural Revolution. By 1980, when love stories were common, accidental bigamy appears in *After the Nightmare Comes the Dawn* and *Not for Love*. In both cases, this results when a spouse thought to have been killed during the Cultural Revolution returns to discover their partner has remarried. In both cases, the new spouse nobly sacrifices herself or himself and leaves. This qualifies as a socialist tragedy, because one person must suffer in order that the other two may have a chance of being happy.

However, as the piquant ironies of the bigamy examples just given indicate, socialist tragedy within a film does not always imply a tragic ending to a film in which both story resolution and narrative closure are negative. In fact, *Bitter Love* is unusually bleak and provocative in its use of socialist tragedy as the outcome of the major action code in the film, namely Ling's life story of attempted patriotic contribution to society. Most examples use socialist tragedy in ways that are less likely than *Bitter Love* to be read as questioning the revolution. There are four patterns. Two concern the positioning of the socialist tragedy story element in the narrative as either a premise or as the outcome of a particular action code that is resolved before the end of the film and often off-screen. A third pattern is to give the tragedy positive connotations, from the point of view of the Party at least. A fourth pattern is use the narrative closure to suggest that although there may be socialist tragedies in the past, at least the future is bright.

First, the story event of socialist tragedy is positioned as a narrative premise for a number of films. In these circumstances, there is nowhere to go but up, and the narrative of the film can focus on overcoming the tragedy or moving beyond it. In *Tear Stain* (1979), Kong Nina's cadre husband cannot be brought back to life, but she can be cured of her madness and her husband's name can be cleared. In *May Love Be Everlasting* (1981), Huyan Ziqian discovers the death of his friend at the beginning of the narrative when he returns to his workplace after the smashing of the Gang of Four. However, this then enables him to meet his friend's widow and the scene is set for the formation of a new family, a redemptive theme that is the main action code of the film. *The Crystal Heart* is slightly more complex, as there are two deaths. The first, which is indeed a premise, is of Yuan Wenping's mother as a result of persecution during the Cultural Revolution. But in this case it only starts a chain of events and complications among the younger generation, including the two men Yuan gets involved with, Lai Zhiqing and Tang Ming.

Yuan Wenping's own death part way through *The Crystal Heart* is typical of the second pattern for softening the representation of socialist tragedy by placing it in the middle of the narrative, and often off-screen. In the case of Yuan Wenping's death, we are told this by another character long after it happened and long after she herself has disappeared from the events represented in the film. In many cases, the death is positioned in the overall narrative structure as the resolution of a relatively minor action code (in terms of the film), which is then transcended by a positive resolution of a more major code at the end of the film.

For example, during her journey to discover what has happened to her former friends in the 1979 film *My Ten Classmates*, Professor Fang Min finds that many have suffered and at least one has been persecuted to death in the Cultural Revolution. However, the film has an ending which echoes its beginning — a closure effect Neupert calls "bracketing," — and it is upbeat.[25] Fang Min is motivated to carry out her research at the beginning of the narrative by the 1977 debate about whether the educated classes can be considered of positive class background. The film ends with her overhearing a radio announcement that the educated classes have been awarded status as members of the proletariat.[26] In *The Child Violinist* (1980), when the title character's father is persecuted to death during the Cultural Revolution part of the way through the narrative, he implores his wife not to let their son work in the music world. But both the son and his elder sister overcome obstacles to enter a conservatory at the end of the narrative. So they demonstrate that in the new society established after the fall of the Gang of Four their father's fears are groundless.

A third pattern also eschewed by *Bitter Love* in its representation of socialist tragedy is to present it at the end of the film, but as a necessary sacrifice for the future of the socialist motherland. This martyrdom pattern was well established in Chinese revolutionary narratives before the late seventies. Probably one of the best-known heroes of this sort was Lei Feng, a soldier who expressed the desire to be a screw in a machine, sacrificed himself to save his colleagues, and was eulogized by Mao himself.[27] However, in the case of *Bitter Love*, nothing positive is achieved by Ling's death.

In contrast, many socialist tragedies are productive martyrdoms. In *Fast as Light* (1979), the heroes die to save their plane from falling into the hands of the Gang. Even in *The Death of the Marshal* (1980), at least he dies as a result of persecution and swearing his undying loyalty to the Party, unlike Ling who dies fleeing from rescuers he mistakes for persecutors and leaving a question mark in the snow. Provided one overlooks the fact that the Party was being run by the Gang and their followers during the Cultural Revolution, the marshal can be seen as a martyr, too.

From this survey, it can be seen that *Bitter Love* is unusual in placing socialist tragedy as both the end of the film and the resolution of the main action code in the story, with little if any hope for the future. But it was not the only film to do so. Among the other films to present socialist tragedy at the end of the narrative is the 1979 film, *Troubled Heart*. We discover that surgeon Luo Bingzhen has died in the final days of the Cultural Revolution when he is called to participate in a national science conference after the fall of the Gang of Four. However, here the fourth pattern is at work: a positive narrative closure to give a positive ending to the film despite the negative resolution of the story. The conference itself is the requisite confident gesture towards the happy future. The doctor's death, which is not presented on-screen, is a sobering note but not a challenge to the upbeat ending. The same bittersweet mixture of positive and negative elements can be found in the 1980 film, *Sea Love*. Although Liqiu discovers Nanxia's death and rushes to the shoreline to mourn him at the end of the film, at least the event sobers her up enough to make her break off her relationship with another man.

Perhaps the only other film to push the socialist tragedy element of story resolution as far as *Bitter Love* is the 1980 film, *Maple*, about the two young members of rebel factions in the early days of the Cultural Revolution. Yet, even this film's narrative closure handles the brutal end of the story more optimistically than that of *Bitter Love* in the published script. Both films have a coda or small epilogue that significantly modifies the socialist tragedy presented at the end of the film.

In *Bitter Love*, after the scene where the rescue helicopter has discovered the question mark in the snow and descended to discover Ling's corpse forming the dot at the base of it, there are three more small scenes. In the first, there is a shot from high up of the Chinese landscape, and over it is Ling Chenguang's patriotic statement, which ends with the phrase, "We have won the right to say, 'I love this land, my motherland.'" The next scene depicts a flock of geese making the outline of the Chinese character for "humankind" in the sky as they fly, and the theme song on the soundtrack reminds us of the beauty of this term. Finally, there is an image of a reed plant standing up in the roaring wind.[28] These images affirm Ling's patriotism. Presumably they should act as a counter to the seeming bleakness of the socialist tragedy. But the word used in Ling's patriotic statement is the problematic term *zuguo* ("ancestral land") discussed earlier in the chapter, rather than *guojia* ("nation-state"). So, instead of affirming his patriotism towards socialist China, it can easily be read as gesturing towards a cultural formation. In these circumstances, the final image of defiance can be read as directed against the socialist regime. There is no affirmation that the future of socialist China is bright.

Maple's coda, on the other hand, seems more surefooted in its moderation of socialist tragedy. The film's focus on violence amongst the rebel factions in the early years of the Cultural Revolution displays loss of life and anarchy created by the Cultural Revolution and in response to the direct calls of the Party leadership. This ran the risk of upsetting the censors. The tale of the two young lovers who end up on opposite sides during the fighting is told by their former art teacher, Wang, as a series of extended flashbacks, and bracketing is used to signal closure. In a pre-credits scene, Lü Danfeng throws herself to her death from a building when her faction is besieged and she refuses to surrender. A man soon revealed to be Wang appears in the next scene throwing down his gun as his voice-over asks how lovers can become enemies. This retrospectively marks the first scene as his flashback. The credits sequence follows. Wang reappears in an orchard with a little girl who addresses him as "Daddy." Her questions lead Wang to say the lovers died because they were misled by Lin Biao and the Gang of Four, and to begin telling the story. The end is signaled when the rooftop suicide scene is repeated, but in an extended form, followed by Wang in the orchard in the present, remembering Li Honggang's fate, which was to be accused of causing Lü's death and executed. A montage flashback represents these events, ending with two red maple leaves floating in the river, symbolizing the fallen lovers.

After this, Wang's daughter reappears for the first time since the beginning of the film to ask her father why he is not crying. As the film shows shots of the white blossoms on the trees, Wang says he is not crying because he sees the rays of the sun. When she asks if "aunty and uncle" are heroes or bad people, he says "no" to both questions and tells her they are history lessons. Then he says, "Let's go home," as the camera cranes up over the orchard and the title "the end" is imposed over the shot. This final shot, then, ends the film on a positive note. The sun is shining, Wang is not crying. The future is bright.

However, even here there is ambiguity that can be mobilized by the disaffected spectator. For it is not specified exactly what the "history lesson" we have just seen is supposed to tell us. Maybe this is why there is one extra sentence of narration as the camera cranes up at the end of the film. This comes after a pause, and, unlike everything else Wang has said, it is not prompted by a question from his little daughter. As they walk off, Wang's voice suddenly adds, "We have already arrived in the white-blossomed springtime again." The very redundancy of this remark, combined with pause and the break with the pattern of questioning from the little girl, throws doubt over this remark for the sensitive viewer. It seems tacked on. Was it demanded by the censor, one is likely to ask?

The ambivalence of these final seconds in *Maple* undermines the positive epilogue. However, it would be wrong to suggest that *Maple* creates ambiguity, moving from outright socialist tragedy to affirmative optimism and then back from that, but that *Bitter Love* is simply negative. Ling's flight and death are the result of a misunderstanding. In fact, his pursuers are his res-cuers and the fall of the Gang of Four has happened. Therefore, Ling's

death cannot really be laid at the hands of the Party and his doubt is based
on misunderstanding rather than proper judgment. However, *Bitter Love*'s
fate reveals the risk of relying on ambiguity. While it can lead to interpretations that save the film, when it suits the authorities it can also lead to interpretations that damn it.

LET THE AUDIENCE DECIDE

The discussion of the possible significations of the endings of *Bitter Love*
and *Maple* demonstrate how vigilant readers can find ambiguity even in
seemingly closed texts. What this ambiguity depends upon is the kind of
active spectatorship that the closed and multiply redundant texts of classical cinema are usually considered to work against. Yet, in some of the
films under consideration, the open story is also deployed, a form which
assumes the active spectator and suggests a certain ambiguity, a certain
quality of leaving it to the viewer to decide what is the most plausible outcome. These films were found acceptable by the authorities at this time. It
is only possible to speculate why. First, none raise possible interpretations
that could be seen as a direct finger of accusation pointed against the Party
and the state, although not all the possible outcomes are optimistic. Second,
the realist rhetoric of the times also legitimates open stories in China, as it
does with the open story art film.[29] Possibly, as Clark says, this type of ending can be seen as "a new concession to the intelligence of post-Cultural
Revolution audiences."[30] What is of significance here is how what is unques-
tionably an open story ending radically disables the didactic paradigm, for
these are films that refuse to give the audience a lesson.

However, it must be acknowledged the false open story film is common.
These are films that have sad narrative endings, but endings that occur historically before the fall of the Gang of Four and in which the lead protagonists do not die. These films depend on the spectator's knowledge of the new
convention in the narrative of socialist history where 1976 has become the
new 1949: the date dividing the line between the bad old days and the good
new society. The open story is "false" in these circumstances because the
films imply that the happy ending that will save the suffering protagonist is
just around the corner.

Most of the films with these false open story endings occur in 1979,
when the range of films had begun to open up, but the focus was still on the
final years of the Cultural Revolution decade. It was possible to end films
with the arrest of characters by the henchmen of the Gang on the eve of their

fall, thus implying that soon they would be freed and things would get better. This occurs in *Wedding*, where the daughters in a family are divided over the Four Modernizations policy in 1975. The supporter of the Four Modernization's fiancé is arrested as they get married to funeral music mourning the death of Zhou Enlai at the end of the film. Even at this sad moment, we continue to see fantasy shots of her fiancé's dream of the chemical plant he wishes to construct, and so this stands as a kind of defiant declaration of faith that in the future all will be well.[31]

Of course, the effectiveness of this false open story is dependent upon the spectator's willingness to give the story a happy ending. While some might be skeptical, there is nothing in the films to justify that. However, one interesting exception could be said, like *Maple*, to undermine the very possibility its closure appears to be proposing. This is *Troubled Laughter*, discussed in previous chapters. However, where *Maple* has a moment of undermining redundancy, *Troubled Laughter's* entire epilogue works to this effect.[32] Clark, with considerable understatement, refers to it as "the forced joy of a fireworks and flower-filled denouement."[33] It begins when Fu Bin, the journalist, is arrested and driven off. His daughter asks when he will be coming back, and he says, "It won't be long." This is repeated several times as an aural flashback during the departure. Shot 684 is a close-up of Fu's face as he looks out of the back window of the van taking him away at his wife and daughter.[34]

There then follows a fantasy sequence in three sections, separated by two montages, and with the final section also divided by a montage. In the first section (shots 685 to 692), he sees not only his wife and daughter following him down the road as he departs, but also a whole crowd of people, including various positive characters we have seen him encounter. This is signified as a fantasy because, in shots 685 and 687, the wife and daughter are alone on the road before the crowd is suddenly jump cut in behind them. At the end, a long shot (692) has one, two, and then three other shots inserted on top of it, a split-screen technique that gets used frequently as one of the many hyperbolic gestures in this sequence (Figure 6.1). The first montage consists of a volcano exploding and fireworks going off (shots 693 and 694) (Figure 6.2). In the second sequence, Fu Bin and his wife are shown repeatedly running to each other in a park and being reunited (shots 695-699). The next montage consists of two shots again (shots 700 and 701). Both are split screens. The first image is split into four, each with open flowers shown (Figure 6.3). The second image is split into nine time-lapse images of flowers opening. In the third section (shots 702 to 709), Fu and his wife are seen on a beach at sunset, hand in hand. The

Figure 6.1 Shot 692, *Troubled Laughter.*

Figure 6.2 Shot 693, *Troubled Laughter.*

scene includes a cutaway to a split screen shot (shot 706) in which five screens are filled with various scenes from celebrations following the fall of the Gang of Four, followed by a single full-screen shot of the celebrations (shot 707) (Figure 6.4).

Figure 6.3 Shot 700, *Troubled Laughter.*

Figure 6.4 Shot 700, *Troubled Laughter.*

Why is this fantasy not simply optimistic and cheery? In what sense does it undermine its own apparent optimism and become more ambiguous? First, it is inscribed as a fantasy and not as a flash-forward to a future event. In the first section, there are the jump cuts. But in the second section, shots 696 to 698 of Fu and his wife running towards each other in the parklands are in slow motion, another technique that appears to question the reality of the shots through the manipulation of time. Furthermore, in some shots their hair is white and they are in the darker clothes associated with older people (shots 695 to 698), whereas in another they are young but in completely white clothes, which it is unlikely anyone would wear in real life (shot 699). This makes it seem as though the journalist is unsure when he and his wife will ever meet again, and given that white is a color associated with death in China, maybe he cannot imagine it in this life. Finally, in the third section, it is clear that the couple is superimposed on a rear screen projection image by the outline around them and the fact that the backdrop shots dissolve into each other while the couple remain the same (shots 703 and 704). Furthermore, his wife asks in shot 704, "Is this for real?" Although he answers that it is, her very asking underlines the possibility that it might not be. At this point, highly ambiguous results have been produced with various cinematic effects, and the false open story film starts to become a genuine open story film.

Given that Fu Bin's arrest has been signified as a wrongful arrest at the hands of the Gang of Four, it would not be acceptable to the authorities to suggest more directly than this that maybe his future release and happiness was not totally assured. This then limits the possibilities for ending the film as a genuine open story film. However, other films were able to produce genuine open stories. In some cases this was done quite straightforwardly, and in one case it was done ostentatiously.

Revival is an example that ends on a highly ambiguous note with the key action code in the story left unresolved. It does so quite straightforwardly without having to resort to the subtleties of *Troubled Laughter*. The major action code in the film concerns the relationship (or lack of relationship) between a young businessman, Tie Dan, and his former girlfriend, Su Xiaomei, a concert pianist. Mistakes and problems that occurred during the Cultural Revolution caused their break-up before, especially because Tie Dan's father blames Xiaomei for the loss of a precious manuscript during those times. Various obstacles are overcome, including his father's hope that he will marry another woman, and it is revealed that Xiaomei was not really responsible for the loss. However, Xiaomei refuses Tie Dan's advances, saying they should not try to force things and just "let life decide" whether they will get together again or not. Tie Dan rushes to the airport when she is leaving, and the frame freezes as he rushes across the tarmac. In this way, the film leaves it open for the spectator to decide whether life has changed them too much to reunite them. No direct finger of blame is being pointed at the Party or the government for heinous crimes, and Tie Dan and Xiaomei are represented as very upwardly mobile young people. Nonetheless, this pensive work has none of the relentless optimism of most films made at this time, and, indeed, it would be difficult to say what didactic lesson should be drawn from it.

Another film which leaves significant action codes unresolved is *The Legend of Tianyun Mountain*, discussed in some detail in previous chapters. By the end of the film, Song Wei's marriage to Wu Yao has broken up, which is for the good, and she has a better understanding of past mistakes. She has also expressed a resolve to work for a better future and there is also news that the Tianyun Mountain development scheme will go ahead again. However, not only has socialist tragedy occurred because Song's friend and Luo Qun's wife Feng Qinglan is dead, but also there is no guarantee at the end of the film that Luo Qun himself really will be rehabilitated or that the opening up of the mountains will really go ahead. The film ends on a somber note when Song Wei visits Feng Qinglan's grave.

Finally, *On a Narrow Street* is an ostentatiously open story film. The second film by Yang Yanjin, who was also one of the directors of *Troubled Laughter*, this was a follow-up to *Romance on Mount Lushan*, and starred the same lead actors. Given the highly stylized and self-referential ending of *Troubled Laughter*, perhaps it is not surprising that *On a Narrow Street* should also have these characteristics. But where the ambiguity of *Troubled Laughter* was teased out in my analysis above, in *On a Narrow Street* it is ostentatiously displayed. In this case, bracketing in the film is provided by the conceit of having Xia, the male lead, attempting to become a screenwriter in the present of the film. He has produced a script based on his experience in the Cultural Revolution rescuing a young woman called Yu, and shows it to a film director at the beginning of the actual film. The narrative returns to their discussions at the end as Xia and the director discuss what would be a plausible ending for their film. The director first suggests a tragic ending. Maybe she's dead? Xia cannot accept this possibility, so the director begins to spin out another possibility. The camera zooms into Xia's face, signaling an imagined sequence.

In this second possibility and first visualized ending, Xia has recovered his sight and become a taxi driver. He discovers Yu at a party, dancing wildly and smoking, when he is called to pick up some guests. Chandeliers and western liquor indicate decadence just as surely in this film as they did in *The Unfailing Beam*, discussed in chapter two. In the back of Xia's taxi with her friends, Yu's corruption is signified when she organizes another false sick note. Later, she tells Xia she discovered after the end of the Cultural Revolution that she was too old to apply for Music College. She feels her opportunities in life have been ruined and she just wants to enjoy herself. The implication of a whole generation that has been ruined is unprecedented in film.

However, the film cuts back to the present and Xia tells the director he cannot accept this ending. Interestingly, he does not say this is because he finds it incredible, but rather because after all that his generation has gone through, they need to believe in some sort of hope for the future. The director hastily backtracks. In other words, at this point the film signifies quite clearly to the spectator the idea of a gap between reality and what people want to believe.

Then, outside, there is the sound of a truck horn. The director has already told Xia he has to help a woman to move her things to a new apartment, and Xia has understood this woman to be the director's fiancée. As he is blind, Xia himself cannot help. In the director's apartment, however, he overhears and recognizes the woman's voice. It is Yu. They meet again. After some misunderstandings, she reveals she is not the director's fiancée. Despite his protestations that she deserves more happiness than he, a blind man, can bring her, she insists they will not be parted again and they walk towards us, arm in arm. At this point, the camera pulls back and reveals lights and other film equipment in the foreground.

Cutting back into the director's apartment, he laughs about this ending. They promise to go on thinking about plausible endings, and Xia leaves to visit his parents. The director is shown back in his apartment wondering what has happened to Yu. The camera zooms into his face, and then cuts to Xia on the train on the way to his parents. The audience may read this as an epilogue, and indeed Yu appears on the train, too. They meet again and exchange experiences. They are both ordinary people leading ordinary lives, now. Just as the audience may be accepting this as the "real" ending of the story, a swish pan shot outside of the train passing pivots left to right to reveal the director, crew, and equipment filming again.

This film, then, not only has an open story. In these two final "false" endings, it undermines the very distinction between story and discourse and between film and reality. This, then, is not just an open story film, but an open text. With no clear sense of a reality independent of narration that can be "represented" accurately or inaccurately, the didactic paradigm is radically disabled. As the train speeds on, Xia's voice-over comments that he still feels this ending is not right. Maybe they should just "let the audience decide" according to their own experiences and imagination. It is hard to imagine a spirit further removed from the determined didacticism of the classical mainland cinema.

Chapter 7

AFTERWORD: FOREIGNER WITHIN, FOREIGNER WITHOUT

I write about mainland Chinese cinema... ultimately as a foreigner.

— Rey Chow

In the preceding chapters, I have attempted to demonstrate that a fundamental move away from the pedagogical structures of the classical Chinese cinema occurred before the appearance of the so-called "Fifth Generation" in the mid-eighties, and therefore earlier than most commentators have previously held. Furthermore, this move constitutes these films as the earliest sustained cinematic manifestation of Chinese postsocialist culture, defined as a culture resulting from loss of faith in the socialist myth but in a society where many of the institutions of socialism continue to operate. However, this cinema does not have this postsocialist status because it is explicitly oppositional and a direct continuation of some of the suppressed Democracy Movement activities, as argued by some others. Instead, it is postsocialist because it uses the ambiguities of cinematic discourse to open up an ambivalent space in which the spectatorial investment may no longer be that of a pupil-spectator seeking enlightenment from and identification with the position of the state, but an engagement based on the building of bonds and renewing of empathetic connections among social peers outside and excluding the hierarchy of the no longer infallible Party-state apparatus.

This conclusion will review the evidence produced to support these claims and their significance in the light of debates about the situated quality of knowledge in relation to the global heritage of colonialism. If Rey Chow, brought up in Hong Kong and currently resident in the United States, finds it necessary or useful to state that she writes about mainland Chinese cinema "as a foreigner,"[1] then I am an even more "distant observer."[2] The issue of knowledge as situated was discussed in the introduction under the rubric of interpretive frameworks. However, in accordance with the conventions of academic writing, subjectivity and self-reflection have not been featured in the main body of the book. Therefore, this seems an appropriate point to return to some consideration of the status of the work produced here.

The introduction argued there is neither authentic knowledge based on experience, nor objective knowledge based on pure scientific distance. Therefore, instead of regarding the situated quality of knowledge as bias or taint, it understands situatedness as a generative precondition for all knowledge production. In that case, what sorts of knowledge have been generated here and in what ways by the status of the author as a foreigner within and without China?

In the introduction, it was acknowledged that the protocols of academic knowledge production in most non-socialist countries require a stance that pretends to neutrality. To maintain this stance rigidly would entail understanding situatedness as merely a manifestation of what Homi Bhabha has discussed as a neutral multicultural diversity rather than contested difference.[3] This would be both a liberal pluralism that fails to attend to connections and contestations between different knowledge positions and a disavowal of the inequalities of power that have subtended the history of knowledge production from the "West" about the "East," namely the Orientalist project whose complicity with imperialism has been made notorious by Said's work.[4] Does the location from which this book is written and the knowledge produced by it necessarily constitute it as an extension of that Orientalist discourse? Ultimately, that judgment will have to be made by others. But, in summing up the work of this book, I would like to venture some initial observations.

The introduction lays out the grounding assumptions of the dissertation as rational and logical outcomes of a series of debates within academia. However, what are the political implications of those assumptions in terms of the cultural politics of globalization and postcoloniality? First, it was noted that all the scholarship from mainland China on the films under consideration here has been produced in a general discursive environment which severely constrains explicit acknowledgment that there have been or are any fundamental differences and areas of contestation within the People's Republic. Of course, it is possible to infer such differences in the case of certain articles, notably those by Chen, Zheng, Zhong and Rao, and by Dai, but they are implicit only.[5] In contrast, this book explicitly entertains such a possibility as part of its grounding assumptions, and the entire manuscript is directing towards demonstrating this hypothesis.

In the introduction, it was acknowledged that the relentless Western search for signs of contention and difference within China can extend Orientalism by demonstrating the seeming superiority of the allegedly more stable liberal democracies. However, this is only necessarily so if East-West differences are understood to be the only relevant differences and both the "East" and the "West" are conceived of as monoliths. Such an understanding refuses to distinguish between various knowledges produced in the West at the behest of the state, at the behest of commercial interests, or to question those forces. It also refuses to distinguish the mainland Chinese Party-state apparatus, the commercial forces it operates in a sometimes tense and sometimes cozy relationship with, and ordinary citizens of the People's Republic. On the other hand, if it is understood that both the "East" and the "West" can be and are riven and dynamized by all manner of internal differences and connections that cut across the East-West divide, then attempts to understand difference in China from outside China may not inevitably be complicit with Western state and commercial neo-imperialisms.

I hope this book might contribute to the larger project of mapping the relationship of cinema to the various forces of modernity and the modern nation-state, East and West, and in particular attempts to counter the oppressive and coercive deployments of the state apparatus. The forces of globalizing transnational capitalism are willing to look across cultures in their search for ever more effective mechanisms for the production of surplus wealth. This is witnessed by the Western fascination with Japanese management techniques and Chinese business strategy, as it is by the entire history of "colonial mimicry" as a strategy of resistance.[6] In these circumstances, it is equally important that all who perceive themselves as in one way or another engaged against the exploitative tendencies and structures of modernity in both its capitalist and socialist forms must also look across cultures for our local options and possibilities.

Second, this book has advanced the concept of "postsocialism" over "Chinese modernism," "Chinese postmodernism," and other options for naming and characterizing the new social and cultural formation that has emerged in post-Mao China. Its ability to account for the specificities of the current Chinese social and cultural formation is the reason for preferring it. In relation to globalized politics, two points need to be made. First, an argument could be mounted that refusing to grant the viability of terms like "modernism" and "postmodernism" in a Chinese context is another act of Orientalist exclusion, drawing a clear line between the "advanced" West and the "backward" East. However, I have not challenged the use of such terms in the post-Mao Chinese context, and indeed I acknowledge many of the reasons for using them. "Postsocialist" is offered as an optimal and more precise term, not as the only viable term. Second, the use of a term like "postsocialism" is provocative in certain ways. Because it could be held to connote that socialism itself is over, waning, or in eclipse, to use such a term within the People's Republic today would risk being accused of "counter-revolutionary activity." This in itself, however, has the advantage of drawing attention to the oppressive conditions of Party and state control that continue to prevail there.

If this project is structured to generate knowledge that would be foreclosed upon under threat of penalty in the People's Republic today, this indicates fundamental differences structuring academic and public discourse in general in English-language liberal democracies and the People's Republic today, differences which cannot be sidestepped and demand decisions. However, these differences are not necessarily best interpreted as an extension of Orientalist structures, with the People's Republic as a last bastion resisting the forces of imperialism. Indeed, the persistent flow of Chinese academics out of the People's Republic and their participation in English-language academic analysis of those things foreclosed upon in public discourse within the People's Republic in itself indicates that English-language academic discourse cannot be understood as a simple extension of the imperialist interests of various European and North American states.

Chapter two has attempted to contribute to the detailing of the discursive characteristics and supporting apparatus of the Chinese classical cinema as a pedagogical discourse. What might be considered contentious here is the use of Hollywood classical cinema as a comparative model. Commentators concerned to protest Orientalism in cinema studies frequently complain about this practice, as Mitsuhiro Yoshimoto uncovers in his survey of the field of Japanese film studies, for example.[7] There, the practices of Hollywood are frequently set up as a backdrop against which not only Japanese difference is produced and then pronounced "modernist" because this difference corresponds to certain characteristics of Euro-American modernism. Yoshimoto quotes Judith Mayne on the problems posed by this tendency: "The classical Hollywood cinema has become the norm against which all other alternative practices are measured. Films which do not engage the classical Hollywood cinema are by and large relegated to irrelevance. Frequently, the very notion of an 'alternative' is posed in the narrow terms of an either-or: either one is within classical discourse and therefore complicit, or one is critical of and/or resistant to it and therefore outside of it." In facing these difficulties, Yoshimoto recommends that "We need to put the Hollywood cinema in specific historical contexts," and notes that "A national cinema as the culture industry exists in a complex web of economic, ideo-logical, and social relations, and the classical Hollywood cinema constitutes only one element of those relations." [8] These observations have been impor-tant guiding admonitions for chapter two, and indeed for the work as a whole. First, Yoshimoto does not fall into the trap of wishful thinking that would ignore the unquestionable fact of the great impact of Hollywood clas-sical cinema in countries like China. There, it captured an very large propor-tion of box office prior to the establishment of the People's Republic and also informed the Soviet socialist realist model that was adopted and adapt-ed by the Chinese Communists after Liberation.[9] Second, he is insistent that the particular significance of classical cinema characteristics in a non-West-ern cinema and the significance of the ways in which that cinema also differs from classical Hollywood cinema both be understood in their local context.

Therefore, chapter two has tried to avoid a purely formal description of textual characteristics or a discussion of the internal structural dynamics of the industry in isolation from the rest of society. Instead, it has been careful to note the specific local version of classical cinema that the Chinese classical cinema is through a social and historically located understanding of its par-ticular characteristics, including those it shares with Hollywood classical cinema. For example, as national (and in the case of Hollywood, transna-tional) mass media dependent on industrial methods of production and dis-tribution and on technology, both are institutions of the modern era. However, the great differences between liberal capitalist societies and state-run command economy societies means that, as specified in chapter two, the Chinese classical cinema places pedagogy above pleasure in its in-stitutional structures and discursive patterns. My effort here is to under-stand local difference in local terms and not as "modernism" or any other Western-inspired "alternative" to Hollywood classical cinema.

Furthermore, at the same time as emphasizing the impact of state socia-lism in shaping the Chinese classical cinema, chapter two has tried to ack-nowledge research that has pointed to local origins for some of the specific and distinctive characteristics of the Chinese classical cinema. Here we see the syncretic process of selection whereby some elements of the past are cho-sen to be adopted and adapted as part of Chinese socialist modernity and usually praised as "tradition," while being combined with introduced things that they are compatible with. Other local elements are rejected as "feudal" things from the "old society." For example, it has been noted in chapter two that the emphasis on the pedagogical function of the arts has a long history stretching back into Confucian ideas of self-cultivation, that socially rather than psychologically-defined characters are common in pre-modern Chinese fiction, and that suspension of the narrative for commentary is a common device in Chinese theater.

The following chapters examine the case for a postsocialist move away from the pedagogical model in terms of various differences from the classical model that help to create ambiguity rather than explicit opposition. They avoid terms like "break" or "rupture" when considering the change that has occurred in the mainland Chinese social and cultural formation since the death of Mao, preferring instead terms like "move away" and "mutation." This is because there is little evidence to suggest a radical revolutionary change in which change is rapid, comprehensive, and based on binary oppositions. Instead, for example, the majority of enterprises in China remain in state ownership to this day while the market economy has developed alongside them. The partial changes in the mainland Chinese cinema in the wake of Mao's death, which do not include industrial structure or ownership, are also part of this partial, slow, and disaggregated process of change characterizing postsocialist China as a whole. Within such a larger understanding, I hope that I have demonstrated the numerous ways in which these films depart from the pedagogical model of the classical cinema. Taken together, these separate areas of difference mutually reinforce each other and support my claim that the post-Mao cycle of films about the Cultural Revolution not only registers the suffering of that era but also breaks with the pedagogical model to produce a new cinematic mode of peer-based empathetic sharing of memories and experiences that marks the emergence of Chinese postsocialism in the cinema.

Notes

NOTES FOR CHAPTER ONE

1. Thomas Elsaesser argues that it took at least thirty years for German culture and cinema to tackle the issue in *New German Cinema* (London: British Film Institute, 1989) 239–278.

2. If the post-*glasnost* 1987 release of Tengiz Abuladze's 1984 film *Repentance* marks the point at with the Soviet Union begins to tackle the history of Stalinism on film more or less explicitly, thirty years had passed before this was possible; Anna Lawton, "Introduction: An Interpretive Survey," in *The Red Screen: Politics, Society, Art in Soviet Cinema* (London: Routledge, 1992), ed. Anna Lawton, 11–13.

3. Rick Berg argues that it took from the 1973 until the nineteen-eighties before America tackled this topic, although he does not consider the 1978 release of films like *Coming Home* and *Deer Hunter*; Rick Berg, "Losing Vietnam: Covering the War in an Age of Technology," in *From Hanoi to Hollywood: The Vietnam War in American Film*, ed. Linda Dittmar and Gene Michaud, (New Brunswick: Rutgers University Press, 1990), 41–68.

4. Chen Huangmei, ed., *Dangdai Zhongguo Dianying* (*Contemporary Chinese Cinema*), 2 vols., (Beijing: *Zhongguo Shehui Kexue Chubanshe* [China Social Sciences Press], 1989), vol.1, 355–7.

5. Tony Rayns, "Chinese Vocabulary: An Introduction to *King of the Children* and the New Chinese Cinema," in *King of the Children and the New Chinese Cinema*, Chen Kaige and Tony Rayns (London: Faber and Faber, 1989), 1.

6. George S. Semsel, Xia Hong and Hou Jianping, ed., *Chinese Film Theory: A Guide to the New Era* (New York: Praeger, 1990), xix. The 1985 date for *Red Sorghum* should be either 1987, when the film was completed, or 1988, when it was released in the People's Republic.

7. The only strict exception would be prior publications detailing the preliminary findings of this book: Chris Berry, "Fragmentation," in "Neither One Thing nor Another: Toward a Study of the Viewing Subject and Chinese Cinema in the 1980's," in *New Chinese Cinemas: Forms, Identities, Politics* (Cambridge: Cambridge University Press, 1994), ed. Nick Browne, Paul G. Pickowicz, Vivian Sobchack, and Esther Yau, 92-94, and Chris Berry, "Seeking Truth From Fiction: Feature Films as Historiography in Deng's China," *Film History* 7, no.1 (1995), 87–99.

8. The following publications were surveyed for this purpose: *Beijing Review*, *China Reconstructs*, *Dazhong Dianying* (*Popular Cinema*), *Dianying Yishu* (*Film Art*), *Guangming Ribao* (*Guangming Daily*), *Renmin Ribao* (*People's Daily*), *Renmin Dianying* (*People's Cinema*), *Shijie Dianying* (*World Cinema*), and *Wenyi Bao* (*Literary Gazette*).

9. Those few works that do not discuss change in the cinema of this period are articles whose particular focus makes this unnecessary. Liu Guiqing discusses the period in a brief page as part of a larger study; "*Xin Shiqi Dianying zhong de Xianshizhuyi*" ("Realism in the Cinema of the New Era"), *Dangdai Dianying* (*Contemporary Cinema*) no.56 (1993), 10-11. Liang Tianming's essay is an auteur study of Yang Yanjin, who did not start working until the end of the Cultural Revolution, making comparison with the past unnecessary; "*Chanshi Yang Yanjin*" ("Explaining Yang Yanjin"), *Dangdai Dianying* (*Contemporary Cinema*) no.38 (1990), 60.

10. The "New Era" is dated as beginning in 1977 in Chen's book, and many others working inside the People's Republic date it as beginning in that year or 1976. In George S. Semsel, Xia Hong and Hou Jianping, the date given is 1979. This is also the usage preferred by Zheng Dongtian in his 1987 article, "*Jinjin Qinian: 1979-1986 Zhongqingnian Daoyan Tansuo Huigu*" ("Only Seven Years: A Look Back at the Explorations of Young and Middle-Aged Directors between 1979 and 1986"), *Dangdai Dianying* (*Contemporary Cinema*) no.16 (1987), 46-54, for example. One date marks the beginning of the period when Hua Guofeng took over, and the other the end of that interregnum and the beginning of Deng Xiaoping's era. However, I have not discovered any explicit discussion of this. In George S. Semsel, Xia Hong and Hou Jianping, and in George S. Semsel, Chen Xihe, and Xia Hong, ed., *Film in Contemporary China: Critical Debates, 1979-1989* (Westport: Praeger, 1993), a more explicit politics of dating occurs. The "New Era" is declared in the latter to have ended "when the PLA fired its first shots at the students demonstrating for democracy in Tiananmen Square on June 4, 1989," 183. A similar statement can be found on 187 of the former.

11. "*Dianying de Fusu*," in Chen, vol.1, 353-358.

12. "*Lishixing de Zhuanzhe*," in Chen, vol.1, 359-373.

13. "*Dadan Kaituo, Chixu Fazhan*," in Chen, vol.1, 374-446. The years 1980 and 1981 are mostly covered on pages 374-392, and 430, 432, and 441. The pattern in Chen's book can also be found, more or less, in Shu Xiaoming, *Zhongguo Dianying Yishushi Jiaocheng* (*A Course in the History of Chinese Film Art*), (Beijing: *Zhongguo Dianying Chubanshe* [China Film Press], 1996); Xi Shanshan, "*Zongguan Xin Shiqi de Dianying Chuangzuo*" ("An Overview of Film Production in the New Era"), *Dangdai Dianying* (*Contemporary Cinema*) no.15 (1986), 3-13; and Yuan Ying "*Dianying de Zijue; Xin Shiqi Dianying Chuangzuo Huigu*" ("Film Consciousness: A Look Back at Film Production in the New Era"), *Dangdai Dianying* (*Contemporary Cinema*) no.15 (1986), 13-20. Régis Bergeron varies on in emphasizing "the turning point" slightly less in *Le Cinéma Chinois 1949-1983*, vol.3, (Paris: *Editions L'Harmattan*, 1984), 189-254. Brief English language accounts

implicitly following a similar pattern include Khan Budong, *"Convales-cence,"* in *Le Cinéma Chinois,* ed. Marie-Claire Quiquemelle and Jean-Loup Passek (Paris: *Centre Georges Pompidou,* 1985), 143-8; and Esther Yau, "China After the Revolution," in *The Oxford History of World Cinema,* ed. Geoffrey Nowell-Smith (Oxford: Oxford University Press, 1996), 698. Yau states that the production of "scar" films continued until 1983, giving *At Middle Age* as an example. However, her usage of the term "scar" seems to exceed the usual, which would only cover films directly representing the ravages of the Cultural Revolution. Films such as *At Middle Age* that represent contemporary social problems, some of which may of course be the aftermath of the Cultural Revolution, are not usually classed as "scar" films.

14. Zheng Dongtian.
15. Zhong Chengxiang and Rao Shuguang, *"Wenhua Fansi zhong de Xin Shiqi Dianying Chuangzuo"* ("Film Production of the New Era in a Time of Cultural Reflection"), *Dangdai Dianying* (*Contemporary Cinema*) no.16 (1987), 34-45.
16. Dai Jinhua, *"Xieta: Chongdu Disidai"* ("A Leaning Tower: Re-Reading the Fourth Generation"), in *Dianying Lilun yu Piping Shouce* (*Handbook of Film Theory and Criticism*), (Beijing: *Kexue Jishu Wenxian Chubanshe* [Scientific and Technological Documents Press], 1993), 3-15.
17. Dai, 5.
18. Rao Shuguang and Pei Yali, *"Shanghen Dianying: Xinnian yu Qingchun de Shenhua ji qi Jieshu"* ("Scar Films: Myths of Faith and Youth and Their End"), in *Xin Shiqi Dianying Wenhua Sichao* (*Thoughts on the Film Culture of the New Era*), (Beijing: *Zhongguo Guangbo Dianshe Chubanshe* [China Radio and Television Press], 1997), 1-16.
19. Rao and Pei, 1-7.
20. Paul Clark, *Chinese Cinema: Culture and Politics Since 1949,* (Cambridge: Cambridge University Press, 1987), 2-3.
21. Clark, 1987, 154-172.
22. Paul Clark, *"La Rivoluzione culturale e le sue conseguenze sulla produzione cinematografica cinese (1966-1981)"* ("The 'cultural revolution' and its effects on Chinese film production"), in *Ombre Elettriche: Saggi e Ricerche sul Cinema Cinese* (Essays and Research on Chinese Cinema), ed. Carlo Pirovano (Milan: Electa, 1982), 99-118.
23. Clark, 1987, 160-6, and Paul Clark, "Two Hundred Flowers on China's Screens," in *Perspectives on Chinese Cinema,* ed. Chris Berry (London: BFI, 1992), 40-61.
24. Ma Ning, "Spatiality and Subjectivity in Xie Jin's Film Melodrama of the New Period," in Browne, Pickowicz, Sobchack, and Yau, 15-39.
25. Ma Ning "Notes on the New Filmmakers," in *Chinese Film: The State of the Art in the People's Republic,* ed. George Semsel (New York: Praeger, 1987), 63-73.
26. Paul G. Pickowicz, "Popular Cinema and Political Thought in Post-Mao China: Reflections on Official Pronouncements, Film, and the Film Audi-ence," in *Unofficial China: Popular Culture and Thought in the People's*

Republic, ed. Perry Link, Richard Madsen, and Paul G. Pickowicz (Boulder: Westview Press, 1989), 39.

27. George S. Semsel, Chen Xihe, and Xia Hong, 185.
28. Mark Poster discusses these differences between Foucault and Althusser in *Foucault, Marxism and History: Mode of Production Versus Mode of Information* (London: Polity Press, 1984), 37-40.
29. Yan Sun, *The Chinese Reassessment of Socialism, 1976-1992* (Princeton: Princeton University Press, 1995), 155.
30. Sun, 162-164.
31. Clark discusses this phenomenon in film culture in "Two Hundred Flowers on China's Screens," 40-61. For a broader discussion, see also Merle Goldman, *Literary Dissent in Communist China* (Cambridge: Harvard University Press, 1967), 158-242.
32. On Democracy Wall, see Andrew J. Nathan, *Chinese Democracy* (New York: Alfred A. Knopf, 1985), 3-44.
33. Sun, 125.
34. Xi, 3.
35. Eve Kosofsky Sedgwick, *Between Men: English Literature and Male Homosocial Desire* (New York: Columbia University Press, 1985), and Eve Kosofsky Sedgwick, *The Epistemology of the Closet* (Berkeley: University of California Press, 1990). For a development and application of Sedgwick's theory that demonstrates the analogy between homophobia, closeting, and subcultural formations on the one hand and political paranoia and suppression of dissent on the other, see also Robert J. Corber, *In the Name of National Security: Hitchcock, Homophobia, and the Political Construction of Gender in Postwar America* (Durham, N.C.: Duke University Press, 1993).
36. Zheng.
37. Zhong and Rao.
38. Rao and Pei.
39. As a measure of this popularity, Bazin gets twenty-two entries in the index to Semsel, Xia and Hou's book on Chinese film theory, 211.
40. Nick Browne, "Introduction," in Browne, Pickowicz, Sobchack, and Yau, 8-9.
41. Dai, 6-7.
42. Edward Said, *Orientalism* (New York: Vintage, 1979).
43. Zhang Xudong, *Chinese Modernism in the Era of Reforms: Cultural Fever, Avant-Garde Fiction, and the New Chinese Cinema* (Durham: Duke University Press, 1997), 92.
44. Xiaobing Tang, "The Function of New Theory: What Does It Mean to Talk about Postmodernism in China?" in *Politics, Ideology and Literary Discourse in Modern China*. ed. Liu Kang and Xiaobing Tang (Durham: Duke University Press, 1993), 278-300.
45. Zhang, 13.
46. Tang, 292-3.
47. For a counter-position from a critic who appears not to have noticed any change at all since the Maoist heyday, see Ellen Johnston Laing, "Is There

Post-Modern Art in the People's Republic of China?" in *Modernity in Asian Art*, ed. John Clark (Sydney: Wild Peony, 1993), 207-221. Laing measures Chinese art against Western postmodernism, and does not allow for the possibility of a different postmodernism in China.

48. See, for example, the essays collected in *Postmodernism and China*, ed. Arif Dirlik and Xudong Zhang (Durham: Duke University Press, 2000).

49. Sheldon Hsiao-peng Lu, "Art, Culture, and Cultural Criticism in Post-New China," *New Literary History* no.28 (1997), 114.

50. For other authors, see for example, Wang Ning, "Confronting Western Influence: Rethinking Chinese Literature of the New Period," *New Literary History* no.24 (1993), 905-926.

51. Tang, 294. Although Tang credits Dirlik for the term, his usage is more similar to that adopted in this book than to Dirlik's. Lu uses the term without any specific periodization, stating in regard to art works that "The incongruent coexistence of an (emergent) materialism and a (fading) revolutionary ethos in Feng's art is indeed the reality of 'postsocialism' in China—the combination of capitalist economy of communist politics," 121.

52. Arif Dirlik, "Post-socialism? Reflections on 'Socialism with Chinese Characteristics'," in *Marxism and the Chinese Experience*, ed. Arif Dirlik and Maurice Meisner (Armonk, NY: M.E.Sharpe, 1989), 362-384.

53. Paul Pickowicz, "Huang Jianxin and the Notion of Postsocialism," in Browne, Pickowicz, Sobchack, and Yau, 57-87.

54. Lu, referring to the 1990's only, also claims that the contemporary Chinese formation is "a 'post-socialist postmodernity,'" 125.

55. Chris Berry, "'Ce que meritait le plus d'être puni était son penis': postsocialisme, distopie et la mort du hêroes," *Cinemas* 3, nos.2-3 (1993), 39-60; Chris Berry and Mary Ann Farquhar, "Post-Socialist Strategies: An Analysis of *Yellow Earth* and *Black Cannon Incident*," in *Cinematic Landscapes: Observations on the Visual Arts and Cinema of China and Japan*, ed. Linda C. Ehrlich and David Desser (Austin: University of Texas Press, 1994), 81-116; and Jean-Francois Lyotard, *The Postmodern Condition: A report on knowledge* (Manchester: Manchester University Press, 1984).

56. Chen, 370-3.

57. Pickowicz, 39

58. Robert Stam, Robert Burgoyne, and Sandy Flitterman-Lewis, *New Vocabularies in Film Semiotics: Structuralism, Post-Structuralism and Beyond*, (London: Routledge, 1992), 28-33.

59. Pickowicz, 48-50.

60. David Bordwell, "The Power of a Research Tradition: Prospects for Progress in the Study of Film Style," *Film History* 6, no.1 (1994), 74-5, n1; Larry Laudan, *Progress and Its Problems; Towards a Theory of Scientific Growth* (Berkeley: University of California Press, 1977).

61. Linda Williams, "Introduction," in *Viewing Positions: Ways of Seeing Film*, ed. Linda Williams (New Brunswick: Rutgers University Press, 1995), 1-20.

62. Mary Ann Doane, "Remembering Women: Psychical and Historical Constructions in Film Theory," in E. Ann Kaplan, ed., *Psychoanalysis and Cinema* (New York: Routledge, 1990), 47.

63. Williams, 3-4.
64. David Bordwell, *Making Meaning: Inference and Rhetoric in the Interpretation of the Cinema,* (Cambridge: Harvard University Press, 1989). See also David Bordwell and Noël Carroll, ed., *Post-Theory: Reconstructing Film Studies* (Madison: University of Wisconsin Press, 1996).
65. Bordwell, 1989, 266.
66. A representative example of this would be the controversy around Edwin Porter's films, as elaborated in Noël Burch, "Porter or Ambivalence," *Screen* 19, no.4 (1978/9), 91-105; David Bordwell and Kristin Thompson, "Linearity, Materialism and the Study of Early American Cinema," *Wide Angle* 5, no.3 (1983), 4-15; and André Gaudreault, "Detours in Film Narrative: The Development of Cross-Cutting," in *Early Cinema: Space, Frame, Narrative,* ed. Thomas Elsaesser (London: BFI Publishing, 1990), 133-150.
67. Burch's arguments about Porter are heavily informed by assumptions about the class composition of audiences, for example.
68. Miriam Hansen, *Babel and Babylon: Spectatorship in American Silent Film* (Cambridge: Harvard University Press, 1991), 93.
69. Jürgen Habermas, *The Structural Transformation of the Public Sphere,* trans. Thomas Burger with Frederick Lawrence (Cambridge: MIT Press, 1989); Jürgen Habermas, "The Public Sphere," *New German Critique* no.3 (1974), 49-55.
70. Oskar Negt and Alexander Kluge, *Public Sphere and Experience: Toward an Analysis of the Bourgeois and Proletarian Public Sphere* (Minneapolis: University of Minnesota Press, 1993).
71. Hansen, 2-7.
72. Hansen, 104.
73. *Modern China* 19, no.2 was devoted to the topic in 1993. An introduction by Frederic Wakeman, Jr., "The Civil Society and Public Sphere Debate: Western Reflections on Chinese Political Culture," considers other English-language writings on the topic to date, 108-138. In addition there has been lively debate on the topic in the pages of Chinese language journals located outside the People's Republic. For example, from the Hong Kong-based critical theory journal, *Ershiyi Shijie (Twenty-First Century),* see Wang Shaoguang, *"Guanyu 'Shimin Shehui' de Jidian Sikao"* ("Reflections on the Notion of 'Civil Society'), *Ershiyi Shijie (Twenty-First Century)* no.6 (1991), 102-114; Shi Yuankang, *"Shimin Shehui yu Zhongben Yimo—Zhongguo Xiandai Daolushang de Zhang'ai"* ("Civil Society and the Policy of 'Emphasizing the Fundamental and Repressing the Secondary'—an Obstacle in China's Road to Modernisation," *Ershiyi Shijie (Twenty-First Century),* no.6 (1991), 105-120; and Yang Nianqun, *"Jindai Zhongguo Yanjiuzhong de 'Shimin Shehui'—Fangfa ji Xiandu"* ("'Civil Society' in Modern China Studies—Methodology and Limitations"), *Ershiyi Shijie (Twenty-First Century),* no.32 (1995), 29-38.
74. Wakeman, Jr., 108-9.
75. Zhang Xudong, 19. Zhang does not specify whether the concept of the public sphere under discussion in China and to which he is referring is the Habermasian concept, one of a range of other definitions, or all of them.

76. Zhang, p.4.
77. Richard Madsen, "The Public Sphere, Civil Society, and Moral Community: A Research Agenda for Contemporary China Studies," *Modern China* 19, no.2 (1993), 184. In the same issue, Heath B. Chamberlain notes the bewildering array of different ways in which the term "civil society" has been used in studies of China, and adds his own for good measure; "On the Search for Civil Society in China," 199-215.
78. Stephanie Hemelryk Donald, *Public Secrets, Public Spaces: Cinema and Civility in China* Lanham, MD: Rowman and Littlefield, 2000), 18.
79. Ben Xu, "*Farewell My Concubine* and its Nativist Critics," *Quarterly Review of Film and Video* 16, no.2 (1997), 160-1.
80. Judith B. Farquhar and James L. Hevia, "The concept of culture in American historiography of China," unpublished paper quoted in Rowe, 140.
81. Rowe, 141.
82. Gilles Deleuze and Félix Guattari, *A Thousand Plateaus: Capitalism and Schizophrenia*, (Minneapolis: University of Minnesota Press, 1987), 3.
83. Jeffrey F. Klenotic, "The Place of rhetoric in 'new' film historiography: the discourse of corrective revisionism," *Film History* 6, no.1 (1994), 45-58.
84. Robert C. Allen and Douglas Gomery, *Film History: Theory and Practice* (New York: Alfred A. Knopf, 1985), iv; cited in Klenotic, 49.
85. Allen and Gomery, chapter 1, "Film History as History," 3-23, summarized in Klenotic, 49-50.
86. Writing in the same issue of *Film History* as Klenotic, Michèle Lagny also pays tribute to Allen and Gomery, but argues that they betray their own "neo-positive" claims to scientific truth in their own history writing, which relies on reductionist assumptions about liberal capitalism as a determination upon film production; Michèle Lagny, "Film History: or Film Expropriated," *Film History* 6, no.1 (1994), 41.
87. See Klenotic, 52-4.
88. Stephen Bottomore, "Out of the World: Theory, Fact and Film History," *Film History* 6, no.1, 12.
89. Klenotic, writing from a background in rhetoric, speaks of this as a dialogic process, 56-7.
90. Hansen, 91.
91. Hansen, 94.

NOTES FOR CHAPTER TWO

1. David Bordwell, Janet Staiger and Kristin Thompson, *The Classical Hollywood Cinema: Film Style and Mode of Production to 1960*, (London: Routledge and Kegan Paul, 1985), 367-77, discuss the persistence of the classical Hollywood cinema. Chris Berry, "The Viewing Subject in *Li Shuangshuang* and *The In-Laws*" traces the persistence of the classical mainland style, in *Perspectives on Chinese Cinema*, ed. Chris Berry, (London: British Film Institute, 1991), 30-9.
2. Paul Clark argues that Chinese films have rarely enjoyed complete domestic market dominance; "Chinese Cinema in 1989 from a Historical Point of

View," *China Screen* 198, no.3. 25. He points out more foreign films than Chinese were distributed up to 1956, and between 1966 and the early 1970s. However, before 1949 Hollywood films dominated Chinese screens alone, but thereafter no single foreign industry held sway. Furthermore, import selection was filtered through the same institutions that controlled and shaped domestic production.

3. See Bordwell, Staiger, and Thompson, 1-11 on the implications of the term "classical" in relation to Hollywood.

4. Rick Altman, "Dickens, Griffith, and Film Theory Today," *South Atlantic Quarterly* 88, no.2, (1989), 321-59.

5. Ma Ning , "Culture and Politics in Chinese Film Melodrama: Traditional Sacred, Moral Economy and the Xie Jin Mode," Ph.D. thesis, (Melbourne: Monash University, 1992).

6. These debates are outlined in Linda Williams, *Playing the Race Card: Melodramas of Black and White from Uncle Tom to O.J. Simpson* (Princeton: Princeton University Press, 2001), 10-44.

7. Ban Wang, *The Sublime Figure of History: Aesthetics and Politics in Twentieth Century China* (Stanford: Stanford University Press, 1997).

8. The Chinese term for "propaganda," "*xuanchuan*," carried none of the negative implications of the English term until quite recently. Its signification encompasses "publicity" and "dissemination," as well as "propaganda."

9. Mei Chen, "1949-1989 China Film Distribution and Exhibition," *China Screen* 1990, no.3, 26.

10. Susan Rubin Suleiman, *Authoritarian Fictions: The Ideological Novel as a Literary Genre*, (New York: Columbia University Press, 1983).

11. Mao Zedong, "On the Ten Major Relationships," *Selected Works*, Volume V, (Beijing: Foreign Languages Press, 1977), 306.

12. Donald J. Munro, *The Concept of Man in Early China*, (Stanford: Stanford University Press, 1969). See especially Chapter 4, "The Path to Privilege."

13. Andrew H. Plaks, "Towards a Critical Theory of Chinese Narrative," in *Chinese Narrative: Critical and Theoretical Essays*, ed. Andrew H. Plaks (Princeton: Princeton University Press, 1977), 309-52, especially 311-14.

14. Ma Ning, 37.

15. Bonnie S. McDougall, *Mao Zedong's "Talks at the Yan'an Conference on Literature and Art": A Translation of the 1943 Text with Commentary* (Ann Arbor: The University of Michigan Center for Chinese Studies, The University of Michigan, 1980).

16. McDougall, 75. McDougall points out that Mao's stance finds its immediate origins in the Soviet Union, but that it is also cognate with much Confucian teaching on the desirable relationship between the arts and the state; 11, 36.

17. Cheng Jihua, *Zhongguo Dianying Fazhanshi (The History of the Development of Chinese Cinema)*, (Beijing: Zhongguo Dianying Chubanshe [China Film Press], 2nd ed., 1981), 402.

18. Paul Clark, *Chinese Cinema: Culture and Politics Since 1949*, (Cambridge: Cambridge University Press, 1987), 34. Clark gives a more detailed account.

19. *Zhongguo Dianying Faxing Fangying Gongsi, Zhongguo Dianying Shuchu Shuru Gongsi* (China Film Distribution and Exhibition Corporation and

China Film Export and Import Corporation), *Dianying Sanshiwu Nian* (*Thirty-Five Years of Film*), (Beijing: *Zhongguo Dianying Faxing Fangying Gongsi, Zhongguo Dianying Shuchu Shuru Gongsi* [China Film Distribution and Exhibition Corporation and China Film Export and Import Corporation], 1986). English edition available.

20. Clark, 1987, 37-8.
21. Clark, 1987, 34. See also Chris Berry, "Now You See It, Now You Don't," *Cinemaya* no.4, (1989), 46-55.
22. Clark, 1987, 45-52.
23. McDougall, 68-74.
24. Clark, 1987,185-186.
25. *Zhongguo Dianying Faxing Fangying Gongsi, Zhongguo Dianying Shuchu Shuru Gongsi*, 94.
26. Mei Chen.
27. Clark, 1987, 36, 61. *Zhongguo Dianying Faxing Fangying Gongsi, Zhongguo Dianying Shuchu Shuru Gongsi*, 94.
28. Although my sample is undeniably small, as a proportion it compares favorably with the sample used by Bordwell, Staiger and Thompson. This consisted of 100 films drawn from total production of over 15,000 films during the period under consideration; 10, 388-9.
29. The figure for production between Liberation and the Cultural Revolution is derived from *Zhongguo Dianying Ziliaoguan, Zhongguo Yishu Yanjiuyuan Dianying Yanjiusuo* (China Film Archive and Film Research Office of the China Arts Research Institute), *Zhongguo Yishu Yingpian Bianmu* (*China Art Filmography*), (Beijing: *Wenhua Yishu Chubanshe* [Culture and Art Publishing House], 1981). It does not include those films specified as stage recordings or animations. It does include various Chinese local opera films, "artistic documentaries" (a euphemism for the amateur productions of the Great Leap Forward), and films "not released" (in most cases, a euphemism for banning). Although he derives his figures from the same source, Clark (1987) lists 617 features for this period, 185-6. No rationale is given.
30. Clark, 1987, 128. Although no feature films appeared, recordings of stage performances of the model revolutionary works sanctioned by Mao's wife, Jiang Qing, were released.
31. Clark, 1987, 29. On the Northeast Film Studio, see Patricia Wilson, "The Founding of the Northeast Film Studio, 1946-1949," in *Chinese Film: The State of the Art in the People's Republic*, ed. George S. Semsel (New York: Praeger, 1987), 15-33.
32. Clark, 1987, 25-34.
33. Yan Minjun, "Wang Bin" and Ren Yin, "Yu Min," *Zhongguo Dianyingjia Xiehui Dianying Lishi Yanjiubu* (Film History Research Section of the China Film Association), *Zhongguo Dianyingjia Liezhuan (Disanji)* (*Biographies of Chinese Filmmakers* [Volume Three]), (Beijing: *Zhongguo Dianying Chubanshe* [China Film Press], 1984), 52-7, 12-19. Clark, 1987, introduces the circumstances of *Bridge*'s production, 42, as does Jay Leyda in *Dianying:*

An Account of Films and the Film Audience in China (Cambridge, MA: MIT Press, 1972), 182.

34. Although director Wang Ping did not spend the war years in Yan'an, according to her biographer, this was because she was a trusted revolutionary since the mid-thirties and undertaking Party activities elsewhere: Bai Ai, "Wang Ping," *Zhongguo Dianyingjia Xiehui Dianying Lishi Yanjiubu* (Film History Research Section of the China Film Association), *Zhongguo Dianyingjia Liezhuan (Diwuji)* (*Biographies of Chinese Filmmakers* [Volume Five]), (Beijing: *Zhongguo Dianying Chubanshe* [China Film Press], 1985), 36-49. This biography also details the production history of *The Unfailing Beam*.

35. Leyda translates the title as *Constant Beam* and places the film in the context of other production during the Great Leap Forward period, 236-7.

36. McDougall, 59-61, 65, 68-9.

37. Born in 1928 in Luoyang, screenwriter Li Zhun was too young to have become associated with either end of Clark's spectrum; Mu Zi, "Li Zhun," *Zhongguo Dianyingjia Xiehui Dianying Lishi Yanjiubu* (Film History Research Section of the China Film Association), *Zhongguo Dianyingjia Liezhuan (Diqiji)* (*Biographies of Chinese Filmmakers* [Volume Seven]), (Beijing: *Zhongguo Dianying Chubanshe* [China Film Press], 1986), 197-205. Director Lu Ren was older and had a more cosmopolitan background: Gu Ming, "Lu Ren," *Zhongguo Dianyingjia Xiehui Dianying Lishi Yanjiubu* (Film History Research Section of the China Film Association), *Zhongguo Dianyingjia Liezhuan (Diliuji)* (Biographies of Chinese Filmmakers [Volume Six]), (Beijing: *Zhongguo Dianying Chubanshe* [China Film Press], 1986), 468-74.

38. The title of *Early Spring in February* is sometimes translated as *February*. Leyda, .313-4, 413, translates it as *Second Lunar Month*, or *Threshold of Spring*. The title of *Stage Sisters* is sometimes translated as *Two Actresses* or *Two Stage Sisters*. Leyda, 252-3, incorrectly identifies the film as a 1964 Changchun Film Studio production and translates it as *Sisters on the Stage*.

39. Ren Yin, "Xie Tieli," *Zhongguo Dianyingjia Xiehui Dianying Lishi Yanjiubu* (Film History Research Section of the China Film Association), *Zhongguo Dianyingjia Liezhuan (Disiji)* (*Biographies of Chinese Filmmakers* [Volume Four]) (Beijing: *Zhongguo Dianying Chubanshe* [China Film Press], 1985), 491-500. Chow Tse-tsung, *The May Fourth Movement*, (Cambridge: Harvard University Press, 1960).

40. Zhao Long, "Xie Jin," *Zhongguo Dianyingjia Xiehui Dianying Lishi Yanjiubu* (Film History Research Section of the China Film Association), *Zhongguo Dianyingjia Liezhuan (Diliuji)* (*Biographies of Chinese Filmmakers* [Volume Six]), (Beijing: *Zhongguo Dianying Chubanshe* [China Film Press], 1985), 481-95. This biography also details the production history of both films.

41. Leyda discusses the checkered history of *Early Spring in February*, 313-4, and quotes criticism of *Stage Sisters*, 341. Marco Müller discusses why the latter film may have been singled out in "Les tribulations d'un cinéaste

chinois en Chine," *Cahiers du Cinéma* 344 (1983), 16-21. Clark (1987) also discusses the criticism of *Early Spring in February*, 112-114, 127.

42. Cited in Gina Marchetti, "*Stage Sisters*—The Blooming of a Revolutionary Aesthetic," *Jump Cut* no. 4 (1989), 101.
43. Bordwell, Staiger and Thompson, 12-3, 16-8.
44. Yu Min's film script for *Bridge* is included in *Zhongguo Dianying Juben Xuanji (Yi) (Selected Chinese Film Scripts* [One]), ed. *Zhongguo Dianying Chubanshe (China Film Press)* (Beijing: *Zhongguo Dianying Chubanshe*, 1959), 1-44. This pre-production script does not correspond exactly to the final film, and is only referenced where in agreement with the film.
45. Xie Tieli's film script for *Early Spring in February* is included in *Zhongguo Dianying Juben Xuanji (Jiu) (Selected Chinese Film Scripts* [Nine]), ed. *Zhongguo Dianying Chubanshe (China Film Press)* (Beijing: *Zhongguo Dianying Chubanshe* [China Film Press], 1981, 65-120. This pre-production script does not correspond exactly to the final film, and is only referenced where in agreement with the film.
46. Bordwell, Staiger and Thompson, 13-16.
47. The literature on "relational" subjectivity in Chinese culture, ancient and modern, is extensive. See, for example: Munro, 23-9, 90-9; Ma Ning 74-148; Plaks, 339-48; Francis L.K. Hsu, "Psychological homeostatis and *jen*: conceptual tools for advancing psychological anthropology," *American Anthropologist*, no.73 (1971), 23-44; Francis L.K. Hsu "The Self in Cross-cultural Perspective," in *Culture and Self: Asian and Western Perspectives*, ed. Anthony J. Marsella, George De Vos, Francis L.K. Hsu, (New York: Tavistock Publications, 1985), 24-55; Sun Lung-kee (Sun Longji), *Zhongguo Wenhua de `Shenceng Jiegou' (The `Deep Structure' of Chinese Culture)*, (Hong Kong: Jixian Publishers, 1983); Sun Lung-kee (Sun Longji), "Contemporary Chinese Culture: Structure and Emotionality," *Australian Journal of Chinese Affairs* no.26 (1991), 1-41, and; Kuo-shu Yang, "Chinese Personality and its Change," and Michael Harris Bond and Kwang-kuo Hwang, "The Social Psychology of Chinese People," in *The Psychology of the Chinese People*, ed. Michael Harris Bond (Hong Kong: Oxford University Press, 1986), 106-170, 213-264.
48. Li Qiang, Lin Ping and Du Yin, "*Yongbu Xiaoshi de Dianwang*" (*The Unfailing Beam*), in *Zhongguo Dianying Juben Xuanji (Si) (Selected Chinese Film Scripts* [Four]), ed. *Zhongguo Dianying Chubanshe (China Film Press)* (Beijing: *Zhongguo Dianying Chubanshe* [China Film Press], 1960), 76 (my translation). This pre-production script does not correspond exactly to the final film, and is only referenced where in agreement with the film.
49. Xie Jin, "*Nülan Wuhao*" (*Woman Basketball Player No.5*), in *Zhongguo Dianying Juben Xuanji (San) (Selected Chinese Film Scripts* (Three), ed. *Zhongguo Dianying Chubanshe (China Film Press)*, (Beijing: *Zhongguo Dianying Chubanshe*, 1959), 491. This pre-production script does not correspond exactly to the final film, and is only referenced where in agreement with the film.
50. Susan Rubin Suleiman, 64-100.

51. David Bordwell, *Narration in the Fiction Film*, (Madison: University of Wisconsin Press, 1985), 235-6.

52. These and further examples can be found in the published post-production script, which is faithful to the film Lu Ren, "*Li Shuangshuang (fenjingtou juben)*," (*Li Shuangshuang [shot breakdown script]*), in *Li Shuangshuang: Cong Xiaoshuo Dao Dianying* (*Li Shuangshuang: From Novel to Film*), ed. *Zhongguo Dianying Chubanshe* (*China Film Press*) (Beijing: *Zhongguo Dianying Chubanshe*, 1963), 69-197.

53. For the scene at the Lu Xun exhibition, see the accurate post-production script: Lin Gu, Xu Jin and Xie Jin, "*Wutai Jiemei (fenjingtou wancheng taiben)*" (*Stage Sisters [post-production shot breakdown script]*), in *Wutai Jiemei: Cong Tigang Dao Yingpian* (*Stage Sisters: from Treatment to Film*), ed. Meng Tao (Shanghai: *Shanghai Wenyi Chubanshe* [Shanghai Arts Press], 1982), 223-4.

54. On "middle characters," see Clark, 66-7. The debate around *Early Spring in February* between September and December 1964 focused on the two characters Xiao Jianqiu and Tao Lan. Examples from the major Shanghai newspaper, *Wenhui Bao*, include: Wang Yigang, "*Xiao Jianqiu de Rendaozhuyi Pouxi*" ("Analysis of Xiao Jianqiu's Humanism"), *Wenhui Bao*, 19 September 1964, 4; Gu Xian, "*Zaochun Eryue Wei Shenme Jieji Fuwu?—Ping Xiao Jianqiu, Tao Lan Liangge Xingxiang Ji Qita*" ("Which Class Does *Early Spring in February* Serve?—A Critique of the Figures Xiao Jianqiu, Tao Lan and Others"), *Wenhui Bao*, 22 September 1964, 2; Mian Si, "*Bu Shi Xuanyang, Shi Shenke Baolu*" ("It's Not Advocacy, But Thorough Exposure"), *Wenhui Bao*, 31 October 1964, 2; Wu Zhongjie, "*Jiujing `Yongxin Shi Haode' Ma?*" ("Did They Really `Mean Well'?"), *Wenhui Bao*, 6 November 1964, 2; Li Jiyan, "*Tao Lan Shi Yige Wanshi Bugong De Nuxing*" ("Tao Lan Is a Cynical, Wanton Female"), *Wenhui Bao*, 6 November 1964, 2; Cai Jianping, "*Shi Xuanyang, Bu Shi Baolu*" ("It Is Advocacy, Not Exposure"), *Wenhui Bao*, 10 November 1964, 2; and Huang Shixian, "*Xiao Jianqiu Shi Yimian Shenme `Qizhi'?*" ("What Is Xiao Jianqiu Really a 'Banner' For?"), *Wenhui Bao*, 27 November 1964, 4.

55. The term "rounded" is derived from E.M. Forster, *Aspects of the Novel* (Harmondsworth: Penguin, 1962. Originally published 1927.)

56. Munro, 168-170.

57. See, for example, Zhi Wei, "*Xuexi Geming Xianbei de Bangyang*" ("Learning From Model Revolutionary Forerunners"), *Renmin Ribao* (*People's Daily*), 2 September 1977, 3. This article was written at the time of the film's post-Cultural Revolution re-release.

58. Examples of articles extolling Li as a model and recording meetings held to learn from her include: Zhou Tong, "`*Wo? Gongshe de Sheyuan!*'" ("`Me? I'm a Member of the Commune!'"), *Gongren Ribao* (*Worker's Daily*), 16 November 1962, 4; *Renmin Ribao* (*People's Daily*), "`*Li Shuangshuang' gei Women Dailai Shenme—Beijing Nanyuan Hongxing Renmin Gongshe Sheyuan Tan Li Shuangshuang*" ("What `Li Shuangshuang' Has Brought Us—Members of the Beijing Nanyuan Red Star People's Commune Discuss *Li Shuangshuang*"), 29 November 1962, 6; Ye Hui (Ed.), "*Zan Li*

Shuangshuang Xue Li Shuangshuang—Baoshan Nongcun Ganbu, Sheyuan Zuotan Jilu Zhaiyao" ("Praise Li Shuangshuang, Study Li Shuangshuang—Extracts from the Record of a Discussion by Rural Cadres and Commune Members from Baoshan"), *Jiefang Ribao (Liberation Daily)*, 29 November 1962, 4; Cui Jingliang et.al. (Eds.), *"Sheyuan Qikua Shuangshuang Hao Reai Jiti Pinde Gao—Xiaoyixian Nongmin Zuotan Yingpian Li Shuangshuang"* ("Commune Members Praise Shuangshuang's Love for the Collective and High Morality—A Discussion of the Film *Li Shuangshuang* Among the Peasants of Xiaoyi County"), *Shanxi Ribao (Shanxi Daily)*, 15 December 1962, 3; and Wu Guofan et.al., *"Women Xihuan Li Shuangshuang Shi de Ren"* ("We Like People of the Li Shuangshuang Type"), *Beijing Ribao (Beijing Daily)*, 10 January 1966, 3.

59. Yu Hui-jung, "Let Our Theatre Propagate Mao Tse-tung's Thought For Ever," *Chinese Literature* 1968, no.7/8, 111. Ellen Johnston Laing cites this as one of the earliest promulgations of the formula: *The Winking Owl: Art in the People's Republic of China* (Berkeley: University of California Press, 1988), 73. The impact of this formula in the cinema is discussed and analyzed in Chris Berry, "Stereotypes and Ambiguities: An Examination of the Feature Films of the Chinese Cultural Revolution," *Journal of Asian Culture*, no.6 (1982), 37-72.

60. Stephen Heath, "Film and System: Terms of Analysis," *Screen* 16, no.1 (1975), 48-50. Altman, notes coincidence, although subordinated to the demands of realism, is not absent in classical cinema, and exists in tension with the demands of realism.

61. David Bordwell, *Narration in the Fiction Film*, (Madison: The University of Wisconsin Press, 1985), 158-9.

62. Suleiman, 149-198.

63. Bordwell, Staiger, and Thompson, 47.

64. Rick Altman suggests suspension is so extensive in the musical that it constitutes another pattern altogether; *The American Film Musical*, (Bloomington: Indiana University Press, 1987), 28. On comedy, see Jerry Palmer, *The Logic of the Absurd: On Film and Television Comedy*, (London: BFI Publishing, 1987), 141-53.

65. Laura Mulvey, "Visual Pleasure and Narrative Cinema," *Screen* 16, no.3 (1975), 6-18.

66. Ma Ning, 158-162.

67. Ma Ning also notes this function of the chorus, 185-6.

68. Bordwell, Staiger, and Thompson, 42-3. In her book devoted to the subject, Maureen Turim explores the great range of uses of the flashback in Hollywood and other cinemas in much greater detail, but her study confirms Bordwell's findings about the usual uses of the flashback in Hollywood classical cinema. Maureen Turim, *Flashbacks in Film: Memory and History*, (New York: Routledge, 1989).

69. William Hinton, *Fanshen: A Documentary of Revolution in a Chinese Village* (Harmondsworth: Penguin, 1966).

70. Bordwell, Staiger and Thompson, 50-9.

71. The debate around "suture" is probably one of the more developed discussions of this characteristic of Hollywood classical cinema. See Jean-Pierre Oudart, "Cinema and Suture," *Screen* 18, no.4, (1977/78), 35-47, and Daniel Dayan, "The Tutor-Code of Classical Cinema," *Film Quarterly* 28, no.1 (1974), 22-31. Nick Browne, "The Spectator-in-the-Text: The Rhetoric of *Stagecoach*," *Film Quarterly* 29, no.2 (1976-6), 26-38 questions some of the assumptions behind these arguments.

72. Examples include: Mulvey; Raymond Bellour, "Hitchcock, the Enunciator," *Camera Obscura*, no.2 (1977), 69-94; Raymond Bellour, "Psychosis, Neurosis, Perversion," *Camera Obscura*, nos. 3-4 (1979), 105-32; Kaja Silverman, *Male Subjectivity at the Margins* (New York: Routledge, 1992); D.N. Rodowick, *The Difficulty of Difference: Psychoanalysis, Sexual Difference, and Film Theory* (New York: Routledge, 1991); and Gaylyn Studlar, *In The Realm of Pleasure: Von Sternberg, Dietrich, and the Masochistic Aesthetic* (Urbana: University of Illinois Press, 1988).

73. If the desire to know can be said to structure libidinal drives such as scopophilia, there is overlap between epistemological and libidinal command.

74. Chris Berry, "Sexual Difference and the Viewing Subject in *Li Shuangshuang* and *The In-Laws*," in Chris Berry, 1991, 30-39.

75. Ma, 184-9.

76. The possibility of multiple identifications based on projection in Western cinema has been explored in essays including Elizabeth Cowie, "Fantasia," *m/f* no.9 (1984), 70-105, and Steve Neale, "Sexual Difference in Cinema," *The Oxford Literary Review* 8, nos.1-2 (1986), 123-132. See also Jacques Laplanche and Jean-Bertrand Pontalis, "Fantasy and the Origins of Sexuality," *The International Journal of Psycho-Analysis* 49, no.1 (1968), 1-18.

77. Ma, 189.

78. Judith Stacey, *Patriarchy and Socialist Revolution in China* (Berkeley: University of California Press, 1983).

79. Chris Berry, 1982.

80. Ma Ning, 160-173.

81. Ma Ning, 101-11.

82. David Bordwell, 1985, 110-2.

83. Roland Barthes, *S/Z* (New York: Hill and Wang, 1974).

84. Tao-Ching Hsu, *The Chinese Conception of Theater* (Seattle: The University of Washington Press, 1985), 490-1.

85. See in particular Ma Ning, 98-111.

86. Ma Ning, 107-9.

87. Ma Ning, 188-190.

88. Teshome Gabriel, *Third Cinema in the Third World* (Ann Arbor: UMI Research Press, 1982), 64

89. Ma Ning, 237.

90. Ma Ning, "Spatiality and Subjectivity in Xie Jin's Film Melodrama of the New Period," in *New Chinese Cinemas: Forms, Identities, Politics* (Cambridge: Cambridge University Press, 1994), ed. Nick Browne, Paul G. Pickowicz, Vivian Sobchack, and Esther Yau, 22.

NOTES FOR CHAPTER THREE

1. Si Ning, *"'Jinqu' yu 'Nanqu' "* ("'Forbidden Zones' and 'Difficult Zones'"), *Dianying Yishu (Film Art)*, 1979, no.1, 46.

2. He Yuhuai, *Cycles of Repression and Relaxation: Politico-Literary Events in China 1976-1989* (Bochum: Universitätsverlag Dr. N. Brockmeyer, 1992), 121-2. The Chinese for this phrase is *zhuti xianxing*, and it is also known as *zhuti juedinglun*, or "the theory of theme as the determining factor." These ideas were attacked frequently after the fall of the Gang. See Cai Shiyong, *"Ticai Mantan"* ("A Few Words about Themes"), *Dianying Yishu (Film Art)* 1979, no.2, 29-30.

3. *'Dianying Yishu Cidian' Bianji Weiyuanhui* (Editorial Committee for the *Film Art Dictionary*), *Dianying Yishu Cidian (Film Art Dictionary)* (Beijing: Zhongguo Dianying Chubanshe [China Film Press], 1986), 143, 67.

4. The transition from *ticai* to genres in the eighties is discussed in Chris Berry, "A Turn for the Better? Genre and Gender in *Girl From Hunan* and Other Recent Mainland Chinese Films," *PostScript* 14, nos.1&2 (1994, 1995), 81-103.

5. Chris Berry, "Now You See It, Now You Don't," *Cinemaya* no.4, (1989), 46-55.

6. Roland Barthes, *Mythologies* (New York: Hill and Wang, 1972).

7. Lyotard calls this "the metanarrative of the march towards socialism" in *The Postmodern Condition: A Report on Knowledge* (Manchester: University of Manchester Press, 1984), 37. There had been some critical approval of the depiction of tragedies under socialism in China during the early 1960's. But no one dared write such works then, and they were resolutely condemned by Jiang Qing during the Cultural Revolution. He Yuhuai, 89-90.

8. Bonnie S. McDougall, *Mao Zedong's "Talks at the Yan'an Conference on Literature and Art": A Translation of the 1943 Text with Commentary* (Ann Arbor: The University of Michigan Center for Chinese Studies, The University of Michigan, 1980), 79-83.

9. For a discussion of the films of this period that explicitly compares them to those of the post-Mao period, see Paul Clark, "Two Hundred Flowers on China's Screens," in *Perspectives on Chinese Cinema*, ed. Chris Berry (London: British Film Institute, 1991), 40-61.

10. Sources on political developments consulted for this chapter are: Peter R. Moody, Jr., *Chinese Politics After Mao: Development and Liberalization 1976 to 1983* (New York: Praeger, 1983); Harry Harding, *China's Second Revolution: Reform After Mao*, (Washington DC: The Brookings Institution, 1987); Immanuel C.Y. Hsu, *China Without Mao: The Search for a New Order* (2nd ed.), (New York: Oxford University Press, 1990); William A. Joseph, *The Critique of Ultra-Leftism in China, 1958-1981* (Stanford: Stanford University Press, 1984); Suzanne Ogden, *China's Unresolved Issues: Politics, Development and Culture* (Englewood Cliffs, NJ: Prentice Hall, 1989); John Gardner, *Chinese Politics and the Succession to Mao*, (London: Macmillan, 1982); Kwan Ha Yim, *China Under Deng* (New York: Facts

On File, 1991); Andrew J. Nathan, *Chinese Democracy* (New York: Alfred A. Knopf, 1985); David S.G. Goodman, "Changes in Leadership Personnel After September 1976," and Gustaaf Vloeberghs, "The Position of Hua Kuo-Feng," in *Chinese Politics After Mao*, ed. Jurgen Domes (Cardiff: University College Cardiff Press, 1979), 37-69 and 71-81; Richard C. Bush "Deng Xiaoping: China's Old Man in a Hurry," and David M. Lampton, "Politics in the PRC: Entering the Fourth Decade," in *China Briefing, 1980*, ed. Robert B. Oxnam & Richard C. Bush (Boulder: Westview Press, 1980), 9-24 and 25-38 respectively; Charles Burton, *Political and Social Change in China Since 1978* (New York: Greenwood Press, 1990); Michael Sullivan, "The Politics of Conflict and Compromise," in *China Since the `Gang of Four'*, ed. Bill Brugger (London: Croom Helm, 1980), pp.20-50; and Roger Garside, *Coming Alive: China After Mao*, (New York: New American Library, 1981). Further references are only given for specific citations.

11. English-language sources on cultural production and policy consulted for this chapter are: He Yuhuai; Kam Louie, *Between Fact and Fiction: Essays on Post-Mao Chinese Literature and Society* (Sydney: Wild Peony Press, 1989); Perry Link, "The Limits of Cultural Reform in Deng Xiaoping's China," *Modern China*, 13, no.2 (1987), 115-176; Sylvia Chan, "Two Steps Forward, One Step Back: Towards a 'Free' Literature," *The Australian Journal of Chinese Affairs* nos.19/20 (1988), 81-126; Anne Wedell-Wedells-borg, "Literature in the Post-Mao Years," in *Reforming the Revolution: China in Transition*, ed. Robert Benewick and Paul Wingrove (London: Macmillan, 1988), 190-206; Xin Xiangrong, "Literature and Art and Politics," *Beijing Review* 27, no.34 (23 August 1982), 3; Anthony J. Kane, "Literary Politics in Post-Mao China," *Asian Survey* 21, no.7 (1981), 775-794; Bonnie S. McDougall, "Dissent Literature: Official and Nonofficial Literature in and about China in the Seventies," *Contemporary China* 3, no.4 (1979), 49-79; Leo Ou-Fan Lee, "Dissent Literature from the Cultural Revolution," *Chinese Literature, Essays, Articles, Reviews* 1, no.1 (1979), 59-79; Joseph S.M. Lau, "The Wounded and the Fatigued: Reflections on Post-1976 Chinese Fiction," *Journal of Oriental Studies* 20, no.2 (1982), 128-42; Richard King, "'Wounds' and 'Exposure': Chinese Literature after the Gang of Four," *Pacific Affairs* 54, no.1 (1981), 82-99; Geremie Barmé, "Flowers or More Weeds? Culture in China Since the Fall of the Gang of Four," *The Australian Journal of Chinese Affairs* no.1 (1979), 125-133; Geremie Barmé, "*Chaotou Wenxue*: China's New Literature," *The Australian Journal of Chinese Affairs* no.2 (1979), 137-148; Peter R. Moody, Jr; Irene Eber, "Old Issues and New Directions in Cultural Activities Since September 1976," in Jurgen Domes, 203-227; Michael Sullivan, "Painting with a New Brush: Art in Post-Mao China" and Leo Ou-fan Lee, "Recent Chinese Literature: A Second Hundred Flowers," in Robert B. Oxnam & Richard C. Bush, 53-64 and 65-74; Sylvia Chan, "The Blooming of a 'Hundred Flowers' and the Literature of the 'Wounded Generation'," in Bill Brugger, 174-201; and Ai-li Chin, "Value Themes in Short Stories, 1976-1977," in *Moving a Mountain: Cultural Change in China*, ed. Godwin

C. Chu and Francis L.K. Hsu (Honolulu: The University Press of Hawaii, 1979), 280-304. Further references will only be given for specific citations.

12. Homi K. Bhabha, "DissemiNation: Time, Narrative and the Margins of the Modern Nation," in *Nation and Narration*, ed. Homi K. Bhabha (London: Routledge, 1990), 291-322.

13. *Renmin Ribao (People's Daily)* editorial, 7 February 1977, cited in Peter R. Moody, Jr., 132.

14. See Immanuel C.Y. Hsu, 12-8, Gardner, 98-119, and Garside, 131-154.

15. Hong Yung Lee, *The Politics of the Chinese Cultural Revolution*, (Berkeley: University of California Press, 1978), 11-26; Tom Fisher, "The Play's the Thing: Wu Han and *Hai Rui* Revisited," *Australian Journal of Chinese Affairs* no.7 (1982), 1-35.

16. Moody, 23.

17. He Yuhuai, 23-4.

18. He Yuhuai, 25-29. Late 1976 and early 1977 issues of *Renmin Dianying (People's Film)* include a multitude of articles rehabilitating the film and detailing Gang crimes against it.

19. He Yuhuai, 48-51. For a detailed analysis of *Counterattack*, see *Beijing Dianying Zhipianchang Pipanzu* (Criticism Group of Beijing Film Studio), *"Huozhenjiashi de Yinmo Wenyi: Dui Yingpian 'Fanji' de Zaipipan"* ("Out-and-out Plotting Art: Further Criticism of the Film, *Counterattack*,") in Anon., *"Sirenbang" Shi Dianying Shiye de Sidi: Wenhuabu Dianying Xitong Jiepi "Sirenbang" Zuixing Dahui Fayan Huibian (The Gang of Four Are Deadly Enemies of the Film Industry: A Compilation of Speeches from the Film System of the Ministry of Culture Rally to Expose and Criticize the Crimes of the Gang of Four)* (Beijing: *Zhongguo Dianying Chubanshe* [China Film Press], 1978), 55-69. Many shorter articles on both films can be found in late 1976 and early 1977 issues of *Renmin Dianying (People's Film)*.

20. Meng Senhui and Si Minsan, *"Nuli jieshi jiejiguanxi de xin bianhua— jiantan caise gushi yingpian Huanteng de Xiaoliang He"* (Vigorously Publicize New Changes in Class Relationships—Also Discuss the Color Feature Film *The Jubilant Xiaoliang River*); *Luwanqu gongren yeyu dianying pinglunzu* (The Workers Amateur Film Criticism Group of Lu Bay District), *"Yongde shi shenme chizi?"* ("By What Measure?"); Lu Lei, *"Wenxue shi zhandoude"* ("Literature is a Military Matter"), *Wenhuibao (Wenhui News)*, 3 August 1976, 3.

21. *Shanghai Dianying Zhipianchang 'Huanteng de Xiaoliang He' Shezhizu (The Jubilant Xiaoliang River Production Unit at Shanghai Film Studio)*, *"Wei 'sirenbang' cuandangduoquan zhizao fangeming yulun de daibiaozuo: yingpian Huanteng de Xiaoliang He paozhi chulong jingguo"* ("A Representative Work to Mould Counter-Revolutionary Public Opinion for the 'Gang of Four' Effort to Usurp Party and State Power: An Account of the Concoction and Release of the Film *The Jubliant Xiaoliang River*"), *Wenhuibao (Wenhui News)*, 24 November 1976, 2. Similar claims were made in *Wenhuibao (Wenhui News)*, *"Jiangsu wenyijie jiepi 'sirenbang' wantu cuandangduoquan paozhi ducao yingpian Huanteng de Xiaoliang he de*

zuixing" ("The Literature and Art Circles in Jiangsu Expose and Criticize the 'Gang of Four' Crime of Concocting the Poisonous Weed Film *The Jubilant Xiaoliang River* in their Vain Effort to Seize Party and State Power"), 19 December 1976, 3, and *Shanghai Dianying Zhipianchang Pipanzu* (Shanghai Film Studio Criticism Group), "*Wei cuandangduoquan dazao yulun de heibiaoben: jiechuan 'sirenbang' paozhi 'Huangteng de Xiaoliang He' de yinmou*" ("A Black Specimen Designed to Whip up Public Opinion for the Effort to Usurp Party and State Power: Exposing 'Gang of Four' Plot in Concocting *The Jubliant Xiaoliang River*"), *Renmin Dianying* (*People's Film*), 1976, no.8, 10-13.

22. The instance with the greatest impact would probably have been the short-lived Hundred Flowers Campaign of 1956. Paul Clark, "Two Hundred Flowers on China's Screens," discusses this in greater detail. The film production figures given in Clark's *Chinese Cinema: Culture and Politics Since 1949* also show a clear negative correlation between film production and periods of intense political campaigns, 185-6.

23. *Zhongguo Dianying Ziliaoguan, Zhongguo Yishu Yanjiuyuan Dianying Yanjiusuo* (China Film Archive and Film Research Office of the China Arts Research Institute), *Zhongguo Yishu Yingpian Bianmu* (*China Feature Filmography*), (Beijing: *Wenhua Yishu Chubanshe* [Culture and Art Publishing House], 1981). My count varies slightly but not significantly from Clark's.

24. Ah Yun, "*Fengyun tubian you digui*" ("Tempered in the Violent Storm"), *Renmin Dianying* (*People's Film*) 1977, no.11, 10.

25. Immanuel C.Y. Hsu, 92-121.

26. Gardner, 62-97.

27. Moody, op.cit., gives a detailed account of the stages in Deng's return to power, pp.41-4.

28. David S.G. Goodman has demonstrated that changes in Party and state leadership during these years constituted a counter-Cultural Revolution, whereby figures deposed in 1966-8 were returned to power.

29. Gardner, 141-172, Nathan, 3-44, Garside, 195-243, and Moody, 65-82. Garside also gives over a chapter to Wei Jingsheng, 243-278.

30. Garside, 182-195.

31. According to Eber, the first films chosen for re-release were mostly revolutionary history films.

32. Liu Xinwu, "*Ban Zhuren*," ("The Class Teacher") *Renmin Wenxue* (*People's Literature*) 1977, no.11, 16-29. Translated as "The Teacher" in Liu Xinwu, et.al, *Prize-Winning Stories From China, 1978-1979* (Beijing: Foreign Languages Press, 1981), 3-26, and as "Class Counsellor" in *The Wounded: New Stories of the Cultural Revolution*, ed. Geremie Barmé and Bennet Lee (Hong Kong: Joint Publishing Company, 1979), 147-178.

33. He Yuhuai, 74-85, Kam Louie, 1-13.

34. Liu Xinwu, "*Aiqing de Weizhi*," *Shiyue* [*October*] no.1 (October 1978), 117-129, translated as "A Place For Love," *Chinese Literature* no.1 (1979), 36-57.

35. Lu Xinhua, "*Shanghen*," ("The Scar") *Wenhuibao* (*Wen Hui News*), 11 August 1978, and translated in Liu Xunwu, et.al, *Prize-Winning Stories*

From China, 1978-1979 (Beijing: Foreign Languages Press, 1981), 108-122, as "The Wound" in *Chinese Literature* 1979, no. 3, 25-38, and as "The Wounded" in Geremie Barmé and Bennet Lee, 9-24.

36. He Yuhuai, 86-102.
37. This voice is attributed to Premier Zhou on page 51 of *Xi'an Dianying Zhipianchang* (Xi'an Film Studio), *Lanse de Haiwan: Secai Gushipian Wancheng Taiben* (*Blue Bay: Color Feature Film Post-Production Script*), (Xi'an: *Xi'an Dianying Zhipianchang* [Xi'an Film Studio], 1978).
38. Immanuel C.Y. Hsu, 127-142.
39. Zhou Enlai, "Zhou Enlai on Questions Related to Art and Literature," *Chinese Literature* 1979, no.6, 83-95. The original Chinese version was published in many places, including *Dianying Yishu* (*Film Art*) 1979, no.1, 1-18.
40. Louie, 3-6, and King.
41. For detailed discussion, see Sylvia Chan (1988); Anthony J. Kane; *Chinese Literature*, "Zhou Yang on Reality in Literature and Other Questions," 1980, no.1, 92-6; Zhou Yang, "On the Hundred Flowers Policy," *China Reconstructs* 29, no.1 (1980), 4-7; Zhou Yang, "Our Achievements, Lessons and Tasks: Extracts of a report to the Fourth Congress of Chinese Writers and Artists," *Chinese Literature* 1980, no.3, 38-51; Xia Yan, "My Opinions," *Chinese Literature* 1980, no.4, 110-4; and Ling Yang, "The Last Three Years," *Beijing Review* 22, no.52 (1979), 7-26. Many texts of speeches are included in Howard Goldblatt, ed., *Chinese Literature for the 1980s: The Fourth Congress of Writers and Artists* (Armonk: M.E. Sharpe, 1982).
42. Zhao Dan, "Rigid Control Ruins Art and Literature," *Chinese Literature* 1981, no.1, 107-114. Also translated as "When Control Is Too Tight, There's No Hope for Literature and Art," by Bett Ting, in *Policy Conflicts in Post-Mao China: A Documentary Survey, with Analysis*, ed. John P. Burns and Stanley Rosen (Armonk: M.E. Sharpe, 1986), 314-7. The Chinese original was published in the People's Daily [*Renmin Ribao*] on October 8, 1980.
43. Peng Ning and He Kongzhou, "*Wenyi Minzhu yu Dianying Yishu*" ("Democracy in Literature and the Arts and Film Art"), *Dianying Yishu* (*Film Art*), 1979, no.1, 28-33.
44. The pre-production script of *Reverberations of Life* has been published. Teng Wenji, *Shenghuo de Chanyin* (*Reverberations of Life*), (Beijing: *Zhongguo Dianying Chubanshe* [China Film Press], 1980).
45. The pre-production script of *My Ten Classmates* has been published. Yang Yingzhang, *Wo de Shige Tongxue* (*My Ten Classmates*), (Beijing: *Zhongguo Dianying Chubanshe* [China Film Press], 1979).
46. The pre-production script of *Loyal Heart* has been published. Su Shuyang, *Dan Xin Pu* (*Loyal Heart*), (Beijing: China Film Press, 1979).
47. The precise details of *The Corner Forgotten by Love* can be followed in the published post-production script; Zhang Qi and Li Yalin, "*Bei Aiqing Yiwang de Jiaoluo (Fenjingtou Juben)*" ("The Corner Forgotten by Love [Shot Breakdown])", in Zhang Xian, *Bei Aiqing Yiwang de Jiaoluo: Cong Xiaoshuo Dao Dianying* (*The Corner Forgotten by Love: From Novel to*

Film), (Beijing: *Zhongguo Dianying Chubanshe* [China Film Press], 1984), 79-180.

48. See the post-production script in Lu Yanzhou et.al., *The Legend of Tianyun Mountain—From Novel to Film* (*Tianyunshan Chuanqi—Cong Xiaoshuo Dao Dianying*), (Beijing: *Zhongguo Dianying Chubanshe* [China Film Press], 1983).

49. The pre-production script of *A Late Spring* has been published. Rao Qu and Tan Su, *Chidao de Chuntian* (*A Late Spring*), (Beijing: *Zhongguo Dianying Chubanshe* [China Film Press], 1981).

NOTES FOR CHAPTER FOUR

1. Seymour Chatman, *Story and Discourse* (Ithaca: Cornell University Press, 1978), 108-9.

2. Chatman, 107.

3. Baruch Hochman, *Character in Literature* (Ithaca: Cornell University Press, 1985), 13-27.

4. The term "rounded" is derived from E.M. Forster, *Aspects of the Novel* (Harmondsworth: Penguin, 1962. Originally published 1927.)

5. See, for example, Zhang Nuanxin and Li Tuo, "*Tan Dianying Yuyan de Xiandaihua,*" ("The Modernization of Film Language"), in *Zhongguo Dianying Lilun Wenxuan*, ed. Luo Yijun (*Chinese Film Theory: An Anthology*) (Beijing: *Wenhua Yishu Chubanshe* [Culture and Art Publishers], 1992), vol.2, 9-34, originally published in *Dianying Yishu* (*Film Art*) 1979, no.3, trans. Hou Jianping, in *Chinese Film Theory: A Guide to the New Era*, ed. George S. Semsel, Xia Hong and Hou Jianping (New York: Praeger, 1990), 10-20.

6. Vladimir Propp, *Morphology of the Folk Tale* (Austin: University of Texas Press, 1977).

7. Peng Ning and He Kongzhou, "*Wenyi Minzhu yu Dianying Yishu*" ("Democracy in Literature and the Arts and Film Art"), *Dianying Yishu* (*Film Art*), 1979, no.1, 30.

8. Chen Huangmei, chief ed., *Dangdai Zhongguo Dianying* (*Contemporary Chinese Cinema*), (Beijing: *Zhongguo Shehui Kexue Chubanshe* [China Social Sciences Press], 1989), vol.2, 359-360.

9. Chen, 368.

10. Chen, 384.

11. For example, Paul Clark, "Two Hundred Flowers on China's Screens," in *Perspectives on Chinese Cinema*, ed. Chris Berry (London: BFI, 1992), 40-61.

12. Rao Shuguang and Pei Yali, *Xin Shiqi Dianying Wenhua Sichao* (*Thoughts on the Film Culture of the New Era*), (Beijing: *Zhongguo Guangbo Dianshe Chubanshe* [China Radio and Television Press], 1997), 5.

13. Wang Fuli, "*Yan Shijiao Wo Yan Song Wei,*" ("Being Taught Strictly to Act Song Wei"), in Lu Yanzhou et.al., *Tianyunshan Chuanqi – Cong Xiaoshuo Dao Dianying* (*The Legend of Tianyun Mountain – From Novel*

to Film), (Beijing: *Zhongguo Dianying Chubanshe* [China Film Press], 1983), 341.

14. Shi Weijian, "*Wo Yan Luo Qun*," ("How I Played Luo Qun"), in Lu Yanzhou et.al., 328-340.

15. Lu Yanzhou, "'*Tianyunshan Chuanqi*' *Chuangzuo de Qianqianhouhou*," ("Before and After the Production of *The Legend of Tianyun Mountain*") in Lu Yanzhou et.al., 277-289.

16. Lu Yanzhou, 278.

17. Ye Nan, "'*Bashan Yeyu*' *Weishenme Meiyou Xie Huairen*" ("Why There Are No Bad Characters in *Evening Rain*"), in Ye Nan et.al., *Bashan Yeyu – Cong Juben Dao Yingpian* (*Evening Rain—From Script to Screen*), (Beijing: *Zhongguo Dianying Chubanshe* [China Film Press], 1982), 179-181.

18. Wu Yonggang and Wu Yigong, "*Huigu yu Sikao: Dai 'Bashan Yeyu' Yishu Zongjie*" ("Looking Back and Thinking: Summing Up the Art of *Evening Rain*," in Ye Nan et.al., 201.

19. Liu Guiqing, "*Xin Shiqi Dianying zhong de Xianshizhuyi*" ("Realism in the Cinema of the New Era"), *Dangdai Dianying* (*Contemporary Cinema*) No.56 (1993), 11.

20. Merle Goldman, *Sewing the Seeds of Democracy in China: Political reform in the Deng Xiaoping Era* (Cambridge: Harvard University Press, 1994), 30.

21. Liu Guiqing, 10.

22. The short story that forms the basis for one of these films has appeared into English: Wang Yaping, "Sacred Duty," (trans. Tang Sheng) in Liu Xinwu et.al., *Prize-Winning Stories from China, 1978-1979* (Beijing: Foreign Languages Press, 1981), 27-57.

23. *Spring Rain* is slightly unusual as the crime police officer Feng Chunhai is ordered to investigate—participation in the 1976 *qingming* demonstrations to commemorate Zhou Enlai—was no longer a crime by the time the film was made. However, there is no doubt that the hero's suffering is linked to the Gang.

24. Paul G. Pickowicz, "Popular Cinema and Political Thought in Post-Mao China: Reflections on Official Pronouncements, Film, and the Film Audience," in *Unofficial China: Popular Culture and Thought in the People's Republic*, ed. Perry Link, Richard Madsen, and Paul G. Pickowicz (Boulder: Westview Press, 1989), 46.

NOTES FOR CHAPTER FIVE

1. *Renmin Ribao* (*People's Daily*), "*Renzhen Taolun yixia Wenyi Chuangzuozhong Biaoxian Aiqing de Wenti*" ("Conscientiously Debate the Issue of the Representation of Love in Literature and Art Work"), 4 November 1981, republished in *Zhongguo Dianyingjia Xiehui* (China Film Association) (compiler), *Zhongguo Dianying Nianjian 1982* (*China Film Yearbook 1982*), (Beijing: *Zhongguo Dianying Chubanshe* [China Film Press], 1983), 41.

2. The two other 1979 films are *Wedding* and *Where Silence Reigns*. The pre-production script of *Reverberations of Life* has been published: Teng Wenji, *Shenghuo de Chanyin (Reverberations of Life)*, (Beijing: *Zhongguo Dianying Chubanshe* [China Film Press], 1980).

3. The films that do not feature romantic love are: *A Loyal Heart, A Handcuffed Passenger, Murder in 405, The Child Violinist, The Tenth Bullet Scar, Jade Butterfly,* and *Ghost* (all 1980); and *Eager to Return, The Investigator* and *The Side Road* (all 1981).

4. For example, Liu Guiqing's overview of realism in the ten years of the new era deplores many of the popular romances of these years on the grounds that they lack realism: *"Xin Shiqi Dianying zhong de Xianshizhuyi"* ("Realism in the Cinema of the New Era"), *Dangdai Dianying (Contemporary Cinema)* no.56 (1993), 12.

5. Chen Huangmei, chief ed., *Dangdai Zhongguo Dianying (Contemporary Chinese Cinema)*, (Beijing: *Zhongguo Shehui Kexue Chubanshe* [China Social Sciences Press], 1989), vol.2, 363-4.

6. Kam Louie, "Love Stories: The Meaning of Love and Marriage in China, 1978-1981," in *Between Fact and Fiction: Essays on Post-Mao Chinese Literature and Society* (Sydney: Wild Peony Press, 1989), 49-75.

7. Louie, 54.

8. Louie, 55-72.

9. Louie, 74.

10. The announcement was made in *Renmin Ribao (People's Daily)* on 16 November 1978, and excerpted in translation in *Beijing Review*, "The Might of the People," 21, no.47 (24 November 1978), 7-11.

11. See also *Beijing Review*, "The Modern Play 'Where the Silence Is'," 21, no.47, (24 November 1978), 11-12 for an English-language discussion of the play and its relation to the Tiananmen Incident.

12. The pre-production script of *The Legend of Tianyun Mountain* has been published: Lu Yanzhou, *Tianyunshan Chuanqi (The Legend of Tianyun Mountain)*, (Beijing: *Zhongguo Dianying Chubanshe* [China Film Press], 1980).

13. *Renmin Ribao (People's Daily)*, *"Renzhen Taolun yixia Wenyi Chuangzuozhong Biaoxian Aiqing de Wenti"*; *Renmin Ribao (People's Daily)*; *"Tigao Shehui Zeren, Zhengque Miaoxie Aiqing"* ("Raise Social Responsibility and Describe Love Correctly), 11 November 1981, 5. An article in *Beijing Review* summarizes the views in these pieces: "On the Presentation of Love," *Beijing Review* 24, no.52, (28 December 1981), 25-6.

14. See "The Pleasures of Adornment and the Dangers of Sexuality" in Emily Honig and Gail Hershatter, *Personal Voices: Chinese Women in the 1980's* (Stanford: Stanford University Press, 1988), 41-80.

15. Louie,.49.

16. Perry Link, "The Limits of Cultural Reform in Deng Xiaoping's China," *Modern China*, 13, no.2 (April 1987), 139.

17. Sylvia Chan, "Two Steps Forward, One Step Back: Towards a 'Free' Literature," *The Australian Journal of Chinese Affairs* no.19/20 (1988), 86. Hu

is quoted to this effect in the 4 November *Renmin Ribao* (*People's Daily*) article.

18. Bao Wenqing, "New Start for Literature and Art: Xia Yan – Difficulties and Prospects," *China Reconstructs* 29, no.2 (February 1980), 21.

19. *Renmin Ribao* (*People's Daily*), 4 and 11 November 1981, and *Beijing Review* 24, no.52, 25.

20. On this underlying ideology of Chinese Studies discourse, see Gloria Davies, "Chinese Literary Studies and Post-Structuralist Positions: What Next?" in *The Australian Journal of Chinese Affairs* no.28 (July 1992), 67-86.

21. Tonglin Lu, *Rose and Lotus: Narrative of Desire in France and China*, (Albany: State University of New York Press, 1991), 11.

22. For further discussion, see E. Perry Link, Jr., *Mandarin Ducks and Butterflies: Popular Fiction in Early Twentieth-Century Chinese Cities* (Berkeley: University of California Press, 1981).

23. Ono Kazuko, *Chinese Women in a Century of Revolution*, (Stanford: Stanford University Press, 1989), 93-111.

24. Leo Ou-Fan Lee notes the prevalence and significance accorded love in the fiction of the 1920's and gives some discussion of the romantic lifestyles and beliefs of May Fourth Movement literati; *The Romantic Generation of Modern Chinese Writers* (Cambridge, MA: Harvard University Press, 1973), 262-274. Tani Barlow discusses the particular instance of Ding Ling, whose 1920's fiction and lifestyle are exemplary instances, in her introductory essay to Ding Ling, *I Myself Am a Woman: Selected Writings of Ding Ling*, (Boston: Beacon Press, 1989), 1-45, see especially 13-4, 21-30.

25. See Judith Stacey, *Patriarchy and Socialist Revolution in China* (Berkeley: University of California Press, 1983).

26. The exceptions are: *South Sea Storm* (1976), in which the main protagonist is separated from his family by military conflict with Vietnam; *Salimake* (1978), in which the eponymous heroine and her fiancé experience relationship difficulties; and *Not a One-Off Story* (1978), in which the main protagonist's devotion to agricultural modernization wins the love of a Party vice-secretary.

27. The films are *Fast as Light*, *Tear Stain*, *My Ten Classmates*, and *Sacred Duty*.

28. The exceptions are: *Fast as Light*, *Spring Rain*, *Loyal Overseas Chinese Family*, *My Ten Classmates*, and *Sacred Duty* (all 1979); *A Handcuffed Passenger*, *Murder in 405*, *Whom Does He Love?* and *Ghost* (all 1980); and *The Side Road* (1981).

29. Other films which could be cited in this regard include: *They Are in Love*, *The Death of the Marshal*, *Sea Love*, *Child Violinist*, *Evening Rain*, *Come Back, Swallow*, *Volleyball Star*, *After the Nightmare Comes the Dawn*, *The Tenth Bullet Scar*, *The Traitor*, *Bamboo*, *Maple*, *The Jade Butterfly*, *A Late Spring*, *Not For Love*, *Rays Penetrating the Clouds*, (all 1980), both versions of *Xu Mao and His Daughters*, *The Investigator*, *May Love Be Everlasting*, *The Spiral*, *Set Sail*, *Whirlpool Song*, *Spirit of the Foil*, *The Corner Forgotten by Love*, *The Rose That Should Not Wither and Die*, and *The Crystal Heart*, (all 1981).

30. The creators of *The Legend of Tianyun Mountain* acknowledge this effect directly. See Xie Jin, Huang Shuqin, and Liao Ruiqun, "On the Direction of *The Legend of Tianyun Mountain*," (*Tianyunshan Chuanqi Daoyan Chanshu*)," in Lu Yanzhou et.al., 299-301.
31. Ma Ning, "The Textual and Critical Difference of Being Radical," *Wide Angle* 11, no.2, (1989), 22-31; Chris Berry, "The Sublimative Text: Sex and Revolution in *Big Road*," *East-West Film Journal* 2, no.2 (1988), 66-87.
32. Robert Thaxton, "The World Turned Downside Up: Three Orders of Meaning in the Peasants' Traditional Political World," *Modern China* 13, no.2, (April 1977), 185-228.
33. Ma Ning, *Culture and Politics in Chinese Film Melodrama: Traditional Sacred, Moral Economy, and the Xie Jin Mode*, Ph.D. Thesis, (Monash University, 1992).

NOTES FOR CHAPTER SIX

1. Deng Xiaoping, "Concerning Problems on the Ideological Front," in *Selected Works of Deng Xiaoping (1975-1982)*, (Beijing: Foreign Languages Press, 1984), 368-9.
2. For example, see Chen Huangmei, chief ed., *Dangdai Zhongguo Dianying* (*Contemporary Chinese Cinema*), (Beijing: *Zhongguo Shehui Kexue Chubanshe* [China Social Sciences Press], 1989), vol.2, 275-8. This is also the approach taken by Régis Bergeron, *Le Cinéma Chinois 1949-1983*, (Paris: *Editions L'Harmattan*, 1984), vol.3, 247-9. For the perspective of the Republic of China government on Taiwan, see Hsüan Mo, "Peiping's Current Policy Toward Literature and Art," *Issues and Studies* 18, no.6 (June 1982), 55-68; Hsüan Mo, "Mainland China's Autocratic Policy Toward Literature and Art: Its Practice and Stratagem," *Issues and Studies* 17, no.12 (December 1981), 33-46; *Issues and Studies*, "A Sharp Reining-In of Artistic Freedom in Mainland China," 17, no.5 (May 1981), 10-12; *Issues and Studies*, "Pai Hua's 'Confession'," 18, no.1 (January 1982), 7-9.
3. Xin Xiangrong draws careful distinctions between this event and the campaigns of the past: "Literary Criticism," *Beijing Review* 24, no.21 (May 25, 1981), 3; "More on Literary Criticism," *Beijing Review* 24, no.35 (August 31, 1981), 3; and "Letting a Hundred Flowers Bloom," *Beijing Review* 24, no.38 (September 21, 1981), 3.
4. Major accounts drawn on for the discussion here include: Sylvia Chan, "Two Steps Forward, One Step Back: Towards a 'Free' Literature," *The Australian Journal of Chinese Affairs* nos.19/20 (1988), 81-126; Paul Clark, *Chinese Cinema: Culture and Politics Since 1949*, (Cambridge: Cambridge University Press, 1987), 167-172; Michael S. Duke, "Resurgent Humanism in Bai Hua's *Bitter Love*," in *Blooming and Contending: Chinese Literature in the Post-Mao Era* (Bloomington: Indiana University Press, 1985), 123-148; Merle Goldman, "The Campaign Against Bai Hua and Other Writers," in *Sewing the Seeds of Democracy in China: Political reform in the Deng Xiaoping Era* (Cambridge: Harvard University Press, 1994), 88-112; Richard King, "Chinese Film Controversy," *Index on Censorship* 10, no.5

(October 1981), 36-7; and Jonathan D. Spence, "Film and Politics: Bai Hua's *Bitter Love*," in *Chinese Roundabout: Essays in History and Culture* (New York: W.W. Norton, 1992), 277-292.

5. Bai Hua and Peng Ning, *"Kulian"* (*Bitter Love*), *Shiyue* (*October*) 1979, no.3, 140-71, 248. After the attacks, this script was republished outside China: Bai Hua and Peng Ning, *"Kulian"* (*Bitter Love*), *Zhengming* no.44 (June 1, 1981), 82-98, and in Bai Hua et.al., *Kulian: Zhongguo Dalu Jubenxuan* (*Bitter Love: A Collection of Mainland Chinese Film Scripts*), (Taipei: *Youshi Wenhua Shiye Gongsi* [Lion Cub Press], 1982), 1-88. It was published again together with an English translation in 1983: Pai Hua and Peng Ning, "Cinematic Script 'Unrequited Love'" in *Pai Hua's Cinematic Script UNREQUITED LOVE With Related Introductory Materials*, ed. T.C. Chang, S.Y. Chen and Y.T. Lin (Taipei: Institute of Current China Studies, 1983), 21-95.

6. Deng Xiaoping, "Opposing Wrong Ideological Tendencies," in Deng, 356-359.

7. Merle Goldman, 92-4.

8. Tang Yin and Tang Dacheng, *"Lun 'Kulian' de Cuowu Qingxiang"* ("On the Incorrect Tendency of *Bitter Love*"), *Wenyi Bao* (*Literary Gazette*), 1981, no.19, 9-16, and republished in *Renmin Ribao* (*People's Daily*) 7 October 1981, 5. Excerpts are given in *Beijing Review*, "On the Film Script 'Unrequited Love'," 24, no.42 (19 October 1981), 28-9, and a full English translation is given in Foreign Broadcast Information Service, "Wenyi Bao Criticizes 'Unrequited Love'," 14 October 1981, K1-9.

9. Bai Hua, *"Guanyu 'Kulian' de Tongxin"* ("A Letter on *Bitter Love*"), *Wenyi Bao* (*Literary Gazette*), 1982, no.1, 29-31. Excerpts are included in *Beijing Review*, "Bai Hua Criticizes Himself," 25, no.2 (11 January 1982), 29, and a full English translation is given in Foreign Broadcast Information Service, "Renmin Ribao Carries Bai Hua Self-Criticism," 29 December 1981, K2-5. The self-criticism was reported to have been written on October 15; Foreign Broadcast Information Service, "Zhongguo Xinwen She on Bai Hua Self-Criticism," 16 November 1981, K1.

10. As reported in *Renmin Ribao* (*People's Daily*), *"Jianchi Liangfenfa Geng Shang Yicenglou,"* ("Persist in the Marxist Principle of Dialectical Reasoning In Order to Move on to the Next Level"), 30 December 1981, 1. An English translation of the story as reported by the Xinhua news agency is given in Foreign Broadcast Information Service, "Hu Yaobang Addresses Film Production Conference," 30 December 1981, K8-11.

11. This account and all further discussion of *Bitter Love* is based on the published script. It has, of course, been impossible to check the film itself to see if it diverges in any significant ways from that script.

12. Tang Yin and Tang Dacheng, 5; Foreign Broadcast Information Service, 14 October 1981, K1.

13. Ibid, and p.K2.

14. Michael S. Duke, 143-4.

15. Bai Hua, 1982, 29; Foreign Broadcast Information Service, 29 December 1981, K2.

16. Tang Yin and Tang Dacheng,.5; Foreign Broadcast Information Service, 14 October 1981, K5.

17. Bai Hua, 1982, 30; Foreign Broadcast Information Service, 29 December 1981, K3, K4.

18. Tang Yin and Tang Dacheng, 5; Foreign Broadcast Information Service, 14 October 1981, K4.

19. Merle Goldman, 1994, 88

20. Tang Yin and Tang Dacheng, *Renmin Ribao*, 5; Foreign Broadcast Information Service, 14 October 1981, K3. My corrections to Foreign Broadcast Information Service translation added in square brackets and based on the *Renmin Ribao* publication.

21. Richard Neupert, *The End: Narration and Closure in the Cinema*, (Detroit: Wayne State University Press, 1995), 12.

22. Neupert, 16-23.

23. Neupert, 32-3.

24. Neupert, 180-181, quotes Ed Branigan and Peter Brooks on this tendency.

25. Neupert, 22.

26. The literary script of this film has been published; Yang Yingzhang, *Wo de Shige Tongxue* (*My Ten Classmates*), (Beijing: *Zhongguo Dianying Chubanshe* [China Film Press], 1979).

27. A brief account of the Lei Feng legend with sources can be found in Zhang Yingjin, "Narrative, Ideology, Subjectivity: Defining a Subversive Discourse in Chinese Reportage," in *Politics, Ideology, and Literary Discourse in Modern China*, ed. Liu Kang and Xiaobing Tang (Durham: Duke University Press, 1993), 241, n.56.

28. Pai Hua and Peng Ning in T.C. Chang, S.Y. Chen and Y.T. Lin, 94-5 (English text,) and 116-117 (Chinese text). Duke gives a close reading of the literary intertexts, both Chinese and foreign, which inform the potential meanings attached to reeds and geese, 134-6.

29. Neupert, 75-6.

30. Clark, 164.

31. The literary script of this film has been published; Hang Ying, Duan Jishun and Yin Zhiming, *Hunli* (*The Wedding*), (Beijing: *Zhongguo Dianying Chubanshe* [China Film Press], 1980).

32. Of course, given the constraints on verbal discourse discussed in chapter one, none of the mainland Chinese analyses of the text interpret it in this way.

33. Clark, 163.

34. *Shanghai Dianying Zhipianchang* (Shanghai Film Studio), *Ku'nao Ren de Xiao: Secai Gushipian Dianying Wancheng Taiben*, (*Troubled Laughter: Color Feature Film Post-Production Script*), (Shanghai: *Shanghai Dianying Zhipianchang* [Shanghai Film Studio], 1979), 156. All following shot numbers are also derived from this accurate source.

NOTES FOR CHAPTER SEVEN

1. Rey Chow, *Primitive Passions: Visuality, Sexuality, Ethnography and Contemporary Chinese Cinema* (New York: Columbia University Press, 1995), 51.
2. Noël Burch, *To the Distant Observer: Form and Meaning in the Japanese Cinema* (Berkeley: University of California Press, 1979).
3. Homi K. Bhabha, *The Location of Culture* (London: Routledge: 1994), 31-9.
4. Edward Said, *Orientalism* (New York: Vintage, 1979).
5. Chen Xihe, *"Tuibian de Jiliu: Xin Shiqi Shinian Dianying Sichao Zouxiang"* (*"A Transforming Torrent: Trends in Film Thought over the Ten Years of the New Era"*), *Dangdai Dianying* (*Contemporary Cinema*), no.15 (1986), 21-31; Zheng Dongtian, *"Jinjin Qinian: 1979-1986 Zhongqingnian Daoyan Tansuo Huigu"* ("Only Seven Years: A Look Back at the Explorations of Young and Middle-Aged Directors between 1979 and 1986"), *Dangdai Dianying* (*Contemporary Cinema*) no.16 (1987), 46-54; Zhong Chengxiang and Rao Shuguang, *"Wenhua Fansi zhong de Xin Shiqi Dianying Chuang-zuo"* ("Film Production of the New Era in a Time of Cultural Reflection"), *Dangdai Dianying* (*Contemporary Cinema*) no.16 (1987),34-45; and Dai Jinhua, *"Xieta: Chongdu Disidai"* ("A Leaning Tower: Re-Reading the Fourth Generation"), in Dai Jinhua, *Dianying Lilun yu Piping Shouce* (*Handbook of Film Theory and Criticism*), (Beijing: *Kexue Jishu Wenxian Chubanshe* [Scientific and Technological Documents Press], 1993), 3-15.
6. Homi K. Bhahbha, "Of Mimicry and Man: The Ambivalence of Colonial Discourse," in *The Location of Culture* (London: 1994), 85-92.
7. Yoshimoto Mitsuhiro, "The Difficulty of Being Radical: The Discipline of Film Studies and the Postcolonial World Order," in Masao Miyoshi and H.D. Harootunian, *Japan in the World* (Durham: Duke University Press, 1993), 338-353.
8. Judith Mayne, *Kino and the Woman Question* (Columbus: Ohio State University Press, 1989), 3. Cited in Yoshimoto, 350.
9. Gina Marchetti, *"Two Stage Sisters* - The Blooming of a Revolutionary Aesthetic," *Jump Cut no.34* (1989), 95-106.

NOTES FOR APPENDIX — 1976

1. Paul Clark lists 300 films for these years in his *Chinese Cinema: Culture and Politics Since 1949* (Cambridge: Cambridge University Press, 1987), 186-7. His figures exclude "musicals." Mine exclude opera films and recordings of stage productions. This may account for the difference.
2. *Zhongguo Dianying Ziliaoguan, Zhongguo Yishu Yanjiuyuan Dianying Yanjiusuo* (China Film Archive and Film Research Office of the China Arts Research Institute), *Zhongguo Yishu Yingpian Bianmu* (*China Feature Filmography*), (Beijing: *Wenhua Yishu Chubanshe* [Culture and Art Publishing House], 1981).

3. *Zhongguo Dianyingjia Xiehui* (China Film Association), (compiler), *Zhong-guo Dianying Nianjian 1981 (1981 China Film Yearbook)*, (Beijing: *Zhongguo Dianying Chubanshe* [China Film Press], 1982).
4. *Zhongguo Dianyingjia Xiehui* (China Film Association), (compiler), *Zhong-guo Dianying Nianjian 1982 (1982 China Film Yearbook)*, (Beijing: *Zhongguo Dianying Chubanshe* [China Film Press], 1983).
5. This slogan was used to describe the move in 1974 and 1975 by the right wing of the Party to have some of those condemned earlier during the Cultural Revolution considered for rehabilitation.
6. In 1975, the Gang of Four launched this counter-attack against the right wing of the Party. Its prime target was Deng Xiaoping; the verdict against him had been reversed and he had been temporarily rehabilitated.
7. The term "rebel faction" goes back to the beginning of the Cultural Revolution in the mid-sixties, when Mao called upon the young Red Guards to rebel against the Party hierarchy with the famous slogan, "it is right to rebel against reactionaries."
8. This term was commonly used against enemies of the Gang of Four, but at this particular time it was being used against Deng Xiaoping, suggesting a possible allegorical dimension to this character.
9. Although the *Zhongguo Yishupian Bianmu (China Feature Filmography)* lists this film as twelve reels, the version I have seen is nearer nine or ten.

NOTES FOR APPENDIX — 1977

1. American readers will be more familiar with Chen Chong's Hollywood name, Joan Chen.

NOTES FOR APPENDIX — 1978

1. The "Tangshan disaster" refers to the 1976 Tangshan earthquake.
2. According to the titles of the film itself, this is a 1977 production. The date given here is derived from *Zhongguo Dianying Ziliaoguan, Zhongguo Yishu Yanjiuyuan Dianying Yanjiusuo*, [China Film Archive and Film Research Office of the China Arts Research Institute], *Zhongguo Yishu Yingpian Bianmu [China Feature Filmography]*, (Beijing: *Wenhua Yishu Chubanshe* [Culture and Art Publishing House], 1981), 1190. This apparent discrepancy may reflect the delay between completion of the film and release, especially because many films were only completed towards the end of each calendar year when quota deadlines had to be met.
3. According to *Zhongguo Dianying Ziliaoguan, Zhongguo Yishu Yanjiuyuan Dianying Yanjiusuo* [China Film Archive and Film Research Office of the China Arts Research Institute], *Zhongguo Yishu Yingpian Bianmu [China Art Filmography]*, (Beijing: *Wenhua Yishu Chubanshe* [Culture and Art Publishing House], 1981), 1215, this is a color print. However, the copy I saw was in black and white.
4. The congress was held in January 1975 and was the site where the push for rapid economic growth and the "Four Modernizations" slogan were first

launched. This call was made in a report by the already sick Premier Zhou Enlai, which was read out for him by Deng Xiaoping.
5. The first of these labels refers to Mao's insistence that intellectuals be both "red and expert" and that mere expertise was not enough. The second label is opposed to communal, mass activity.

NOTES FOR APPENDIX — 1979

1. This was directed by Mao and the Gang against Deng Xiaoping, who was being supported by Zhou Enlai in his efforts to return to power.
2. During 1974 and 1975, various people condemned during the Cultural Revolution were rehabilitated when moderate figures such as Deng Xiaoping and Zhou Enlai recovered some power. However, they were soon deposed, and a full "counterattack" began.
3. Zhou Enlai's death in 1976 triggered anti-Gang activities by young people claiming to commemorate the Premier, much as Hu Yaobang's death provided a pretext for the 1989 democracy movement. Those participating in 1976 were also killed in Tiananmen Square or hunted down afterwards.
4. The pseudonym used by a real Gang militant writing group during the Cultural Revolution.
5. The 1976 Qingming refers to the events discussed in note 3.
6. As opposed to a red expert.
7. Cadre school is where officials were sent for political reeducation and reform through labor during the Cultural Revolution.

Bibliography

Ah, Yun. *"Fengyun tubian you digui"* ("Tempered in the Violent Storm"). *Renmin Dianying (People's Film)* no.11 (1977): 10.

Allen, Robert C. and Douglas Gomery. *Film History: Theory and Practice.* New York: Alfred A. Knopf, 1985.

Altman, Rick. "Dickens, Griffith, and Film Theory Today." *South Atlantic Monthly* 88, no.2 (1989): 321-59.

Altman, Rick. *The American Film Musical.* Bloomington: Indiana University Press, 1987.

Anon. *"Sirenbang" Shi Dianying Shiye de Sidi: Wenhuabu Dianying Xitong Jiepi "Sirenbang" Zuixing Dahui Fayan Huibian* (The "Gang of Four" Are Deadly Enemies of the Film Industry: A Compilation of Speeches from the Film System of the Ministry of Culture Rally to Expose and Criticize the Crimes of the "Gang of Four"). Beijing: *Zhongguo Dianying Chubanshe* (China Film Press), 1978.

Bai Hua et al. *Kulian: Zhongguo Dalu Jubenxuan (Bitter Love: A Collection of Mainland Chinese Film Scripts)*. Taipei: *Youshi Wenhua Shiye Gongsi* (Lion Cub Press), 1982.

Bai Hua. *"Guanyu 'Kulian' de Tongxin"* ("A Letter on *Bitter Love*"). *Wenyi Bao (Literary Gazette)*, 1982, no.1: 29-31.

Bai Hua and Peng Ning. *"Kulian"* (*Bitter Love*). *Zhengming*, no.44 (June 1, 1981),: 82-98.

Bai Hua and Peng Ning. *"Kulian"* (*Bitter Love*). *Shiyue* (*October*) 1979, no.3: 140-71, 248.

Bao Wenqing. "New Start for Literature and Art: Xia Yan — Difficulties and Prospects." *China Reconstructs* 29, no.2 (1980): 19-22.

Barmé, Geremie. "Flowers or More Weeds? Culture in China Since the Fall of the Gang of Four." *The Australian Journal of Chinese Affairs*, no.1 (1979): 125-133.

Barmé, Geremie. *"Chaotou Wenxue:* China's New Literature," *The Australian Journal of Chinese Affairs*, no.2 (1979): 137-148.

Barmé, Geremie and John Binford, ed. *Seeds of Fire.* Hong Kong: Far Eastern Economic Review Ltd., 1986.

Barmé, Geremie and Bennet Lee, ed. *The Wounded: New Stories of the Cultural Revolution.* Hong Kong: Joint Publishing Company, 1979.

Barthes, Roland. *S/Z*. New York: Hill and Wang, 1974.

Barthes, Roland. *Mythologies*. New York: Hill and Wang, 1972.

Beijing Review. "Bai Hua Criticizes Himself." *Beijing Review*,25, no.2 (11 January 1982): 29.

Beijing Review. "On the Presentation of Love." *Beijing Review* 24, no.52 (28 December, 1981): 25-6.

Beijing Review. "On the Film Script 'Unrequited Love.'" *Beijing Review* 24, no.42 (19 October 1981): 28-9.

Beijing Review. "The Modern Play 'Where the Silence Is.'" *Beijing Review* 21, no.47 (24 November 1978), 11-12.

Beijing Review. "The Might of the People." *Beijing Review* 21, no.47 (24 November 1978): 7-11.

Bellour, Raymond. "Psychosis, Neurosis, Perversion." *Camera Obscura* nos.3-4 (1979): 105-32.

Bellour, Raymond. "Hitchcock, the Enunciator." *Camera Obscura* no.2 (1977): 69-94.

Benewick, Robert and Paul Wingrove, ed. *Reforming the Revolution: China in Transition*. London: Macmillan, 1988.

Berg, Rick. "Losing Vietnam: Covering the War in an Age of Technology." In *From Hanoi to Hollywood: The Vietnam War in American Film*, edited by Linda Dittmar and Gene Michaud, 41-68. New Brunswick: Rutgers University Press, 1990.

Bergeron, Régis. *Le Cinéma Chinois 1949-1983*. 3 vols. Paris: *Editions L'Harmattan*, 1984.

Berry, Chris. "Seeking Truth From Fiction: Feature Films as Historiography in Deng's China." *Film History* 7, no.1 (1995): 87-99.

Berry, Chris. "A Turn for the Better? Genre and Gender in *Girl From Hunan* and Other Recent Mainland Chinese Films." *PostScript* 14, nos.1&2 (1994, 1995): 81-103.

Berry, Chris. "Neither One Thing nor Another: Toward a Study of the Viewing Subject and Chinese Cinema in the 1980s." In *New Chinese Cinemas: Forms, Identities, Politics*, edited by Nick Browne, Paul G. Pickowicz, Vivian Sobchack, and Esther Yau, 88-113. Cambridge: Cambridge University Press, 1994.

Berry, Chris. "'Ce que méritait le plus d'être puni était son penis': postsocialisme, distopie et la mort du hêroes." *Cinemas* 3, nos.2-3 (1993): 39-60.

Berry, Chris, ed. *Perspectives on Chinese Cinema*. London: British Film Institute, 1991.

Berry, Chris. "Now You See It, Now You Don't." *Cinemaya* no.4 (1989): 46-55.

Berry, Chris. "The Sublimative Text: Sex and Revolution in *Big Road*." *East-West Film Journal* 2, no.2 (1988): 66-87.

Berry, Chris. "Stereotypes and Ambiguities: An Examination of the Feature Films of the Chinese Cultural Revolution." *Journal of Asian Culture* no.6 (1982): 37-72.

Berry, Chris and Mary Ann Farquhar. "Post-Socialist Strategies: An Analysis of *Yellow Earth* and *Black Cannon Incident*." In *Cinematic Landscapes: Observations on the Visual Arts and Cinema of China and Japan*, edited by Linda C. Ehrlich and David Desser, 81-116. Austin: University of Texas Press, 1994.

Bhabha, Homi K. *The Location of Culture*. London: Routledge: 1994.

Bhabha, Homi K. "DissemiNation: Time, Narrative and the Margins of the Modern Nation." In *Nation and Narration*, edited by Homi K. Bhabha, 291-322. London: Routledge, 1990.

Bond, Michael Harris, ed. *The Psychology of the Chinese People*. Hong Kong: Oxford University Press, 1986.

Bordwell, David. "The Power of a Research Tradition: Prospects for Progress in the Study of Film Style." *Film History* 6, no.1 (1994): 59-79.

Bordwell, David. *Making Meaning: Inference and Rhetoric in the Interpretation of the Cinema*. Cambridge: Harvard University Press, 1989.

Bordwell, David. *Narration in the Fiction Film*. Madison: The University of Wisconsin Press, 1985.

Bordwell, David and Kristin Thompson. "Linearity, Materialism and the Study of Early American Cinema." *Wide Angle* 5, no.3 (1983): 4-15.

Bordwell, David and Noël Carroll, ed. *Post-Theory: Reconstructing Film Studies*. Madison: University of Wisconsin Press, 1996.

Bordwell, David, Janet Staiger and Kristin Thompson. *The Classical Hollywood Cinema: Film Style and Mode of Production to 1960*. London: Routledge and Kegan Paul, 1985.

Bottomore, Stephen. "Out of This World: Theory, Fact and Film History." *Film History* 6, no.1 (1994): 7-25.

Browne, Nick, Paul G. Pickowicz, Vivian Sobchack, and Esther Yau, ed. *New Chinese Cinemas: Forms, Identities, Politics*. Cambridge: Cambridge University Press, 1994.

Browne, Nick. "The Spectator-in-the-Text: The Rhetoric of *Stagecoach*." *Film Quarterly* 29, no.2 (1976-7): 26-38.

Brugger, Bill, ed. *China Since the `Gang of Four.'* London: Croom Helm, 1980.

Burch, Noël. *To the Distant Observer: Form and Meaning in the Japanese Cinema*. Berkeley: University of California Press, 1979.

Burch, Noël. "Porter or Ambivalence." *Screen* 19, no.4 (1978/9): 91-105.

Burton, Charles. *Political and Social Change in China Since 1978*. New York: Greenwood Press, 1990.

Cai, Jianping. "*Shi Xuanyang, Bu Shi Baolu*" ("It Is Advocacy, Not Exposure"). Wenhui Bao, 10 November 1964: 2.

Cai, Shiyong. "*Ticai Mantan*" ("A Few Words about Themes"). *Dianying Yishu (Film Art)* 1979, no.2: 29-30.

Chamberlain, Heath B. "On the Search for Civil Society in China." *Modern China* 19, no.2 (1993): 199-215.

Chan, Sylvia. "Two Steps Forward, One Step Back: Towards a 'Free' Literature." *The Australian Journal of Chinese Affairs* nos.19/20 (1988): 81-126.

Chang, T.C., S.Y. Chen and Y.T. Lin, ed. *Pai Hua's Cinematic Script UNREQUIT-ED LOVE With Related Introductory Materials.* Taipei: Institute of Current China Studies, 1983.

Chatman, Seymour. *Story and Discourse.* Ithaca: Cornell University Press, 1978.

Chen, Huangmei, ed. *Dangdai Zhongguo Dianying (Contemporary Chinese Cinema),* 2 vols. Beijing: *Zhongguo Shehui Kexue Chubanshe* (China Social Sciences Press), 1989.

Chen, Kaige, and Tony Rayns. *King of the Children and the New Chinese Cinema.* London: Faber and Faber, 1989.

Chen, Mei. "1949-1989 China Film Distribution and Exhibition." *China Screen* 1990, no.3: 26-7.

Chen, Xihe. *"Tuibian de Jiliu: Xin Shiqi Shinian Dianying Sichao Zouxiang"* ("A Transforming Torrent: Trends in Film Thought over the Ten Years of the New Era"). *Dangdai Dianying (Contemporary Cinema),* no.15 (1986): 21-31.

Cheng, Jihua, et.al. *Zhongguo Dianying Fazhanshi (The History of the Development of Chinese Cinema),* 2 vols. Beijing: *Zhongguo Dianying Chubanshe* (China Film Press), 1981.

Chinese Literature. "Zhou Yang on Reality in Literature and Other Questions." *Chinese Literature* 1980, no.1: 92-6.

Chow, Rey. *Primitive Passions: Visuality, Sexuality, Ethnography, and Contemporary Chinese Cinema.* New York: Columbia University Press, 1995.

Chow, Tse-tsung. *The May Fourth Movement.* Cambridge: Harvard University Press, 1960.

Chu, Godwin C., and Francis L.K. Hsu, ed. *Moving a Mountain: Cultural Change in China.* Honolulu: The University Press of Hawaii, 1979.

Clark, Paul. "Two Hundred Flowers on China's Screens." In *Perspectives on Chinese Cinema,* edited by Chris Berry, 40-61. London: BFI, 1992.

Clark, Paul. "Chinese Cinema in 1989 from a Historical Point of View." *China Screen* 1989, no.3: 25.

Clark, Paul. *Chinese Cinema: Culture and Politics Since 1949.* Cambridge: Cambridge University Press, 1987.

Clark, Paul. *"La Rivoluzione culturale e le sue conseguenze sulla produzione cinematografica cinese (1966-1981)."* In *Ombre lettriche: Saggi e Richerche sul Cinema Cinese,* edited by Carlo Pirovano, 99-118. Milan: Electa, 1982.

Corber, Robert J. *In the Name of National Security: Hitchcock, Homophobia, and the Political Construction of Gender in Postwar America.* Durham, N.C.: Duke University Press, 1993.

Cowie, Elizabeth. "Fantasia." *m/f* 9 (1984): 70-105.

Cui, Jingliang et.al., ed. *"Sheyuan Qikua Shuangshuang Hao Reai Jiti Pinde Gao — Xiaoyixian Nongmin Zuotan Yingpian Li Shuangshuang"* ("Commune Members Praise Shuangshuang's Love for the Collective and High Morality — A Discussion of the Film *Li Shuangshuang* Among the Peasants of Xiaoyi County"). *Shanxi Ribao (Shanxi Daily),* 15 December 1962: 3.

Dai, Jinhua. *Dianying Lilun yu Piping Shouce (Handbook of Film Theory and Criticism).* Beijing: *Kexue Jishu Wenxian Chubanshe* (Scientific and Technological Documents Press), 1993.

Davies, Gloria. "Chinese Literary Studies and Post-Structuralist Positions: What Next?" *The Australian Journal of Chinese Affairs* no.28 (1992): 67-86.

Dayan, Daniel. "The Tutor-Code of Classical Cinema." *Film Quarterly* 28, no.1 (1974): 22-31.

Deleuze, Gilles, and Félix Guattari. *A Thousand Plateaus: Capitalism and Schizophrenia.* (Minneapolis: University of Minnesota Press, 1987).

Deng, Xiaoping. *Selected Works of Deng Xiaoping (1975-1982).* Translated by the Bureau for the Compilation and Translation of Works of Marx, Engels, Lenin and Stalin Under the Central Committee of the Communist Party of China. Beijing: Foreign Languages Press, 1984.

'Dianying Yishu Cidian' Bianji Weiyuanhui (Editorial Committee for the *Film Art Dictionary*). *Dianying Yishu Cidian (Film Art Dictionary).* Beijing: *Zhongguo Dianying Chubanshe* (China Film Press), 1986.

Ding, Ling. *I Myself Am a Woman: Selected Writings of Ding Ling.* Boston: Beacon Press, 1989.

Dirlik, Arif. "Post-socialism? Reflections on 'Socialism with Chinese Characteristics'." In *Marxism and the Chinese Experience,* edited by Arif Dirlik and Maurice Meisner, 362-384. Armonk, NY: M.E.Sharpe, 1989.

Dirlik, Arif and Xudong Zhang, ed. *Postmodernism and China.* Durham: Duke University Press, 2000.

Doane, Mary Ann. "Remembering Women: Psychical and Historical Constructions in Film Theory." In *Psychoanalysis and Cinema,* edited by E. Ann Kaplan, 46-63. New York: Routledge, 1990.

Domes, Jurgen, ed. *Chinese Politics After Mao.* Cardiff: University College Cardiff Press, 1979.

Donald, Stephanie Hemelryk. *Public Secrets, Public Spaces: Cinema and Civility in China.* Lanham, MD: Rowman and Littlefield, 2000.

Duke, Michael S. *Blooming and Contending: Chinese Literature in the Post-Mao Era.* Bloomington: Indiana University Press, 1985.

Elsaesser, Thomas. *New German Cinema: A History.* London: British Film Institute, 1989.

Fisher, Tom. "The Play's the Thing: Wu Han and *Hai Rui* Revisited." *Australian Journal of Chinese Affairs* no.7 (1982): 1-35.

Foreign Broadcast Information Service. "Hu Yaobang Addresses Film Production Conference." 30 December 1981: K8-11.

Foreign Broadcast Information Service. "Renmin Ribao Carries Bai Hua Self-Criticism." 29 December 1981: K2-5.

Foreign Broadcast Information Service. "Zhongguo Xinwen She on Bai Hua Self-Criticism." 16 November 1981:.K1.

Foreign Broadcast Information Service. "Wenyi Bao Criticizes 'Unrequited Love'." 14 October 1981: K1-9.

Forster, E. M. *Aspects of the Novel.* Harmondsworth: Penguin, 1962.

Gabriel, Teshome. *Third Cinema in the Third World.* Ann Arbor: UMI Research Press, 1982.

Gardner, John. *Chinese Politics and the Succession to Mao.* London: Macmillan, 1982.

Garside, Roger. *Coming Alive: China After Mao*. New York: New American Library, 1981.

Goldblatt, Howard, ed. *Chinese Literature for the 1980s: The Fourth Congress of Writers and Artists*. Armonk: M.E. Sharpe, 1982.

Goldman, Merle. *Sewing the Seeds of Democracy in China: Political reform in the Deng Xiaoping Era*. Cambridge: Harvard University Press, 1994.

Goldman, Merle. *Literary Dissent in Communist China*. Cambridge: Harvard University Press, 1967.

Gu, Xian. "*Zaochun Eryue Wei Shenme Jieji Fuwu? — Ping Xiao Jianqiu, Tao Lan Liangge Xingxiang Ji Qita*" ("Which Class Does *Early Spring in February* Serve? — A Critique of the Figures Xiao Jianqiu, Tao Lan and Others"). *Wenhui Bao*, 22 September 1964: 2.

Habermas, Jürgen. *The Structural Transformation of the Public Sphere*. Translated by Thomas Burger and Frederick Lawrence. Cambridge: MIT Press, 1989.

Habermas, Jürgen "The Public Sphere." *New German Critique* no.3 (1974): 49-55.

Hang, Ying, Duan Jishun and Yin Zhiming. *Hunli (The Wedding)*. Beijing: *Zhongguo Dianying Chubanshe* (China Film Press), 1980.

Hansen, Miriam. *Babel and Babylon: Spectatorship in American Silent Film*. Cambridge: Harvard University Press, 1991.

Harding, Harry. *China's Second Revolution: Reform After Mao*. Washington DC: The Brookings Institution, 1987.

He, Yuhuai. *Cycles of Repression and Relaxation: Politico-Literary Events in China 1976-1989*. Bochum: Universitatsverlag Dr. N. Brockmeyer, 1992.

Heath, Stephen. "Film and System: Terms of Analysis." *Screen* 16, no.1 (1975): 7-77.

Hinton, William. *Fanshen: A Documentary of Revolution in a Chinese Village*. Harmondsworth: Penguin, 1966.

Hochman, Baruch. *Character in Literature*. Ithaca: Cornell University Press, 1985.

Honig, Emily and Gail Hershatter. *Personal Voices: Chinese Women in the 1980s*. Stanford: Standford University Press, 1988.

Hsu, Francis L.K. "The Self in Cross-cultural Perspective." In *Culture and Self: Asian and Western Perspectives*, edited by Anthony J. Marsella, George De Vos, Francis L.K. Hsu, 24-55. New York: Tavistock Publications, 1985.

Hsu, Francis L.K. "Psychological homeostatis and *jen*: conceptual tools for advancing psychological anthropology." *American Anthropologist* no.73 (1971): 23-44.

Hsu, Immanuel C.Y. *China Without Mao: The Search for a New Order*. New York: Oxford University Press, 1990.

Hsu, Tao-Ching. *The Chinese Conception of Theatre*. Seattle: The University of Washington Press, 1985.

Hsüan, Mo. "Peiping's Current Policy Toward Literature and Art." *Issues and Studies* 18, no.6 (1982): 55-68.

Hsüan, Mo. "Mainland China's Autocratic Policy Toward Literature and Art: Its Practice and Stratagem." *Issues and Studies* 17, no.12 (1981): 33-46.

Huang, Shixian. "*Xiao Jianqiu Shi Yimian Shenme 'Qizhi'?*" ("What Is Xiao Jianqiu Really a 'Banner' For?"). *Wenhui Bao*, 27 November 1964: 4.

Issues and Studies. "Pai Hua's 'Confession'." *Issues and Studies* 18, no.1 (1982): 7-9.

Issues and Studies. "A Sharp Reining-In of Artistic Freedom in Mainland China." *Issues and Studies* 17, no.5 (1981): 10-12.

Joseph, William A. *The Critique of Ultra-Leftism in China, 1958-1981.* Stanford: Stanford University Press, 1984.

Kane, Anthony J. "Literary Politics in Post-Mao China." *Asian Survey* XXI, no.7 (1981): 775-794.

Khan, Budong. *"Convalescence."* In *Le Cinéma Chinois,* edited by Marie-Claire Quiquemelle and Jean-Loup Passek, 143-8. Paris: *Centre Georges Pompidou,* 1985.

King, Richard. "Chinese Film Controversy." *Index on Censorship* 10, no.5 (1981): 36-7.

King, Richard. "'Wounds' and 'Exposure': Chinese Literature after the Gang of Four." *Pacific Affairs* 54 no.1 (1981): 82-99.

Klenotic, Jeffrey F. "The place of rhetoric in 'new' film historiography: the discourse of corrective revisionism." *Film History* 6, no.1 (1994): 45-58.

Lagny, Michèle. "Film History: or Film Expropriated." *Film History* 6, no.1 (1994): 26-44.

Laing, Ellen Johnston. "Is There Post-Modern Art in the People's Republic of China?" In *Modernity in Asian Art,* edited by John Clark, 207-221. Sydney: Wild Peony, 1993.

Laing, Ellen Johnston. *The Winking Owl: Art in the People's Republic of China.* Berkeley: University of California Press, 1988.

Laplanche, Jacques, and Jean-Bertrand Pontalis. "Fantasy and the Origins of Sexuality." *The International Journal of Psycho-Analysis* 49, no.1 (1968): 1-18.

Lau, Joseph S.M. "The Wounded and the Fatigued: Reflections on Post-1976 Chinese Fiction." *Journal of Oriental Studies* 20, no.2 (1982): 128-42.

Lawton, Anna, ed. *The Red Screen: Politics, Society, Art in Soviet Cinema.* London: Routledge, 1992.

Lee, Hong Yung. *The Politics of the Chinese Cultural Revolution.* Berkeley: University of California Press, 1978.

Lee, Leo Ou-Fan. "Dissent Literature from the Cultural Revolution." *Chinese Literature, Essays, Articles, Reviews* 1, no.1 (1979): 59-79

Lee, Leo Ou-Fan. *The Romantic Generation of Modern Chinese Writers.* Cambridge, MA: Harvard University Press, 1973.

Leyda, Jay. *Dianying: An Account of Films and the Film Audience in China.* Cambridge, MA: MIT Press, 1972.

Li, Jiyan. *"Tao Lan Shi Yige Wanshi Bugong De Nüxing"* ("Tao Lan Is a Cynical, Wanton Female"). *Wenhui Bao,* 6 November 1964: 2.

Liang, Tianming. *"Chanshi Yang Yanjin"* ("Explaining Yang Yanjin"). *Dangdai Dianying (Contemporary Cinema)* no.38 (1990): 59-68.

Ling, Yang. "The Last Three Years," *Beijing Review* 22, no.52 (1979): 7-26.

Link, Perry, Richard Madsen, and Paul G. Pickowicz, ed. *Unofficial China: Popular Culture and Thought in the People's Republic.* Boulder: Westview Press, 1989.

Link, Perry "The Limits of Cultural Reform in Deng Xiaoping's China." *Modern China*, 13, no.2 (1987): 115-176.

Link, E. Perry, Jr. *Mandarin Ducks and Butterflies: Popular Fiction in Early Twentieth-Century Chinese Cities*. Berkeley: University of California Press, 1981.

Liu, Guiqing. "*Xin Shiqi Dianying zhong de Xianshizhuyi*" ("Realism in the Cinema of the New Era"). *Dangdai Dianying (Contemporary Cinema)* no.56 (1993): 10-15.

Liu, Xinwu, et.al. *Prize-Winning Stories from China, 1978-1979*. Beijing: Foreign Languages Press, 1981.

Liu, Xinwu. "*Aiqing de Weizhi*." *Shiyue (October)* no.1 (1978): 117-129. Translated as "A Place For Love." *Chinese Literature* no.1 (1979): 36-57.

Louie, Kam. *Between Fact and Fiction: Essays on Post-Mao Chinese Literature and Society*. Sydney: Wild Peony Press, 1989.

Lu, Lei. "*Wenxue shi zhandoude*" ("Literature is a Military Matter"). *Wenhuibao (Wenhui News)*, 3 August 1976: 3.

Lu, Sheldon Hsiao-peng. "Art, Culture, and Cultural Criticism in Post-New China." *New Literary History* no.28 (1997): 111-133.

Lu, Tonglin. *Rose and Lotus: Narrative of Desire in France and China*. Albany: State University of New York Press, 1991.

Luwanqu gongren yeyu dianying pinglunzu (The Workers Amateur Film Criticism Group of Lu Bay District). "*Yongde shi shenme chizi?*" ("By What Measure?"). *Wenhuibao (Wenhui News)*, 3 August 1976: 3.

Lu, Yanzhou, et.al. *Tianyunshan Chuanqi — Cong Xiaoshuo Dao Dianying (The Legend of Tianyun Mountain — From Novel to Film)*. Beijing: *Zhongguo Dianying Chubanshe* (China Film Press), 1983.

Lu, Yanzhou. *Tianyunshan Chuanqi (The Legend of Tianyun Mountain)*. Beijing: *Zhongguo Dianying Chubanshe* (China Film Press), 1980.

Luo, Yijun, ed. *Zhongguo Dianying Lilun Wenxuan (Chinese Film Theory: An Anthology)*, 2 vols. Beijing: *Wenhua Yishu Chubanshe* (Culture and Art Publishers), 1992.

Lyotard, Jean-Francois. *The Postmodern Condition: A Report on Knowledge*. Manchester: University of Manchester Press, 1984.

Ma, Ning. "Culture and Politics in Chinese Film Melodrama: Traditional Sacred, Moral Economy and the Xie Jin Mode." Ph.D. thesis. Melbourne: Monash University, 1992.

Ma, Ning. "The Textual and Critical Difference of Being Radical." *Wide Angle* 11, no.2, (1989): 22-31.

Madsen, Richard. "The Public Sphere, Civil Society, and Moral Community: A Research Agenda for Contemporary China Studies." *Modern China* 19, no.2 (1993): 183-198.

Mao, Zedong. "On the Ten Major Relationships." In *Selected Works*, Volume V, 284-307. Beijing: Foreign Languages Press, 1977.

Marchetti, Gina. "*Two Stage Sisters* — The Blooming of a Revolutionary Aesthetic." *Jump Cut* no.34 (1989): 95-106.

Mayne, Judith. *Kino and the Woman Question*. Columbus: Ohio State University Press, 1989.

McDougall, Bonnie S. *Mao Zedong's "Talks at the Yan'an Conference on Literature and Art": A Translation of the 1943 Text with Commentary*. Ann Arbor: The University of Michigan Center for Chinese Studies, The University of Michigan, 1980.

McDougall, Bonnie S. "Dissent Literature: Official and Nonofficial Literature in and about China in the Seventies." *Contemporary China* 3, no.4 (1979): 49-79.

Meng, Senhui, and Si Minsan. *"Nuli jieshi jiejiguanxi de xin bianhua — jiantan caise gushi yingpian Huanteng de Xiaoliang He"* (Vigorously Publicize New Changes in Class Relationships — Also Discuss the Color Feature Film *The Jubilant Xiaoliang River*). *Wenhuibao (Wenhui News)*, 3 August 1976: 3.

Meng, Tao, ed. *Wutai Jiemei: Cong Tigang Dao Yingpian (Two Stage Sisters: from Treatment to Film)*. Shanghai: *Shanghai Wenyi Chubanshe* (Shanghai Arts Press), 1982.

Mian, Si. *"Bu Shi Xuanyang, Shi Shenke Baolu"* ("It Is Not Advocacy, But Thorough Exposure"). *Wenhui Bao*, 31 October 1964: 2.

Moody, Peter R., Jr. *Chinese Politics After Mao: Development and Liberalization 1976 to 1983*. New York: Praeger, 1983.

Müller, Marco. *"Les tribulations d'un cineaste chinois en Chine."* *Cahiers du cinema* no.344 (1983): 16-21.

Mulvey, Laura. "Visual Pleasure and Narrative Cinema." *Screen* 16, no.3 (1975): 6-18.

Munro, Donald J. *The Concept of Man in Early China*. Stanford: Stanford University Press, 1969.

Nathan, Andrew J. *Chinese Democracy*. New York: Alfred A. Knopf, 1985.

Neale, Steve. "Sexual Difference in Cinema." *The Oxford Literary Review* 8, nos.1-2 (1986): 123-132.

Negt, Oskar, and Alexander Kluge. *Public Sphere and Experience: Toward an Analysis of the Bourgeois and Proletarian Public Sphere*. Minneapolis: University of Minnesota Press, 1993.

Neupert, Richard. *The End: Narration and Closure in the Cinema*. Detroit: Wayne State University Press, 1995.

Ogden, Suzanne. *China's Unresolved Issues: Politics, Development and Culture*. Englewood Cliffs, NJ: Prentice Hall, 1989.

Kazuko, Ono. *Chinese Women in a Century of Revolution*. Stanford: Stanford University Press, 1989.

Oudart, Jean-Pierre. "Cinema and Suture." *Screen* 18, no.4 (1977/78): 35-47.

Oxnam, Robert B., and Richard C. Bush, ed. *China Briefing, 1980*. Boulder: Westview Press, 1980.

Palmer, Jerry. *The Logic of the Absurd: On Film and Television Comedy*. London: BFI Publishing, 1987.

Peng, Ning, and He Kongzhou. *"Wenyi Minzhu yu Dianying Yishu"* ("Democracy in Literature and the Arts and Film Art"). *Dianying Yishu (Film Art)*, 1979, no.1: 28-33.

Plaks, Andrew H., ed. *Chinese Narrative: Critical and Theoretical Essays*. Princeton: Princeton University Press, 1977.

Poster, Mark. *Foucault, Marxism and History: Mode of Production Versus Mode of Information*. London: Polity Press, 1984.

Propp, Vladimir. *Morphology of the Folk Tale*. Austin: University of Texas Press, 1977.

Rao, Shuguang, and Pei Yali. *Xin Shiqi Dianying Wenhua Sichao (Thoughts on the Film Culture of the New Era)*. Beijing: *Zhongguo Guangbo Dianshe Chubanshe* (China Radio and Television Press), 1997.

Rao, Qu, and Tan Su. *Chidao de Chuntian (A Late Spring)*. Beijing: *Zhongguo Dianying Chubanshe* (China Film Press), 1981.

Renmin Ribao (People's Daily). "*Jianchi Liangfenfa Geng Shang Yicenglou*," ("Persist in the Marxist Principle of Dialectical Reasoning In Order to Move on to the Next Level"). 30 December 1981: 1.

Renmin Ribao (People's Daily). "*Tigao Shehui Zeren, Zhengque Miaoxie Aiqing*" ("Raise Social Responsibility and Describe Love Correctly). 11 November 1981: 5.

Renmin Ribao (People's Daily). "*Renzhen Taolun yixia Wenyi Chuangzuozhong Biaoxian Aiqing de Wenti*" ("Conscientiously Debate the Issue of the Representation of Love in Literature and Art Work"). 4 November 1981.

Renmin Ribao (People's Daily). "'*Li Shuangshuang' gei Women Dailai Shenme — Beijing Nanyuan Hongxing Renmin Gongshe Sheyuan Tan Li Shuangshuang*" ("What 'Li Shuangshuang' Has Brought Us — Members of the Beijing Nanyuan Red Star People's Commune Discuss *Li Shuangshuang*"). 29 November 1962: 6.

Rodowick, D.N. *The Difficulty of Difference: Psychoanalysis, Sexual Difference, and Film Theory*. New York: Routledge, 1991.

Rowe, William T. "The Problem of 'Civil Society' in Late Imperial China." *Modern China* 19, no.2 (1993): 139-157.

Said, Edward. *Orientalism*. New York: Vintage, 1979.

Sedgwick, Eve Kosofsky. *Between Men: English Literature and Male Homosocial Desire*. New York: Columbia University Press, 1985.

Sedgwick, Eve Kosofsky. *The Epistemology of the Closet*. Berkeley: University of California Press, 1990.

Semsel, George, ed. *Chinese Film: The State of the Art in the People's Republic*. New York: Praeger, 1987.

Semsel, George S., Chen Xihe, and Xia Hong, ed. *Film in Contemporary China: Critical Debates, 1979-1989*. Westport: Praeger, 1993.

Semsel, George S., Xia Hong and Hou Jianping, ed. *Chinese Film Theory: A Guide to the New Era*. New York: Praeger, 1990.

Shanghai Dianying Zhipianchang (Shanghai Film Studio). *Ku'nao Ren de Xiao: Secai Gushipian Dianying Wancheng Taiben, (Troubled Laughter: Color Feature Film Post-Production Script)*. Shanghai: *Shanghai Dianying Zhipianchang* (Shanghai Film Studio), 1979.

Shanghai Dianying Zhipianchang 'Huanteng de Xiaoliang He' Shezhizu (The Jubilant Xiaoliang River Production Unit at Shanghai Film Studio). *"Wei 'sirenbang' cuandangduoquan zhizao fangeming yulun de daibiaozuo: yingpian Huanteng de Xiaoliang He paozhi chulong jingguo"* ("A Representative Work to Mould Counter-Revolutionary Public Opinion for the 'Gang of Four' Effort to Usurp Party and State Power: An Account of the Concoction and Release of the Film *The Jubliant Xiaoliang River"*). *Wenhuibao (Wenhui News)*, 24 November 1976: 2.

Shanghai Dianying Zhipianchang Pipanzu (Shanghai Film Studio Criticism Group). *"Wei cuandangduoquan dazao yulun de heibiaoben: jiechuan 'sirenbang' paozhi 'Huangteng de Xiaoliang He' de yinmou"* ("A Black Specimen Designed to Whip up Public Opinion for the Effort to Usurp Party and State Power: Exposing 'Gang of Four' Plot in Concocting *The Jubliant Xiaoliang River"*). *Renmin Dianying (People's Film)*, 1976, no.8: 10-13.

Shi, Yuankang. *"Shimin Shehui yu Zhongben Yimo — Zhongguo Xiandai Daolushang de Zhang'ai"* ("Civil Society and the Policy of 'Emphasizing the Fundamental and Repressing the Secondary' — an Obstacle in China's Road to Modernisation." *Ershiyi Shijie (Twenty-First Century)*, no.6 (1991): 105-120.

Shu, Xiaomin. *Zhongguo Dianying Yishushi Jiaocheng (A Course in the History of Chinese Film Art)*. Beijing: *Zhongguo Dianying Chubanshe* (China Film Press), 1996.

Si, Ning. *"'Jinqu' yu 'Nanqu'"* ("'Forbidden Zones' and 'Difficult Zones'"). *Dianying Yishu (Film Art)*, 1979, no.1: 46.

Silverman, Kaja. *Male Subjectivity at the Margins*. New York: Routledge, 1992.

Spence, Jonathan D. *Chinese Roundabout: Essays in History and Culture*. New York: W.W. Norton, 1992.

Stacey, Judith. *Patriarchy and Socialist Revolution in China*. Berkeley: University of California Press, 1983.

Stam, Robert, Robert Burgoyne, and Sandy Flitterman-Lewis. *New Vocabularies in Film Semiotics: Structuralism, Post-Structuralism and Beyond*. London: Routledge, 1992.

Studlar, Gaylyn. *In The Realm of Pleasure: Von Sternberg, Dietrich, and the Masochistic Aesthetic*. Urbana: University of Illinois Press, 1988.

Su, Shuyang. *Dan Xin Pu (Loyal Heart)*. Beijing: China Film Press, 1979.

Suleiman, Susan Rubin. *Authoritarian Fictions: The Ideological Novel as a Literary Genre*. New York: Columbia University Press, 1983.

Sun, Lung-kee (Sun Longji). "Contemporary Chinese Culture: Structure and Emotionality." *Australian Journal of Chinese Affairs* no.26 (1991): 1-41.

Sun, Lung-kee (Sun Longji). *Zhongguo Wenhua de `Shenceng Jiegou' (The `Deep Structure' of Chinese Culture)* Hong Kong: Jixian Publishers, 1983.

Sun, Yan. *The Chinese Reassessment of Socialism, 1976-1992*. Princeton: Princeton University Press, 1995.

Tang, Xiaobing. "The Function of New Theory: What Does It Mean to Talk about Postmodernism in China?" In *Politics, Ideology and Literary Discourse in Modern China*, edited by Liu Kang and Xiaobing Tang, 278-300. Durham: Duke University Press, 1993.

Tang, Yin, and Tang Dacheng. *"Lun 'Kulian' de Cuowu Qingxiang"* ("On the Incorrect Tendency of *Bitter Love*"). *Wenyi Bao* (*Literary Gazette*), 1981, no.19: 9-16.

Teng, Wenji. *Shenghuo de Chanyin* (*Reverberations of Life*). Beijing: *Zhongguo Dianying Chubanshe* (China Film Press), 1980.

Thaxton, Robert. "The World Turned Downside Up: Three Orders of Meaning in the Peasants' Traditional Political World." *Modern China* 13, no.2 (1977): 185-228.

Turim, Maureen. *Flashbacks in Film: Memory and History*. New York: Routledge, 1989.

Wakeman Jr., Frederic. "The Civil Society and Public Sphere Debate: Western Reflections on Chinese Political Culture." *Modern China* 19, no.2 (1993): 108-138.

Wang, Ban. *The Sublime Figure of History: Aesthetics and Politics in Twentieth Century China*. Stanford: Stanford University Press, 1997.

Wang, Ning. "Confronting Western Influence: Rethinking Chinese Literature of the New Period." *New Literary History* no.24 (1993): 905-926.

Wang, Shaoguang. *"Guanyu 'Shimin Shehui' de Jidian Sikao"* ("Reflections on the Notion of 'Civil Society'). *Ershiyi Shijie* (*Twenty-First Century*) no.6 (1991): 102-114.

Wang, Yigang. *"Xiao Jianqiu de Rendaozhuyi Pouxi"* ("Analysis of Xiao Jianqiu's Humanism"). *Wenhui Bao*, 19 September 1964: 4.

Wedell-Wedellsborg, Anne. "Literature in the Post-Mao Years." In *Reforming the Revolution: China in Transition*, edited by Robert Benewick and Paul Wingrove, 190-206. London: Macmillan, 1988.

Wenhuibao (*Wenhui News*). *"Jiangsu wenyijie jiepi 'sirenbang' wantu cuandangduoquan paozhi ducao yingpian Huanteng de Xiaoliang he de zuixing"* ("The Literature and Art Circles in Jiangsu Expose and Criticise the 'Gang of Four' Crime of Concocting the Poisonous Weed Film *The Jubilant Xiaoliang River* in their Vain Effort to Seize Party and State Power"). 19 December 1976: 3.

Williams, Linda. *Playing the Race Card: Melodramas of Black and White from Uncle Tom to O.J. Simpson*. Princeton: Princeton University Press, 2001.

Williams, Linda, ed. *Viewing Positions: Ways of Seeing Film*. New Brunswick: Rutgers University Press, 1995.

Wu, Guofan, et al. *"Women Xihuan Li Shuangshuang Shi de Ren"* ("We Like People of the Li Shuangshuang Type"). *Beijing Ribao* (*Beijing Daily*), 10 January 1966: 3.

Wu, Zhongjie. *"Jiujing `Yongxin Shi Haode' Ma?"* ("Did They Really `Mean Well'?"). *Wenhui Bao*, 6 November 196: 2.

Xi, Shanshan. *"Zongguan Xin Shiqi de Dianying Chuangzuo"* ("An Overview of Film Production in the New Era"). *Dangdai Dianying* (*Contemporary Cinema*) no.15 (1986): 3-13.

Xi'an Dianying Zhipianchang (Xi'an Film Studio). *Lanse de Haiwan: Secai Gushipian Wancheng Taiben* (*Blue Bay: Color Feature Film Post-Production Script*). Xi'an: *Xi'an Dianying Zhipianchang* (Xi'an Film Studio), 1978.

Xia, Yan. "My Opinions." *Chinese Literature* 1980, no.4: 110-4.

Xin, Xiangrong. "Literature and Art and Politics." *Beijing Review* 27, no.34 (August 23, 1982): 3.

Xin, Xiangrong. "Letting a Hundred Flowers Bloom." *Beijing Review* 24, no.38 (September 21, 1981): 3.

Xin, Xiangrong. "More on Literary Criticism." *Beijing Review* 24, no.35 (August 31, 1981): 3.

Xin, Xiangrong. "Literary Criticism." *Beijing Review* 24, no.21 (May 25, 1981): 3.

Xu, Ben. "*Farewell My Concubine* and its Nativist Critics." *Quarterly Review of Film and Video* 16, no.2 (1997): 155-170.

Yang, Nianqun. "*Jindai Zhongguo Yanjiuzhong de 'Shimin Shehui' — Fangfa ji Xiandu*" ("'Civil Society' in Modern China Studies — Methodology and Limitations"). *Ershiyi Shijie (Twenty-First Century)*, no.32 (1995): 29-38.

Yang, Yingzhang. *Wo de Shige Tongxue (My Ten Classmates)*. Beijing: *Zhongguo Dianying Chubanshe* (China Film Press), 1979.

Yau, Esther. "China After the Revolution." In *The Oxford History of World Cinema*, edited by Geoffrey Nowell-Smith, 698. (Oxford: Oxford University Press, 1996).

Ye, Hui, ed. "*Zan Li Shuangshuang Xue Li Shuangshuang — Baoshan Nongcun Ganbu, Sheyuan Zuotan Jilu Zhaiyao*" ("Praise Li Shuangshuang, Study Li Shuangshuang — Extracts from the Record of a Discussion by Rural Cadres and Commune Members from Baoshan"). *Jiefang Ribao (Liberation Daily)*, 29 November 1962: 4.

Ye, Nan, et al. *Bashan Yeyu — Cong Juben Dao Yingpian (Evening Rain — From Script to Screen)*. Beijing: *Zhongguo Dianying Chubanshe* (China Film Press), 1982.

Yim, Kwan Ha. *China Under Deng*. New York: Facts On File, 1991.

Yoshimoto, Mitsuhiro. "The Difficulty of Being Radical: The Discipline of Film Studies and the Postcolonial World Order." In *Japan in the World*, edited by Masao Miyoshi and H.D. Harootunian, 338-353. Durham: Duke University Press, 1993.

Yu, Hui-jung. "Let Our Theatre Propagate Mao Tse-tung's Thought For Ever." *Chinese Literature* 1968, nos.7/8: 111.

Yuan, Ying. "*Dianying de Zijue; Xin Shiqi Dianying Chuangzuo Huigu*" ("Film Consciousness: A Look Back at Film Production in the New Era"). *Dangdai Dianying (Contemporary Cinema)* no.15 (1986): 13-20.

Zhang, Xian. *Bei Aiqing Yiwang de Jiaoluo: Cong Xiaoshuo Dao Dianying (The Corner Forgotten by Love: From Novel to Film)*. Beijing: *Zhongguo Dianying Chubanshe* (China Film Press), 1984.

Zhang, Xudong. *Chinese Modernism in the Era of Reforms: Cultural Fever, Avant-Garde Fiction, and the New Chinese Cinema*. Durham: Duke University Press, 1997.

Zhang, Yingjin. "Narrative, Ideology, Subjectivity: Defining a Subversive Discourse in Chinese Reportage." In *Politics, Ideology, and Literary Discourse in Modern China* edited by Liu Kang and Xiaobing Tang, 211-242. Durham: Duke University Press, 1993.

Zhang, Zhaolong, ed. *Zhongguo Dianying Nianjian 1991 (1991 China Film Yearbook)*. Beijing: *Zhongguo Dianying Chubanshe* (China Film Press), 1993.

Zhao, Dan. "Rigid Control Ruins Art and Literature," *Chinese Literature* 1981, no.1: 107-114. Also translated as "When Control Is Too Tight, There's No Hope for Literature and Art," by Bett Ting, In John P. Burns and Stanley Rosen, ed., *Policy Conficts in Post-Mao China: A Documentary Survey, with Analysis*, 314-7. Armonk: M.E. Sharpe, 1986.

Zheng, Dongtian. *"Jinjin Qinian: 1979-1986 Zhongqingnian Daoyan Tansuo Huigu"* ("Only Seven Years: A Look Back at the Explorations of Young and Middle-Aged Directors between 1979 and 1986"). *Dangdai Dianying (Contemporary Cinema)* no.16 (1987): 46-54.

Zhi, Wei. *"Xuexi Geming Xianbei de Bangyang"* ("Learning From Model Revolutionary Forerunners"). *Renmin Ribao (People's Daily)*, 2 September 1977: 3.

Zhong, Chengxian, and Rao Shuguang. *"Wenhua Fansi zhong de Xin Shiqi Dianying Chuangzuo"* ("Film Production of the New Era in a Time of Cultural Reflection"). *Dangdai Dianying (Contemporary Cinema)* no.16 (1987): 34-45.

Zhongguo Dianying Chubanshe (China Film Press), ed. *Li Shuangshuang: Cong Xiaoshuo Dao Dianying (Li Shuangshuang: From Novel to Film)*. Beijing: *Zhongguo Dianying Chubanshe*, 1963.

Zhongguo Dianying Chubanshe (China Film Press), ed. *Zhongguo Dianying Juben Xuanji (Yi) (Selected Chinese Film Scripts* [One]). Beijing: *Zhongguo Dianying Chubanshe*, 1959.

Zhongguo Dianying Chubanshe (China Film Press), ed. *Zhongguo Dianying Juben Xuanji (San) (Selected Chinese Film Scripts* [Three]). Beijing: *Zhongguo Dianying Chubanshe*, 1959.

Zhongguo Dianying Chubanshe (China Film Press), ed. *Zhongguo Dianying Juben Xuanji (Si) (Selected Chinese Film Scripts* [Four]). Beijing: *Zhongguo Dianying Chubanshe*, 1960.

Zhongguo Dianying Chubanshe (China Film Press), ed. *Zhongguo Dianying Juben Xuanji (Jiu) (Selected Chinese Film Scripts* [Nine]). Beijing: *Zhongguo Dianying Chubanshe*, 1981.

Zhongguo Dianying Faxing Fangying Gongsi, Zhongguo Dianying Shuchu Shuru Gongsi (China Film Distribution and Exhibition Corporation and China Film Export and Import Corporation). *Dianying Sanshiwu Nian (Thirty-Five Years of Film)*. Beijing: *Zhongguo Dianying Faxing Fangying Gongsi, Zhongguo Dianying Shuchu Shuru Gongsi* (China Film Distribution and Exhibition Corporation and China Film Export and Import Corporation), 1986.

Zhongguo Dianying Ziliaoguan, Zhongguo Yishu Yanjiuyuan Dianying Yanjiusuo (China Film Archive and Film Research Office of the China Arts Research Institute). *Zhongguo Yishu Yingpian Bianmu (China Art Filmography)*. Beijing: *Wenhua Yishu Chubanshe* (Culture and Art Publishing House), 1981.

Zhongguo Dianyingjia Xiehui Dianying Lishi Yanjiubu (Film History Research Section of the China Film Association). *Zhongguo Dianyingjia Liezhuan (Disanji) (Biographies of Chinese Film Makers* [Volume Three]). Beijing: *Zhongguo Dianying Chubanshe* (China Film Press), 1984.

Zhongguo Dianyingjia Xiehui Dianying Lishi Yanjiubu (Film History Research Section of the China Film Association). *Zhongguo Dianyingjia Liezhuan (Disiji)* (*Biographies of Chinese Film Makers* [Volume Four]). Beijing: *Zhongguo Dianying Chubanshe* (China Film Press), 1985.

Zhongguo Dianyingjia Xiehui Dianying Lishi Yanjiubu (Film History Research Section of the China Film Association). *Zhongguo Dianyingjia Liezhuan (Diwuji)* (*Biographies of Chinese Film Makers* [Volume Five]). Beijing: *Zhongguo Dianying Chubanshe* (China Film Press), 1985.

Zhongguo Dianyingjia Xiehui Dianying Lishi Yanjiubu (Film History Research Section of the China Film Association). *Zhongguo Dianyingjia Liezhuan (Diliuji)* (*Biographies of Chinese Film Makers* [Volume Six]). Beijing: *Zhongguo Dianying Chubanshe* (China Film Press), 1985.

Zhongguo Dianyingjia Xiehui Dianying Lishi Yanjiubu (Film History Research Section of the China Film Association). *Zhongguo Dianyingjia Liezhuan (Diqiji)* (*Biographies of Chinese Film Makers* [Volume Seven]). Beijing: *Zhongguo Dianying Chubanshe* (China Film Press), 1986.

Zhou, Enlai. "Zhou Enlai on Questions Related to Art and Literature." *Chinese Literature* 1979, no.6: 83-95.

Zhou, Tong. "`Wo? Gongshe de Sheyuan!'" ("`Me? I'm a Member of the Commune!'"). *Gongren Ribao* (*Worker's Daily*), 16 November 1962: 4.

Zhou, Yang. "On the Hundred Flowers Policy." *China Reconstructs* 29, no.1 (1980): 4-7.

Zhou, Yang. "Our Achievements, Lessons and Tasks: Extracts of a report to the Fourth Congress of Chinese Writers and Artists." *Chinese Literature* 1980, no.3: 38-51.

FILMOGRAPHY

Note: This listing organized alphabetically by English-language title includes all the Chinese films discussed in the dissertation, excluding those films covered in the appendix. Abbreviations: sc, screenplay; dir, direction.

At Middle Age (Ren Dao Zhongnian), Changchun Film Studio, 1982, sc: Chen Rong, dir: Wang Qimin, Sun Yu.

Big Road (Dalu), Lianhua Film Studio (Shanghai), 1934, sc, dir: Sun Yu.

Bridge (Qiao), Northeast Film Studio, 1949, sc: Yu Min, dir: Wang Bin.

Crossroads (Shizijietou), Mingxing Film Studio (Shanghai), 1937, sc, dir: Yuan Muzhi.

Eager to Return (Guixin Sijian), August First Film Studio, 1979, sc: Li Keyi, dir: Li Jun.

Early Spring in February (Zaochun Eryue), Beijing Film Studio, 1963, sc, dir: Xie Tieli.

Hibiscus Town (Furongzhen), Shanghai Film Studio, 1986, sc: Ah Cheng, Xie Jin, dir: Xie Jin.

Li Shuangshuang, Haiyan Film Studio (Shanghai), 1962, sc: Li Zhun, dir: Lu Ren.

The Life of Wu Xun (Wu Xun Zhuan), Kunlun Film Studio, 1950, sc, dir: Sun Yu.

October Victory (Shiyue de Shengli), August First Film Studio, 1977, dir: Li Jun, Wang Shaoyan, Shen Shan, Jing Mukui, Jia Shi, Ren Pengyuan.

The Pioneers (Chuangye), Changchun Film Studio, 1974. sc: collective, transcribed by Zhang Tianmin, dir: Yu Yanfu.

Red Sorghum (Hong Gaoliang), Xi'an Film Studio, 1987, sc: Chen Jianyu, Zhu Wei, Mo Yan, dir: Zhang Yimou.

Spring Shoots (Chunmiao), Shanghai Film Studio, 1975, sc: collective, transcribed by Zhao Zhiqiang, Yang Shiwen, and Cao Lei, dir: Xie Jin, Yan Bili, Liang Tingduo.

Street Angel (*Malu Tianshi*), Mingxing Film Studio (Shanghai), 1937,
    sc, dir: Shen Xiling.

Two Stage Sisters (*Wutai Jiemei*), Tianma Film Studio (Shanghai), 1965,
    sc: Lin Gu, Xu Jin, Xie Jin, dir: Xie Jin.

The Unfailing Beam (*Yong bu Xiaoshi de Dianbo*), August First Film
    Studio, 1958, sc: Lin Jin, dir: Wang Ping.

Woman Basketball Player No.5 (*Nulan Wuhao*), Tianma Film Studio
    (Shanghai), 1957, sc, dir: Xie Jin.

Yellow Earth (*Huang Tudi*), Guangxi Film Studio, 1984, sc: Zhang
    Ziliang, dir: Chen Kaige.

Appendix

THE FILMS

This appendix provides some details about the eighty-one films viewed for analysis in this book. A list of possible films was compiled by consulting published synopses of all feature films completed between 1976 and 1981 and excluding any set outside the Cultural Revolution decade (1966 to 1976). Although some unreleased films were in the filmographies consulted, others were not. *Bitter Love (Kulian*, 1981) is a well-known example, but there may be more. Where unreleased films are included here, this is indicated after the title.

Some films on the initial list were excluded. Eight were unavailable for viewing: *Song of the Mango Fruit (Mangguo zhi ge*, Changchun Film Studio, 1976); *Thousands of Rosy Clouds (Hongxia wan duo*, Pearl River Film Studio, 1976); *The Main Subject (Zhuke*, Guangxi Zhuang Autonomous Region Film Study Group, 1976); *Arduous Journey (Wanli zhengtu*, Beijing Film Studio, 1977); *Earthquake, (Zhen*, August First Film Studio, 1977); *Donggang Spy (Donggang die ying*, Shanghai Film Studio, 1978); *Troubled Times (Bu pingjing de rizi*, Pearl River Film Studio, 1978); and *Willow Dark, Flower Bright (Liu an hua ming*, Beijing Film Studio, 1979). Others were struck off after viewing confirmed that they were not set in the Cultural Revolution. In most cases, there was ambiguity in the synopsis.

Including the eight unavailable films, the total number of films covering the Cultural Revolution decade is 89 out of the approximately 305 features produced during this period, or 29 per cent.[1] For films made from 1976 to 1979, details here are drawn from the *China Feature Filmography*.[2] For films made in 1980, the source is the *1981 China Film Yearbook*,[3] and for 1981, the *1982 China Film Yearbook*.[4] Films are listed in the order they appear in in these publications, which may signify a certain hierarchy among Chinese film studios based on seniority. For fuller details, please consult these volumes.

1976

1. *Wild Goose Calls on the Lakeshore* (*Yan ming hu pan*), Changchun Film Studio, 1976, Color, 11 reels. Screenplay: Zhang Xiaotian, Wang Weichen. Director: Gao Tianhong. Cinematography: Tang Yunsheng. Cast: Zhang Liwei (as Lan Haiying), Shi Kefu (as Zhang Houde), Ye Zhikang (as Song Changyou), and Wang Haoming (as Lan Haitao).

In 1971, concealed class enemy Lin Daquan seizes control of the cooperative medical station and closes it down. Lan Haiying, an educated youth sent down to the countryside, exposes Lin's corruption. When Haiying sees through his plots, Lin tries to murder a woman and shift the blame onto her. Haiying saves the woman and exposes the class enemy. The brigade's cooperative medical station is consolidated and develops.

2. *New People of the Mountain Villages* (*Shan cun xin ren*), Changchun Film Studio, 1976, Color, 12 reels. Screenplay: collective, written up by Zhao Yuxiang. Direction: Jiang Shusen, Jing Jie. Cinematography: Shu Xiaoxin, Chen Chang'an. Cast: Zhang Jinling (as Fanghua).

In a mountain village, the educated youth Fanghua writes a criticism of the hydroelectric station head's capitalist thinking and corruption of young people. He tries to fool the masses with a false self-criticism, and also to poison the children of a landlord who know about problems in his background. Fanghua exposes his background problem and destroys his plot. The hydroelectric station is built.

3. *Shanhua* Beijing Film Studio, 1976, Color, Wide-screen, 13 reels. Screenplay: Sun Qian, Ma Feng, Guo Ende, Yang Maolin, Xie Junjie (written up by Sun Qian and Ma Feng). Direction: Cui Wei, Sang Fu. Cinematography: Gao Hongtao, Yu Zhenyu. Cast: Xie Fang (as Gao Shanhua), Zhang Ping (as Hu Genmao), and Xiang Kun (as Sun Guangzong).

Sun Guangzong tires to persuade head of White Pebble Beach Brigade Hu Genmao to "contract casual labor from outside so as to sabotage agricultural production." Party Secretary Gao Shanhua blocks this and gets into a conflict with her adopted father, Hu Genmao. However, the masses and the Commune Secretary support her. By recalling sufferings, Shanhua helps her adopted father. Following thoroughgoing class struggle, Sun sees his attempted crimes come to nothing.

4. *Counterattack* (*Fanji*, unreleased), Beijing Film Studio, 1976, Color, 13 reels. Screenplay: *Counterattack* production team collective (written up by Mao Feng). Director: Li Wenhua. Cinematography: Zheng Yuyuan. Cast: Yu Yang (as Jiang Tao), and He Haichuan (as Han Ling).

First Party Secretary Han Ling pursues rectification as part of the effort to realize the Four Modernizations. His opponents feel that everything he does is part of the "Drive to Reverse Verdicts."[5] They stick up big character posters stating "The Capitalist Roader Faction Is Still In Power." Their leader, Jiang Tao, is thrown into jail, but the struggle continues. Jiang is released and the "Counter-Attack Against the Rightist Reversal of Verdicts" begins.[6]

5. *Jewel of the Sea* (*Haishang mingzhu*), Beijing Film Studio, 1976, Color, 10 reels. Screenplay: Zhang Xianglin. Direction: Lin Yang, Wang Haowei. Cinematography: Wang Zhaolin. Cast: Wang Suya (as Ling Yanzi), Chen Qiang (as Guo Laoda), and Shao Wanlin (as Cui Min).

Ling Yanzi, new bride in the household of Phoenix Island Brigade Party Branch Secretary Guo Laoda, discovers Vice-Brigade Head Cui Min illegally selling nylon yarn. Yanzi puts up a big character poster to expose Cui's plot. Cui unties the cultivation brigade's largest boat and lets it run aground and be destroyed. Yanzi resolutely pursues class struggle After the "newborn capitalist element" of Cui has been dug out, the aquatic cultivation experiments are successful again and there is a bumper harvest of kelp.

6. *The Jubilant Xiaoliang River* (*Huanteng de Xiaoliang he*), Shanghai Film Studio, 1976, Color, Wide-screen, 11 reels. Screenplay: Wang Lixin, Gao Xing. Direction: Liu Qiong, Shen Yaoting. Cinematography: Shen Xilin, Qu Jiazhen. Cast: Ma Changyu (as Zhou Changlin, dubbed by Bi Ke), and Wen Xiying (as Vice-Director Xia).

Team Leader Zhou Changlin is a "rebel faction member."[7] He seeks to harness the Xiaoliang river so as to develop the collective economy, but runs into opposition from County Vice-Director Xia. Zhou is victorious and Xia is criticized as an "unrepentant capitalist roader."[8]

7. *Song of the New Wind* (*Xin feng ge*), Shanghai Film Studio, 1976, Color, 12 reels.[9] Screenplay: Zhang Youde, Duan Quanfa, Fan Junzhi. Direction: Zhao Huanzhang, Lu Ren. Cinematography: Zhu Yongde, Wu Lielian. Cast: Zhao Jing (as Song Wenying), and Feng Chunchao (as Li Changju).

New bride Song Wenying discovers her brother-in-law Li Changju has been using his position as head of the brick kiln to carry out illegal trade. She criticizes him for taking on aspects of a bourgeois lifestyle. Li will not admit defeat and gets his brother to have Song transferred away from the brickyard. She flatly refuses and thoroughly criticizes Li's errors.

> 8. *The Secret of the Ahxia River (Ahxia he de mimi)*, Shanghai Film Studio, 1976, Color, 10 reels. Screenplay: collective, written up by Cao Zhonggao and others. Direction: Yan Bili, Shen Fu, Wu Zhennian. Cinematography: Qiu Yiren, Shen Miaorong. Cast: Liang Jinyang (as Sun Daliang, dubbed by Liu Guoying), Zhao Xixiong (as Drashi, dubbed by Cao Lei), Yang Peiguo (as Ma Jiajia, dubbed by Zhang Yan), and Feng Chunzhao (as Ma Hade).

Han Chinese, Tibetan, and Hui Moslem youths Sun Daliang, Drashi, and Ma Jiajia discover logs that have been floated along the Ahxia river. Shuiyun Brigade Head Ma Hade conspires with a gang of thieves to steal logs set aside for the military. When Ma is meeting with his co-conspirators, the three youths cleverly rush in and expose the plot.

> 9. *South Sea Storm (Nanhai fengyun)*, August First Film Studio, 1976, Color, 10 reels. Screenplay: Lu Zhuguo. Direction: Jing Mukui, Zhang Yongshou. Cinematography: Cai Jiwei, Gao Jiuling. Cast: Tang Guoqiang (as Yu Hualong).

Yu Hualong's family is out fishing when the marauding South Vietnamese battleship No.10 attacks and separates them. After Yu is saved by our navy, he joins up and becomes a naval captain. Ten years later, the Saigon reactionary clique dispatches warship No.10 again. Yu leads the fleet into battle, making the enemy flee in panic. The Yu family is reunited. Later, the navy recovers our Freshwater Island, and the five-starred red flag flies over the treasure islands of the South Sea again.

> 10. *Red Plum in the Mountains (Shanli hong mei)*, Pearl River Film Studio, 1976, Color, 10 reels. Screenplay: *Red Plum in the Mountains* production collective, written up by Qiao Dianyuan. Director: Si Meng. Cinematography: Wang Yunhui, Liu Hongming. Cast: Zheng Youmin (as Shanmei), Ye Jiangdong (as Wei Ruxue), and Yang Xiuzhang (as Liu Lianfa).

In 1971, Shanhe Brigade Party Branch Secretary Shanmei returns from visiting Dazhai and revises plans for repairing irrigation ditches. Corrupted by the profiteer Liu Lianfa, County Revolutionary Committee Vice-Director

Wei Ruxue orders a halt to the repair work. Shanmei exposes Wei's incorrect line, surviving a murder attempt.

> 11. *Faith* (*Jituo*), Emei Film Studio, 1976, Color, 11 reels. Screenplay: Gao Ying, Yin Qi, Yang Yingzhang. Direction: Ye Ming, Zhang Yi. Cinematography: Gu Wenhou, Feng Shilin. Cast: Rong Xiaomi (as Wang Xiaolei), Liu Zinong (as Li Shouyi), and Tian Yuan (as Du Shiyou).

The educated youth and Red Guard Wang Xiaolei is sent to Manfei village. There, she blocks Secretary Du Shiyou's speculation and profiteering. Director Li, who appointed Du, feels Wang should mind her own business. The Party Committee supports Xiaolei. Li suppresses a weather warning, causing flooding in Manfei. Cornered and desperate, Du flees. Xiaolei pursues and catches him with the assistance of the militia.

1977

1. *Bear Print* (*Xiongji*), Changchun Film Studio, 1977, Color, 13 reels. Screenplay: Gong Zhuo. Director: Zhao Xinshui. Cinematography: Chen Chang'an, Gao Hongbao. Cast: Shi Weizhi (as Li Xin), Tang Ke (as Yao Bingzhang), and Ahbulizi (as Bideluofu).

In 1971, a spy slips across the northeastern border and enters River City, where he contacts the undercover agent "Sable." Sable gets him appointed as a driver on the "814" war preparedness project. Li Xin, intelligence section head of the River City public security bureau, cleverly pretends to be Sable, and finally proves that the real Sable is former Special Intelligence Bureau Head Yao Bingzhang. Yao also orders the spy to steal the plans for our war preparedness project. The public security bureau seizes Sable and the spy. However, the enemy is unwilling to concede defeat and sends Bideluofu, a spy who left the country twenty years ago, to Beijing again.

2. *Youth* (*Qingchun*), Shanghai Film Studio, 1977, Color, Wide-screen, 12 reels. Screenplay: Li Yunliang, Wang Lian. Director: Xie Jin. Cinematography: Shen Xilin, Qu Jiazhen. Cast: Chen Chong (as Yamei),[1] and Yu Ping (as Xiang Hui).

Deaf-mute Yamei is treated by Xiang Hui during the Cultural Revolution, recovers her speech and hearing, and becomes a communications soldier. Xiang Hui is a veteran Red Army woman who took part in the Long March. She was injured and her health is not good. One day, Yamei comes across her medical record and is deeply moved. Xiang Hui's condition worsens, but her revolutionary will encourages Yamei. Finally, Yamei enters the party and becomes an outstanding communications soldier.

3. *New Song of the Wei River* (*Weishui xin ge*), Xi'an Film Studio, 1977, Color, 9 reels. Screenplay: Chen Zhongshi. Director: Liu Bin. Cinematography: Lin Jing. Cast: Li Anqin (as Liu Donghai), Cun Li (as Liu Tianyin), and Tan Tuo (as Liu Jingzhai).

Liu Donghai becomes Party Secretary in Liujiaqiao Brigade, and a high tide of "Learning From Dazhai" rises under his leadership. The landlord element Liu Jingzhai lures fourth brigade leader Liu Tianyin into sideline production. Taking class struggle as the lead, Liu Donghai criticizes capitalism and exposes the class enemy's evil plot, thus leading the brigade's "Learn From Dazhai" movement to success.

4. *October Storm* (*Shiyue de fengyun*), Emei Film Studio, 1977, Black and White, 11 reels. Screenplay: Yan Yi. Director: Zhang Yi. Cinematography: Li Erkang. Cast: Li Rentang (as He Fan), and Liu Zinong (as Ma Chong).

After Chairman Mao passes away, Ma Chong, Secretary in charge of industry in a certain municipality, takes advantage of armaments factory Party Secretary He Fan's hospitalization to order the factory to restart production of obsolete weapons. He Fan stops production of the weapons the minute he leaves hospital. Ma Chong threatens He Fan. Because he is unpanicked and stands his ground, He Fan is suspended from duties. The Gang of Four is smashed, and Ma Chong and Zhang Lin are arrested.

1978

1. *Emergency* (*Yanjun de licheng*), Changchun Film Studio, 1978, Color, 12 reels. Screenplay: Zhang Xiaotian, Shi Xiyu, Li Jie. Direction: Su Li, Zhang Jianyou. Cinematography: Wu Guojiang, Han Hanxia. Cast: Zhao Zhilian (as Cheng Shaojie), and Zheng Zaishi (as Fang Lei).

On the orders of the Gang of Four, Jiangbing Highway Bureau Director Cheng Shaojie dubs Party Secretary Fang Lei a "capitalist roader." However, with Fang Lei's help, the "Great Wall" locomotive team is able to send a wagonload of emergency materials to the Tangshan disaster.[1] Cheng Shaojie then tries to sabotage locomotives and rig a life-threatening accident. A member of the Great Wall team dies protecting the locomotives. At this time, members of the Ministry of Railways rush to give everyone the news of the smashing of the Gang of Four.

2. *Lights* (*Deng*), Changchun Film Studio, 1978, Color, 10 reels. Screenplay: Yan Yi. Director: Yin Yiqing. Cinematography: Wang Lei. Cast: Zhang Zhen (as Chu Ge).

In 1974, Engineer Chu Ge of a navigation light factory on the Yangtse River is ignoring his terminal illness and developing remote control river navigation lights. Henchmen of the Gang of Four accuse him of being a negative model who "puts production above everything." Chu is arrested and interrogated illegally, but released when this is reported to the State Council. Under the care of the Party, he finally achieves success.

3. *Salimake*, Beijing Film Studio, 1978, Color, 10 reels. Screenplay: Yao Yuanhuan, Shen Ying. Direction: Yu Lan, Li Wei. Cinematography: Luo Dean. Cast: Song Xiaoying (as Salimake), Paerhati (as Kuaiken), and Liu Long (as Tuluhala).

Salimake sets up a "horseback primary school" so all the children of Hongjitan may go to school. Reactionary herd owner Tuluhala's plot to poach protected species is discovered by the schoolchildren. Tuluhala accuses Salimake of taking the so-called "capitalist line in education." The commune secretary supports the school. Tuluhala pressures his son Kuaiken to fix things for him, but educated by the "horseback primary school," Kuaiken exposes his father instead.

4. *Hard Struggle* (*Fengyu licheng*), Beijing Film Studio, 1978, Color, 11 reels. Screenplay: Cui Wei, Yu Shan. Director: Cui Wei. Cinematography:

Nie Jing. Cast: Gao Weiqi (as Lu Yunzhi), and Chi Jianhua (as Yao Xing-bang).

In 1975, Revolutionary Committee Chair Lu Yunzhi leads a repair team inspecting railway track. Gang of Four henchman Yao Xingbang sabotages Lu's work. He even attempts to cause train accidents, one of which is averted at the risk of Lu's life. Yao flees, but sends his bodyguard to kidnap Lu. With the help of the track guard and the masses, the repair team frees Lu Yunzhi and victoriously reaches the final station in its repair work.

> 5. *The Amnesiac* (*Shiqu jiyi de ren*), Shanghai Film Studio, 1978, Color, 9 reels.[2] Screenplay: Yan Shiwen, Si Minsan, Zhou Yang. Direction: Huang Zuolin, Yan Bili. Cinematography: Ma Linfa, Ying Fukang. Cast: Wu Xiqian (as Ye Chuan).

For the Four Modernizations, East Wind Chemical Equipment Plant Party Secretary Ye Chuan takes on the task of experimental mass production. However, he is falsely accused of being a "capitalist roader" and cruelly beaten up. The State Council calls him to a meeting in Beijing. His persecutors try to get a doctor to damage Ye's memory, but the doctor heals him. They ask a writer to describe him as a "capitalist roader," but the writer meets secretly with Ye, gathers supporters, and destroys the evil plot.

> 6. *In the Vanguard* (*Zou zai zhanzheng qianmian*), August First Studio, 1978, Color, 11 reels.Screenplay: Li Pingfen, Lu Wei, Xu Qingdong, Yang Tao. Direction: Hao Guang, Wei Long. Cinematography: Yang Zhaoren, Gao Jiuling. Cast: Li Moran (as Yan He).

In 1975, the "Red Fourth Platoon" fails to extinguish railway carriage lights on time during nighttime exercises because of the long-running interference of the Lin Biao anti-Party clique and the Gang of Four. Military District Vice-Commander Yan He personally takes over training. Obstruction by a Gang of Four special reporter and a Soviet spy forces the suspension of the platoon's anti-tank review. However, guided by the Central Military Commission, the platoon victoriously carries out exercises commemorating the 40th anniversary of the Long March.

> 7. *Eventful Years* (*Zhengrong suiyue*), August First Studio, 1978, Black and White, 11 reels.[3] Screenplay: Gu Ertan, Fang Hongyou. Direction: Jing Mukui, Wang Feng. Cinematography: Ding Shanfa. Cast: Zhang Hui (as Gong Fang), Chen Xi (as Li Mengliang), and Yang Fan (as Kong Jing).

In Fall 1976, Gang of Four agent and Party Committee Secretary Li Mengliang suddenly announces that the illegally imprisoned commander of "Project 903," Gong Fang, is to be released. Gang of Four agent Kong Jing wants Li to restore Gong to his post, secretly sabotage Project 903, and then pin the blame on Gong. Gong does not give in. On the eve of Chairman Mao's death, he is illegally detained again. When Li hears the news of the fall of the Gang, he tries to burn Gong to death in an attempt to kill witnesses, but Gong is rescued in the nick of time.

8. *Blue Skies Defense Line* (*Lantian fangxian*), Pearl River Film Studio, 1978, Color, 11 reels. Screenplay: Lu Wei, Lin Hangsheng, Wang Peigong. Director: Wang Weiyi. Cinematography: Liu Hongming. Cast: Zhu Shimao (as Yang Ping), and Shi Jin (as Quan Fu).

The Chiang Kai-shek military forces in Taiwan dispatch an air force plane codenamed "Blackbird," which lands on China's Baisha Island. They also hide jamming equipment on a Taiwan fishing vessel. The PLA discovers this equipment, but old boatman Quan Fu is too afraid of the consequences in Taiwan to tell the PLA the truth. Officer Yang Ping realizes the jamming equipment in Quan's boat is a red herring and so lets him go. On his return, Quan is suspected and there is an attempt to kill him. Yang Ping leads his men to save Quan, who then exposes the Taiwanese regime's plot.

9. *Thank You, Comrade* (*Tongzhi ganxie ni*), Pearl River Film Studio, 1978, Color, 10 reels. Screenplay: Li Bing, Hu Qingshu. Direction: *Thank You, Comrade* Direction group, under the guidance of Chen Ying. Cinematography: Li Shengwei, Liang Xiongwei. Cast: Liu Xiaoqing (as Yang Jie).

The leaders are selecting model workers from the East Wind Cleaning Squad to enter university. Some educated young people who have been influenced by traditional thinking and people with serious capitalist ideological problems look down upon sanitation workers. Squad Party Branch Secretary Yang Jie also had a mistaken attitude once, but her consciousness was raised. The Party selects her to go to university, but she insists on staying in the squad.

10. *Blue Bay* (*Lanse de haiwan*), Xi'an Film Studio, 1978, Color, 11 reels. Screenplay: Wu Yinxun, Zhou Minzhen. Direction: Yan Xueshu, Yi Shui. Cinematography: Zhang Faliang, Chen Wancai. Cast: Xin Jing (as Ling Yong), and Cao Jingyang (as Wen Minghong).

Chief Commander Ling Yong and the workers of the Blue Bay Harbor worksite labor to construct a 20,000-ton wharf in 1974. However, to sabotage construction, Office Director Wen Minghong publicizes a well deviation and a casting accident. The Central Committee calls Ling to Beijing for the Fourth National People's Congress, and Premier Zhou has an audience with him. Ling returns and gives a report about the Fourth National People's Congress and Premier Zhou Enlai's good news report.[4] He also criticizes Wen Minghong.

> 11. *Not a One-Off Story* (*Bing fei yige ren de gushi*), Emei Film Studio, 1978, Color, 11 reels. Screenplay: Zhao Danian. Director: Zhang Fengxiang. Cinematography: Gu Wenhou. Cast: Shi Weijian (as Zhang Heng), and Leng Mei (as Li Nong),

Agricultural machinery engineer Zhang Heng has devoted himself wholly to scientific research and is unmarried at forty. When the Gang of Four persecutes intellectuals and destroys science, he persists, giving them an opportunity to attack him as a "reactionary expert roader" and an "individualist struggler."[5] He is sent to undergo reform through agricultural labor. After he has been in Green Slope Brigade for a while, Vice-Secretary Li Nong asks him to help with the wheat harvester. When the Central Committee of the Party smashes the Gang of Four, his combine harvester is successfully trial produced and, through class struggle and scientific experimentation, he and Li Nong develop a sincere love.

1979

> 1. *Troubled Heart (Kunan de xin)*, Changchun Film Studio, 1979, Color, 11 reels. Screenplay: Zhang Xian. Director: Chang Zhenhua. Cinematography: An Zhiguo. Cast: Kang Tai (as Luo Bingzhen), Li Junhai (as Xu Jiamao), and Song Chunli (as Xiao Qiao).

In 1975, surgeon Luo Bingzhen is recalled from the countryside and resumes his "new valve" experiments. The Gang of Four fans the "anti-restorationist" wind.[1] Nurse Xiao Qiao writes a criticism of Luo while she is supposed to be tending a patient, who dies. Workers propaganda team head Xu Jiamao tries to pin the blame on Luo. Luo resists, but Xu seizes him. After the Gang has been smashed, Luo is invited to a national science conference, but the good doctor has died long ago.

> 2. *Fast as Light (Shunjian)*, Changchun Film Studio, 1979, Color, 11 reels. Screenplay: Peng Ning, He Kongzhou, Song Ge. Director: Zhao Xinshui. Cinematography: Wu Benli. Cast: Ma Qun (as Wei, the Steelworker), Liang Boluo (as Shi Feng), and Zhu Decheng (as Song Xiaolei).

Air force plane designer Shi Feng is designing lights for the "Crocodile" aircraft. He sees a "criminal" risk his life to save Song Xiaolei, but Song follows orders to handcuff the old man. Shi discovers the old man, Wei, saved him during the war, but when they meet he is too terrified to recognize him. A plane comes from Beijing carrying Lin Biao's special messenger with the "blow up the train order." The plot is foiled, but the desperate Gang of Four followers try to escape in the Crocodile. Wei, Song, and Shi die stopping them.

> 3. *Wedding (Hunli)*, Beijing Film Studio, 1979, Color, 10 reels. Screenplay: Hang Ying, Duan Jishun, Yin Zhiming. Director: Duan Jishun. Cinematography: Zhang Shicheng. Cast: Liu Xiaoqing (as Sheng Min), Zhang Lianwen (as Yue Zhipeng), Zhu Yurong (as Sheng Jie), Xu Min (as Gao Yu).

In 1975, Yue Zhipeng is enthusiastic about the Four Modernizations and helps install imported chemical equipment together with his girlfriend Sheng Min. However, the Gang of Four plans sabotage and Premier Zhou dies. Project vice-commander Gao Yu and Sheng Min's sister Sheng Jie celebrate their marriage regardless. Yue reports the situation to the State Council, and so the Gang orders Gao to attack Yue. When Gao comes to arrest Yue, he and Sheng Min are getting married to the accompaniment of funeral music.

4. *Tear Stain* (*Leihen*), Beijing Film Studio, 1979, Color, 12 reels. Screenplay: Sun Quan, Ma Feng. Director: Li Wenhua. Cinematography: Wu Shenghan, Chen Youxiang. Cast: Li Rentang (as Zhu Keshi), Xie Fang (as Kong Nina), Yang Wei (as Lü Mingyuan), and Guo Xiaojun (as Cao Jianjian).

After the smashing of the Gang of Four, new Party Secretary Zhu Keshi discovers that the water conservancy project is not supported by the masses. Former Party Secretary Cao Yi's death during the Cultural Revolution and his wife Kong Nina's "insanity" also arouses his suspicions. Zhu rehabilitates the original head of the public security bureau, Lü Mingyuan, to his post. Together, they discover Kong Nina went mad after being struggled, and they also discover the truth about Cao Yi's killing, clearing his record. They abandon the water conservancy project and destroy the enemy's evil plans.

5. *Wind and Waves* (*Fenglang*), Shanghai Film Studio, 1979, Color, 10 reels.Screenplay: Gao Xing, Shi Yong. Direction: Zhao Huanzhang, Hu Chengyi. Cinematography: Zhu Yongde, Wu Liekang. Cast: Qin Yi (as Xiao Yuhua).

In 1975, Haibin Fishing Boat Factory Party Committee Secretary Xiao Yuhua proposes a new fishing vessel, to develop the fishing industry. Gang of Four henchmen try to turn Xiao's son against her to sabotage the plan. Soon after, the Fourth National Congress opens and Premier Zhou calls for the "Four Modernizations." The Gang henchmen try to force Xiao's other son to design a battleship, but he sees through their plot. Despite all efforts to stop them, they seize Xiao and both her sons by the sea. However, a great wave wells up, symbolizing coming victory.

6. *Troubled Laughter* (*Kunao ren de xiao*), Shanghai Film Studio, 1979, Color, 9 reels. Screenplay: Yang Yanjin, Bi Jing. Director: Yang Yanjin, Deng Yimin. Cinematography: Ying Fukang, Zheng Hong. Cast: Li Zhiyu (as Fu Bin), Pan Hong (as his wife), and Yuan Yue (as Secretary Song).

In 1975, when the Gang of Four is active, rehabilitated reporter Fu Bin is unable to tell the truth and unwilling to lie. Sent to interview Municipal Secretary Song during the "counter-attack against the reversal of rightist verdicts" being directed at an old medical professor,[2] Fu witnesses the professor's humiliation but also Secretary Song's insistence that the professor treat him. Fu decides to write the truth, but his wife wants him to think about the consequences. Fu feigns illness, but eventually makes his true feelings known, and is arrested.

> 7. *A Silent Place* (*Yu wusheng chu*), Shanghai Film Studio, 1979, Color, 10 reels. Screenplay: Zong Fusheng. Director: Lu Ren. Cinematography: Zhang Yuanmin, Ji Hongsheng. Cast: Zhang Xiaozhong (as Ouyang Ping), Yang Baoling (as Meilin), Zhu Yuwen (as He Yun), and Zhao Shusen (as He Shifei).

In 1976, terminally ill old cadre Meilin, who was persecuted by the Gang of Four, and her son Ouyang Ping visit her old comrade-in-arms, He Shifei. He betrayed Meilin with false evidence and fears exposure. His daughter He Yun is Ouyang's girlfriend. When she discovers that he has become a counter-revolutionary because he has collected a poem commemorating Premier Zhou at Tiananmen, she is upset.[3] Meilin encourages Ouyang to go to jail. He's wife, seeing how Meilin has suffered, exposes him. He Yun breaks with her father as Ouyang Ping is about to be arrested and courageously stands by him.

> 8. *Roar, Yellow River!* (*Nuhou ba! Huanghe*), August First Film Studio, 1979, Color, 11 reels. Screenplay: Wang Xingpu. Direction: Shen Yan, Jia Shihong. Cinematography: Chen Ruiling, Gao Jiuling. Cast: Zhang Ruifang (as He Dan), Liu Shanxian (as He Xiaoxi), and Gao Ming (as Xiao Yuchi).

He Dan is "tempering herself through manual labor" in 1975, when she is recalled to Beijing. She is upset to discover her daughter, Xiaoxi, has abandoned learning cello to join the Ministry of Culture's "First Blast" essay-writing group.[4] He Dan also refuses to write a piece supporting the Gang of Four. This enrages Gang representatives in the Ministry, who bribe Xiaoxi's boyfriend Xiao Yuchi to write an essay, intending to publish it under He's name. When mother and daughter see this essay attacking Premier Zhou, they both denounce Xiao Yuchi.

> 9. *So Near Yet So Far* (a.k.a. *Sakura, Ying*), Beijing Film Academy Studio, 1979, Color, 11 reels. Screenplay: Zhan Xiangchi. Direction: Zhan Xiangchi, Han Xiaolei. Cinematography: Cao Zuobing. Cast: Cheng Xiaoying (as Morishita Mitsuko), Li Lin (as Xiulan, [Morishita Mitsuko as a child]), Jiang Yanhui (as Takazaki Yoko), Fu Yuzhong (as Tetsu), Xu Huanshan (as Chen Jianhua), Xu Bing (as Techu [Chen Jianhua as a child]).

In 1945, vanquished Japan repatriated many Japanese refugees from China. Japanese woman Takazaki Yoko left her baby daughter, Mitsuko, with the Chinese woman Chen Sao, who gives the baby a bracelet. After 1949, Mitsuko returns to Japan. In 1975, she comes to Beijing. Chinese engineer Chen Jianhua guesses from her excellent Chinese and the bracelet that she is his Japanese sister, and wants to meet her. However, his wife recalls the Cultural Revolution. To avoid being dubbed a Japanese spy again, Chen avoids his sister. Mitsuko guesses what is going on and, to protect her relatives, returns home with a heavy heart. After the smashing of the Gang of Four, Mitsuko comes to China again and finds her brother and mother are waiting to welcome her.

> 10. *Spring Rain* (*Chunyu xiaoxiao*), Pearl River Film Studio, 1979, Color, 9 reels. Screenplay: Su Shuyang. Direction: Ding Yinnan, Hu Bingliu. Cinematography: Wei Duo. Cast: Zhang Liwei (as Gu Xiuming), Zhang Jie (as Feng Chunhai), Huang Wenkui (as Chen Yang).

After the 1976 Qingming, nurse Gu Xiuming tends a young patient on a train from Beijing.[5] Her policeman husband, Feng Chunhai, is ordered to board the same train and arrest Chen Yang, a "counter-revolutionary." Gu has discovered her patient is Chen, and is as determined to save him as her husband is to fulfill his orders. However, the people's revolutionary struggle leads Feng to break the fetters of Gang of Four thinking. He gives his wife a travel pass so she can break the blockade and help Chen escape.

> 11. *Loyal Overseas Chinese Family* (*Haiwai chizi*), Pearl River Film Studio, 1979, Color, 12 reels. Screenplay: Hu Bing. Direction: Ou Fan, Xing Jitian. Cinematography: Huang Yonghu. Cast: Chen Chong (as Huang Sihua).

Huang Sihua has a good singing voice, so she auditions for a cultural troupe. However, she is not admitted because she is the daughter of an overseas Chinese with "foreign connections." Her father went abroad as a child and had a tough life. Patriotism brought him and his wife together and after 1949, they returned to China to build socialism. Later, Lin Biao and the Gang of Four's henchmen dubbed him a "capitalist roader" and spy. When the Central Committee smashes the Gang of Four, Huang Sihua gets her life in the arts.

> 12. *Reverberations of Life* (*Shenghuo de chanyin*), Xi'an Film Studio, 1979, color, 11 reels. Screenplay: Teng Wenji. Direction: Teng Wenji,

Wu Tianming. Cinematography: Liu Changxu, Zhu Dingyu. Cast: Shi
Zhongqi (as Zheng Changhe), Leng Mei (as Xu Shanshan),.

After the fall of the Gang of Four, violinist Zheng Changhe performs a concerto written out of his own suffering. A girl in the audience, Xu Shanshan,
recalls events of 1976. Just before Qingming, Gang of Four lackeys were
chasing Zheng and she hid him. She had witnessed him bravely perform his
violin concerto in memory of Premier Zhou. A drum roll like thunder calls
Xu back from her memories and a beam of light appears before her eyes.

13. *My Ten Classmates* (*Wo de shige tongxue*), Emei Film Studio, 1979,
Color, 10 reels. Screenplay: Yang Yingzhang. Director: Ye Ming. Cine-
matography: Feng Shilin. Cast: Yang Yaqin (as Fang Min), Ren Shen (as
Yu Qingdong), Huang Daliang (as Yan Song), Zhao Youliang (as Li
Dazhi), Li Guilan (as Shen Yujie), and Jin Di (as Luo Congfen).

In 1977, Professor Fang Min decides to find out what has happened to her
classmates. Scientist Yu Qingdong was criticized by the Gang of Four as a
"typical white expert."[6] Zhou Mengjia is working for rural modernization
at an agricultural technology popularization station. Yan Song works in a
mountain weather station. Li Dazhi is experimenting into the elimination of
waste gasses at his factory, and was imprisoned by Gang lackeys. Teacher
Shen Yujie was criticized by the Gang as one who "places knowledge above
everything" and has died. Luo Congfen backed the Gang, has had an easy
life, and has become an important figure in the Ministry of Culture and Education. She is directly implicated in Shen's death.

14. *Sacred Duty* (*Shensheng de Shiming*), Emei Film Studio, 1979, black
and white, 10 reels. Screenplay: Wang Yaping, Li Caiyong. Direction:
Mao Yuqin, Teng Jinxian. Cinematography: Wang Wenxiang, Xie Erx-
iang. Cast: Gao Fu (as Wang Gongbo), Fu Hengzhi (as Bai Shun), Wang
Ruoli (as Lin Fang), Jiang Lili (as Yang Qiong).

Veteran policeman Wang Gongbo has just returned from cadre school
in 1975.[7] He discovers suspicious points in Bai Shun's case and decides to
reinvestigate. Just as Wang locates Bai's wife, Lin Fang, and his accuser,
Yang Qiong, the "counterattack on the reversal of Rightist verdicts" begins,
and Gang elements try to send him back to cadre school. Wang disregards
the risk and educates Yang, who reveals the truth. The Gang's henchmen try
to eliminate Yang but Wang sacrifices his own life to save him, fulfilling the
sacred duty of a policeman.

1980

> 1. *They Are in Love* (*Tamen zai xiang'ai*), Beijing Film Studio, 1980, color, 10 reels. Screenplay: Yang Jinyan, Wang Qi. Direction: Qian Gang, Zhao Yuan. Cinematography: Sun Changyi. Cast: Zhang Ping (as Chen Hao), Da Shichang (as Chen Zhan), Xiao Wei (as Su Yi), Guo Xuxin (as Chen Nan), Xu Yushun (as Wang Hui), Qiu Ge (as Chen Ping), Yang Hailian (as Zhang Lang).

The Gang of Four persecutes cadre Chen Hao and his three sons. Eldest son Chen Zhan is an eye doctor. Because he criticizes the Gang, he is labeled a counter-revolutionary and exiled to Xinjiang. His relationship with Su Yi is broken. After the Gang smashed, they are reunited and work for the Four Modernizations in Xinjiang. Second son Chen Nan is beaten and injured. Nevertheless, he learns three languages and wins the love of schoolteacher Wang Hui. Youngest son Chen Ping is a good-for-nothing seduced by female delinquent Zhang Lang. However, after she dumps him, he turns over a new leaf.

> 2. *A Loyal Heart* (*Dan xin pu*), Beijing Film Studio, 1980, Color, 11 reels. Screenplay: Su Shuyang. Directed by Xie Tian and Zheng Guoquan. Cinematography: Huang Xinyi. Cast: Zheng Rong (as Fang Lingxuan), Xiu Zongdi (as Zhuang Jisheng),

In 1975, ailing Premier Zhou attends to old Chinese medicine specialist Fang Lingquan's research on a new heart medicine during the Fourth National People's Congress. Gang of Four henchman Zhuang Jisheng causes an accident leading the lab to be sealed. Fang gradually realizes Zhuang intends to use this to slander Premier Zhou, and becomes despondent. Suddenly, the phone rings. When he answers, he hears Premier Zhou's concerned voice. He directs that this research must be given higher priority and additional personnel. Neither evil nor difficulty can frighten a loyal heart. The new medicine is born. However, news of Premier Zhou's death comes. Fang determines to continue fighting for a new dawn.

> 3. *A Handcuffed Passenger* (*Dai shoukao de "luke"*), Beijing Film Studio, 1980, Color, 11 reels. Screenplay: Ji Ming, Ma Lin. Director: Yu Xiang. Cinematography: Zhang Qinghua. Cast: Ding Xiang (as Liu Jie), Shao Wanlin (as Su Zhe), Ma Shuzhao (as Zhang Qiang), Ge Cunzhuang (as Ge Shiquan).

Early in the Cultural Revolution, a lab worker is killed and rocket fuel A-1 is stolen. Old policeman Liu Jie is found at the scene and flees. Security brigade Vice-head Ge Shiquan sends the victim's husband, Su Zhe, and young detective Zhang Qiang after Liu. Zhang was Liu's student and still believes in him. In fact, Liu is tailing Su, and sees him meet a woman from a "rebel faction." Liu tells Zhang, who realizes Su killed his own wife and stole the A-1, too. Su flees south, Liu on his tail. Su tries to kill Liu on a train, which Zhang forces to stop in Anshan. The local police chief is Liu's old colleague, and they follow Su to the border, preventing the A-1 from being smuggled out. However, Liu is still wanted by Ge and taken off in handcuffs.

> 4. *Death of the Marshal* (*Yuanshuai zhi si*), 1980, Beijing Film Studio, Color, 10 reels. Screenplay: He Xingtong, Yu Li. Directors: Shi Yifu, Que Wen. Cinematography: Xu Xiaoxian, Tu Jiakuan. Cast: Li Rentang (as Marshal He), Zhu Yanping (as Ma Honghu), Zhao Na (as Wu Tonghua).

Marshal He returns to Xiang'exi, to inspect military exercises in 1964. Company Commander Ma Honghu, and Wu Tonghua, descendant of a revolutionary martyr, grew up under He's care. After the Cultural Revolution breaks out, Lin Biao and his followers begin to persecute He. Ma's father sells out to them, slanders He, and tricks Honghu into criticizing He. However, Wu stands firm and cares for He. The couple breaks up. He's persecutors put him in solitary, deliberately making his diabetes worse. Honghu sees the light, but too late. He's dying words are: "I want to go on for the Party; He Long always obeys the Party..."

> 5. *Murder in 405* (*405 mosha an*), 1980, Shanghai Film Studio, Black and White, 10 reels. Screenplay: Yu Benzheng, Shen Yaoting. Director: Shen Yaoting. Cinematography: Zhang Guifu, Zhao Linghong. Cast: Xu Min (as Qian Kai), Zhong Xinghuo (as Chen Minghui).

Ding Juan finds her boyfriend dead in his room. Detectives Qian Kai and Chen Minghui discover tiny feathers in the victim's wound, a fingerprint on a tea glass, two V-shaped marks in the toilet, and the phrase "Ah Lan, I'll never let you go" in the victim's notebook. There are two Ah Lan's. One is a gambler who owed the victim money and was seen running from the scene of the crime. The other is a TV cameraman, whose fingerprint matches that on the glass. But the feathers are from a bird only found somewhere the TV cameraman has never been. The other Ah Lan has tennis shoes that leave V-shaped prints. Under interrogation, he admits going to rob the victim, but claims to have hid in the toilet and later discovered the victim's corpse. Eventually, the detectives are able to catch the real murderer and prove that the head of police is behind the crime.

6. *Sea Love* (*Hai zhi lian*), 1980, Shanghai Film Studio, Black and White, 10 reels. Screenplay: Li Yunliang, Yang Shiwen, Wang Lian. Director: Zhao Huanzhang. Cinematography: Zhu Yongde, Cheng Shiyu. Cast: Mao Yongming (as Jeifang), Ma Xiaowei (as Nanxia), Wang Guojing (as Jianguo), Meng Ling (as Huanqing), Hong Xuemin (as Xiyue), Zhao Jing (as Liqiu).

Jiefang, Nanxia, Jianguo and Huanqing were all born in the same year as New China. In the early seventies, Jiefang joins the navy, Nanxia and Huanqing do marine research work, and Jianguo goes down to the countryside. Nanxia and a worker called Liqiu fall in love. Huanqing becomes a Gang of Four follower, struggles with Nanxia's father, and gets promoted. He also slanders Nanxia as a counter-revolutionary. Liqiu is forced to dump Nanxia and gets involved with Jianguo. Her younger sister, Xiyue falls in love with Jiefang. However, Huanqing is attracted to her and slanders Jiefang. Xiyue sees through this and marries Jiefang. Because Nanxia refuses to slander Jiefang, Huanqing threatens his life. Hearing this on the eve of her wedding to Jianguo, Liqiu rushes to the hospital, but Nanxia is already dead. She breaks off with Jianguo and mourns Nanxia as his wife.

7. *Romance on Lushan Mountain* (*Lushan lian*), 1980, Shanghai Film Studio, Color, 9 reels. Screenplay: Bi Bicheng. Director: Huang Zumo. Cinematography: Shan Liangguo, Zheng Xuan. Cast: Zhang Yu (as Zhou Jun), Guo Kaimin (as Geng Hua).

After the smashing of the Gang of Four, Zhou Jun, daughter of a former KMT general who is now an American overseas Chinese, visits Mount Lushan for the second time. Five years earlier, she met Geng Hua, whose father was being persecuted by the Gang. Their common patriotism caused them to fall in love. However, the stormy times forced them to separate. Reunited, they discover their fathers were enemies. But prejudice is overcome and they become a couple.

8. *The Child Violinist* (*Qin tong*), 1980, Shanghai Film Studio, Color, 11 reels. Screenplay: Zhao Danian. Director: Fan Lai. Cinematography: Li Zongling, Wang Yi. Cast: Xiang Mei (as Yu Ping), Wu Cihua (as Liu Xin), Gao Yang and Ding Yi (as Jingjing), Mao Weiyu (as Li Duihou).

Overseas Chinese singer Yu Ping and orchestra conductor Liu Xin are married and have a baby son, Jingjing. Liu's classmate Fang Wei is jealous. When the Cultural Revolution begins, Fang catches Liu playing the "bourgeois" violin and he attacks him so badly that he dies. Liu's final wish is that his son should not go into music. Down in the countryside, sent-down violinist Li Duihou discovers Jingjing's talent and persuades Yu to let him teach Jingjing. In 1977, the conservatorium is enrolling students, and Li sends Jingjing to audition. Fang Wei is Head of Admissions. Afraid his crime will be exposed, he chases Jingjing out. But in the end, the facts are revealed and Jingjing is admitted.

> 9. *Evening Rain (Bashan ye yu)*, 1980, Shanghai Film Studio, Color, 9 reels. Screenplay: Ye Nan. Directors: Wu Yonggang, Wu Yigong. Cinematography: Cao Weiye. Cast: Li Zhiyu (as Qiu Shi).

Designated a criminal by the Gang of Four six years ago, the poet Qiu Shi boards a ferry bound for Wuhan escorted by a man and a woman. In the third class section, five others join them. A sad girl is selling herself to discharge a debt. A woman teacher has unintentionally brought disaster upon others with her reports. An old Beijing Opera performer has been struggled so badly that he is permanently nervous. An old woman has come to hold a memorial ceremony for her son who died in the Cultural Revolution. A young worker seeks to express his love. A young girl in rags has slipped in, too. Everyone feels sorry for Qiu and dislikes his arrogant woman guard. The sad girl throws herself overboard, but Qiu saves her. The woman guard sees the error of her ways, figures out the young girl is Qiu's long lost daughter, and helps the two of them to escape.

> 10. *Come Back, Swallow (Yan guilai)*, Shanghai Film Studio, 1980, Wide-screen, Color, 10 reels. Screenplay: Shi Yong, Meng Senhui, Si Minsan. Director: Fu Jinggong. Cinematography: Qiu Yiren, Zhou Zaiyuan. Cast: Ma Xiaowei (as Xie Feng), Zhang Xiaolei (as Wu Lan).

Xie Feng and Wu Lan are in love. Xie Feng's father discovers Wu Lan's mother was someone he labeled a Rightist twenty years ago. When Wu breaks her leg Dr. Lin Hanhua is also upset to discover who her mother is. Back then, Lin and Wu's mother were married, but when she was accused of being a Rightist, she left him to protect him. Wu knows nothing of this. Soon after, her mother comes to visit and everything comes out. She is their daughter. When Xie finds out this was his father's fault, he is filled with guilt and tells Wu, who breaks off with him in shock. Xie's father criticizes his past actions, and he and Wu's mother decide to overcome the past for the sake of their children.

> 11. *The Legend of Tianyun Mountain (Tianyun shan chuanqi)*, Shanghai Film Studio, 1980, Wide-screen, Color, 12 reels. Screenplay: Lu

Yanzhou. Director: Xie Jin. Cinematography: Xu Qi. Cast: Wang Fuli (as Song Wei), Shi Weijian (as Luo Xiang), Shi Jianlan (as Feng Qinglan), Zhong Xinghuo (as Wu Yao).

Party Committee Organization Bureau Vice-Head Song Wei hears of an un-rehabilitated Rightist on Tianyun Mountain called Luo Xiang, whose appeals have been blocked. In the fifties, Song and Feng Qinglan joined the Tianyun Mountain investigation team, where Luo had taken over political work from Wu Yao. Song and Luo fell in love. In 1957, the Anti-Rightist Movement begins. Luo is unjustly accused, and Wu persuades Song to "make a clean break" with him. Later, she marries Wu. Feng cannot believe Luo really is an "anti-Party, anti-socialist element," and marries him. They all suffer during the Cultural Revolution, even Wu. Afterwards, Wu is restored to power, but refuses to rectify Luo's verdict. Song successfully appeals the case higher up. But when the news arrives, Feng has already died of overwork.

12. *Volleyball Star* (*Paiqiu zhi hua*), Changchun Film Studio, 1980, Color, 9 reels.Written and directed by Lu Jianhua. Cinematography: Fang Weice, He Shouxin. Cast: Guo Zhenqing (as Wu Zhenya), Huang Daliang (as Tian Dali), Pan Yuehua (as Xiaoli), Guo Min (as Wu Lingling), Wang Duoyang (as Wu Lingling, as a child).

Famous volleyball coach Wu Zhenya's assistant Tian Dali goes to the North, where he discovers ice skater Ling Xue. She develops a close relationship with Tian's five year-old girl, Xiaoli, who lost her mother long ago. Tian sends Ling to Wu for further training. Wu is attacked during the Cultural Revolution. Tian firmly defends him, but is beaten to death. After the smashing of the Gang of Four, Wu returns to volleyball. His daughter Lingling is the main spiker. Poisonously influenced by the Gang, she clashes with him. The stress brings back Wu's old illness. Memories of the Gang educate Lingling and the team, who redouble their efforts. It turns out that Tian Dali is still alive and he is reunited with Xiaoli and Ling Xue.

13. *After the Nightmare Comes the Dawn* (*Emeng xinglai shi zaochen*), Pearl River Film Studio, 1980, Color, 9 reels.Screenplay: Wang Bei. Director: Wang Shi. Cinematography: Shi Fengqi, Xia Lixing. Cast: Yu Ping (as Chen Jinglan), Ma Yi (as Zhou Chuan).

During the Gang of Four years, shipyard head Zhou Chuan is imprisoned and his wife is persecuted to death. Their daughter Juanjuan is bullied and alone. Her teacher is sympathetic, but as a result is falsely accused of a crime.

On his release, Zhou helps Teacher Chen. They are drawn to each other, marry, and give Juanjuan a little brother. The Gang is finally deposed but then Chen discovers Zhou's first wife is still alive. Suffering deeply, she leaves before dawn.

> 14. *Whom Does He Love? (Ta ai shui?)*, Pearl River Film Studio, 1980, Color, 9 reels. Screenplay: Bi Bicheng. Director: Xian Bibao. Cinematography: Liang Xiongwei, Bai Yunshen. Cast: Pan Zhiyuan (as Yang Ming), Che Xiuqing (as Xiao Ying).

In 1975, ambitious Yang Ming sticks close to Ning Yan, daughter of the Chairman of the Ministry of Culture Revolutionary Committee. Her father is suspended when Deng Xiaoping takes over the Central Committee's day-to-day work. The pre-Cultural Revolution head of the Ministry returns. Yang drops Ning and turns to the new head's daughter, Xiao Ying, who falls for him. In 1976, the movement to "oppose the rightist overturning of verdicts" begins and Yang dumps Xiao, swinging back to Ning again. Xiao learns a bitter lesson.

> 15. *The Tenth Bullet Scar (Di Shige Dan Kong)*, Xi'an Film Studio, 1980, Color, 11 reels. Screenplay: Cong Weixi, Yi Shui. Director: Yi Shui. Cinematography: Cao Jinshan. Cast: Cao Huiqu (as Lu Hong), Bao Xun (as Lu Xiaofan), Chen Lizhong (as Granny).

After ten years hard labor, police chief Lu Hong's first case concerns his son Xiaofan's participation in blowing up a bridge. Xiaofan was an honest child with soft little hands that once caressed his father's nine bullet scars. Now he has become a criminal, this is like another bullet. When the Gang of Four was running wild, Lu and his wife were struggled. Xiaofan ran wild. His aunt, who was in league with a "rebel troop" commander, corrupted him. Lu Hong sentences his son according to the law. Xiaofan does not understand why his own father is so cruel. On a prison visit, Granny tells Xiaofan how, during the War of Resistance Against Japan, Lu recuperated from his wounds in the home of a Party underground worker called Shi Daniang. Her son betrayed Lu, so Shi killed him herself. Xiaofan sees the error of his ways.

> 16. *The Traitor (Panguozhe)*, Xi'an Film Studio, 1980, Color, 9 reels. Screenplay: Ji Xing, Ji Yao. Director: Zhang Qicheng. Cinematography: Niu Han. Cast: Ma Jingwu (as Niu Yusheng), Shen Guanchu (as Li Jun), Na Renhua (as Tian Tian).

Returned overseas Chinese snake expert Niu Yusheng is sent to deal with a plague of snakes on the southwest border in 1975. Niu concludes a new black-eyed snake's venom can form a new antidote. Li Jun is under orders to observe Niu. Li's sweetheart Tian Tian acts as a guide, discovers Li spying on Niu, and is upset. One day, Niu chases a black- eyed snake across the borderline. Li aims his gun to force the "traitor" to return. Tian Tian breaks off their relationship. Discovering another black-eyed snake, Niu struggles fiercely to get its venom, but it spits venom into his eye. Niu thinks how he has been persecuted and separated from his wife and daughter. But it turns out the doctor who treats him is his wife, and she tells him Tian Tian is their daughter. Back in the forest, a snake has bitten Tian Tian, but Niu rushes and saves her. The family is reunited, but Li Jun comes with orders to arrest Niu.

17. *Bamboo* (*Zhu*), Emei Film Studio and Youth Film Studio, 1980, Color, 9 reels. Written and directed by Wang Suihan, Situ Zhaodun. Cinematography: Liao Jiaxiang, Yu Defu. Cast: Li Lan (as Zhu Hua), Cui Xinqin (as Zhu Zi), Li Yulong (as Teacher Xiao Guan), Zhao Chunming (as Ah Fu).

Her revolutionary hero parents under attack, Zhu Hua is sent by her mother Zhu Zi to the family home to take part in manual labor. Meeting a young man called Teacher Xiao Guan by a pond, she is reminded of her parents' story. Zhu Zi saw a young underground messenger for the Party called Ah Fu washing his wounds by a pond and fell in love with him. Soon after their marriage, Ah Fu was captured. Later, Zhu Zi was also thrown into jail. The enemy knocked Ah Fu unconscious, but allowed Zhu Zi to look after him in the hope of overhearing secrets. All these ploys failed, but eventually Ah Fu was killed and Zhu Zi escaped. Zhu Hua and Xiao Guan fall in love, but Zhu Hua is arrested because of her mother's background. At the end of the year, the victory bugle sounds and Zhu Zi is happily reunited with her mother and Xiao Guan.

18. *Maple* (*Feng*), Emei Film Studio, 1980, Color, 10 reels. Screenplay: Zheng Yi. Director: Zhang Yi. Cinematography: Li Erkang, Wang Wenxiang. Cast: Xu Feng (as Lu Danfeng), Wang Erli (as Li Honggang).

When the Cultural Revolution begins in 1966, students and lovers Lu Danfeng and Li Honggang join the Red Guards. Under the influence of ultra-leftism, one joins the "Red Flag" faction, the other the "Jinggang Mountains" faction. Honggang is captured by the "Jinggang Mountains" faction. Danfeng sets him free, but afterwards denounces her own disloyalty. Honggang fights "Jinggang Mountains," but worries about Danfeng. When "Jinggang Mountains" is making a last stand, Danfeng fires at Honggang. He leads the final attack. Reunited, they each remain resolute, trying to convince the other to surrender. In despair, Danfeng throws herself off the building. Bitter, Honggang withdraws from the struggle. But two years later, "Jinggang Mountains" takes power, Honggang is dubbed a counterrevolutionary who forced Lu Danfeng to her death, and he is executed.

> 19. *Jade Butterfly* (*Yuse hudie*), Emei Film Studio, 1980, Color, 10 reels. Screenplay: Zhao Danian, Fan Jihua. Direction: Zhang Fengxiang, Yang Gaisen. Cinematography: Zhang Shicheng, Gao Lixian. Cast: Yu Yana (as Chonen Nakako), Huang Daliang (Wang Dong), Wang Danfeng (as Takeuchi Kimio), Xiang Kun (as Professor Qiu Tong).

Chonen Nakako comes to Beijing in 1976, in search of the jade butterfly. Her translator Wang Dong refuses to meet butterfly specialist Professor Qiu Tong. On her return to Japan, Nakako mentions Qiu to her mother, Takeuchi Kimio. Forty years ago, when Qiu was a student in Japan, he and Kimio married and had a son. Forced to leave during the war, he took their son with him, naming him Wang Dong, which means looking eastwards towards where his mother was. Kimio was misinformed that Qiu had died. To reunite the family, Kimio and Nakako come to Beijing after the smashing of the Gang of Four.

> 20. *A Late Spring* (*Chidao de chuntian*), Emei Film Studio, 1980, Color, 9 reels. Screenplay: Rao Qu, Tan Su. Direction: Ma Shaohui, Tai Gang. Cinematography: Mai Shuhuan. Cast: Zhang Jiatian (as Zhao Cheng), Xiang Hong (as Zeng Xiaobei).

Zhao Cheng and Zeng Xiaobei are separated. During the Cultural Revolution, Zhao was beaten by Red Guards, including Xiaobei. Later, Xiaobei, labeled the daughter of a "capitalist roader," is sent to labor in the same brigade. Zhao beats up a cadre who attempts to rape Xiaobei. When he is under threat, she saves him, and they fall in love. Xiaobei is transferred back to the city. After the smashing of the Gang of Four, Zhao comes to town for the university entrance examinations. Zhao gets good results, but as the son of a Rightist, he is not admitted. However, he persists and is successful the next year. The lovers are reunited.

> 21. *Not for Love* (*Bu shi weile aiqing*), Emei Film Studio, 1980, Color, 10 reels. Screenplay: Yang Tao, Cui Changwu. Director: Yin Xianglin.

Cinematography: Li Dagui. Cast: Peilan Nikelaida (as Wilma), Yan Shikui (as Pu Dahai), Liu Dong (as Hong Mei), Li Shixi (as Han Yu).

Pu Dahai, the fiancé of Wilma, is arrested because of his participation in the 1976 Tiananmen activities to commemorate Premier Zhou. Wilma is the orphan of a foreign communist who fought with the Chinese Communist Party. Overwhelmed with grief, she throws herself into a lake, but is rescued and cared for by railway worker Han Yu. His girlfriend Hong Mei becomes jealous, threatens Wilma, and even slanders Han Yu as a counter-revolutionary. He and Wilma fall in love. On their wedding night after the smashing of the Gang of Four, news arrives that the "dead" Pu Dahai has been released from jail. Han reluctantly leaves Wilma.

22. *Rays Penetrating the Clouds* (*Touguo yunceng de xiaguang*), Xiaoxiang Film Studio, 1980, Color, 9 reels. Screenplay: Liu Cheng. Director: Ouyang Shanzun. Cinematography: Shen Miaorong. Cast: Bi Jianchang (as Zheng Yan), Pan Hong (as White Sister), Song Yining (as Black Sister), Liang Yuru (as Hailao).

During the Cultural Revolution, author Zheng Yan falls in love with a doctor called White Sister. Her father, a salvage worker, is opposed, because Zheng is a pencil-pusher. White Sister leaves home but Zheng refuses her. Later, Zheng meets Black Sister and Hailao. When Hailao finds out that Zheng's marriage was blocked by his future father-in-law, he is indignant. Just as White Sister rushes to meet him, Zheng's premonitions come true, and he is arrested. When will this young couple finally be reunited? Only when the sun's rays penetrate the clouds.

23. *Ghost* (*Youling*), 1980, Xiaoxiang Film Studio, Color, 10 reels. Screenplay: Chen Zhaoming, Zhang Jinbiao. Director: Chen Fangqian. Cinematography: Yun Wenyao. Cast: Shao Huifang (as Xia Zhenglan), Wang Mingsheng (as Lu Hanzhang), Yu Shaokang (as Zhao Yuxiong), Zhao Zuguo (as Wen Wanjun), Ren Dao (as Wu Sen).

Ballet dancer Xia Zhenglan and doctor Lu Hanzhang marry just before the Gang of Four is smashed. Lu drinks from a glass Xia has given him and dies, having been poisoned. Veteran policeman Zhao Yuxiong investigates with two assistants. They discover poison in the toothpaste and a torn-up letter with a woman's signature in Lu's office. Xia tries to drown herself. At the hospital Zhao finds matron Wen Wanjun congenial but cold. Late one night, Zhao survives an attack. Municipal Revolutionary Committee Vice-Chairman Wu Sen advises him to rest. Wen starts to get nervous. Wu tries to kill her, but she survives and tells the police everything. It turns out Wu is affiliated to the Gang and Lu knew too much. Xia killed herself because she knew the Gang would never leave her alone.

1981

1. *Xu Mao and his Daughters* (*Xu Mao he ta de nüermen*), 1981, Beijing Film Studio, Color, 10 reels. Written and directed by Wang Yan. Cinematography: Zou Zhixun. Cast: Li Wei (as Xu Mao), Li Xiuming (as Xu Xiuyun), Yang Zaibao (as Jin Dongshui), Lu Guilan (as Yan Shaochun), Zhang Lianwen (as Zheng Bairu).

In 1975, Xu Mao's daughter, Xiuyun, refuses an arranged marriage, because she cares deeply for her dead sister's child and husband, Jin Dongshui. Yan Shaochun from the County government comes to implement rectification, giving people new hope. Accountant Zheng Bairu, an opportunistic rebel divorced from Xiuyun, senses the changing climate and begs her to remarry, but she refuses. He gossips about Xiuyun and Dongshui. Xiuyun attempts suicide, but Shaochun and Dongshui save her. Shaochun suspends Zheng from his job and restores Dongshui to his. Xu Mao eventually agrees to Xiuyun and Dongshui's marriage. However, the movement against the reversal of rightist verdicts begins, and Shaochun has to leave.

2. *Home at Last* (*Guisu*), 1981, Beijing Film Studio, Color, 11 reels. Screenplay: Zhao Lingfang. Director: Dong Kena. Cinematography: Zhang Shicheng. Cast: Xu Huanshan (as Yang Zhihe), Zhao Ruping (as Chang Laoyue), Qiu Yingshi (as Gao Zhankui), Tan Tianqian (as Li Niuhai).

Yang Zhihe, fleeing from famine, sells himself to become a KMT soldier. On the way to Taiwan in 1949 he befriends the other soldiers Chang Laoyue, Gao Zhankui, and Li Niuhai. Li dies of homesickness. Gao goes into business, but kills himself when he goes bankrupt. Chang starts a restaurant. Yang becomes a KMT colonel, but misses his wife. He returns secretly to the mainland, searching for her and Chang's wife. He meets a young marine, who is actually Chang's daughter-in-law. Chang's family is happy. He discovers that Gao's wife is dead and that his sons have suffered so during the Cultural Revolution they almost dare not accept their KMT father's ashes. He discovers his own wife is vice-head of a machinery plant, and her daughter is the marine he met earlier. Knowing how the KMT treats people who go home, he is confused and leaves. His wife rushes to the dock. He still leaves, but promises to return later.

3. *Laughter in Moon Bay* (*Yueliangwan de xiaosheng*), 1981, Shanghai Film Studio, Color, 9 reels. Screenplay: Jin Haitao, Fang Yihua. Director: Xu Suling. Cinematography: Zhang Er. Cast: Zhang Yan (as Jiang

Maofu), Kou Zhenhai (as Jiang Guigen), Zhong Xinghuo (as Qing Liang), Gu Yuqin (as Qing Lanhua).

Jiang Maofu is a skilled fruit tree grower and a bit richer than most, so he becomes a "capitalist-roader." Qing Liang from the neighboring village refuses to engage his daughter Lanhua to Maofu's son, Guigen. Later, the provincial newspaper cites Maofu as an example of "prosperity" and a model. Lanhua and Guigen are engaged and their fathers become friends. But then the Gang of Four begins to criticize the "rightist tendency to reverse verdicts," and the wedding is called off. When the Gang of Four falls, the verdict on Maofu is reversed again, but he is still depressed. Guigen convinces Maofu things have changed, and the marriage is on again.

> 4. *The Investigator* (*Jianchaguan*), 1981, Shanghai Film Studio, Color, 9 reels. Screenplay: Luo Hualing, Li Zaizhong, Zhao Zhiqiang. Director: Xu Weijie. Cinematography: Qu Jiazhen. Cast: Li Moran (as Xu Li), Wang Weiping (as Zhang Hua), Huang Daliang (as Xu Wentao), Gu Deyin (as Bureau Vice-Head Liang).

In 1977, Xu Li issues an arrest warrant for Zhang Hua in the unsolved Mo Xiaoli rape case. When he sees Zhang's photo, he remembers Zhang was the Red Guard who saved him during the Cultural Revolution and so does not believe he is really a criminal. However, Zhang has fled and fallen to his death. After various twists, Xu is shocked to discover the main criminal may be his own son. Further investigations run into opposition from Public Security Bureau Vice-Head Liang and his wife. Xu's son throws himself off a cliff, but Xu insists the investigations continue.

> 5. *On a Narrow Street* (*Xiao jie*), 1981, Shanghai Film Studio, Color, 11 reels. Screenplay: Xu Yinghua. Director: Yang Yanjin. Cinematography: Ying Fukang, Zhang Hong. Cast: Guo Kaimin (as Xia), Zhang Yu (as Yu).

Blind man Xia pours out his past to a film director. During the ten turbulent years, Xia got to know a delicate young man called Yu. When Yu fell into some water, the secret that he was really a girl was revealed. When her mother was suddenly made a "black gang" element, her hair was chopped off and she had to pretend to be a boy. Xia wanted to make her happy! However, in his efforts to help, he was beaten and went blind. Then they lost touch. Xia considers what may have become of her — so deeply wounded that she became depraved? A violinist? An ordinary factory worker?

6. *May Love Be Everlasting* (*Dan yuan ren chang jiu*), 1980, Changchun Film Studio, Color, 11 reels. Screenplay: Zhang Tianmin. Direction: Bai Dezhang, Xu Xunxing. Cinematography: Tu Jiakuan. Cast: Li Qiyuan (as Huyan Ziqian), Huang Daliang (as Ou Yi).

After the smashing of the Gang of Four, Communist Party member Huyan Ziqian returns to the geology research institute. His friend Ou Yi has died during the chaos, leaving behind a widow and family. The widow's adoptive father encourages him to marry her. She has been unwilling to remarry for fear of its effect on the old man. They decide to establish a family anew, and take in an orphan boy. However, the boy turns out to be the son of the man who drove Ou Yi to death. After some resistance, Huyan is able to persuade his new wife to accept the boy.

7. *Xu Mao and his Daughters* (*Xu Mao he tade nüermen*), 1980, August First Film Studio, Color, 9 reels. Screenplay: Zhou Keqin, Xiao Mu. Director: Li Jun. Cinematography: Yang Guangyuan. Cast: Jia Liu (as Xu Mao).

See Beijing Film Studio version above for synopsis.

8. *The Spiral* (*Luoxuan*), 1981, August First Film Studio, Wide-screen, Color, 9 reels. Screenplay: Huang Ying. Director: Bo Fujin. Cinematography: Bo Fujin, Wang Jianguo. Cast: Zhao Xiuling (as Zhang Lei), Liu Linian (as Liang Dapeng), Sun Jitang (as Gao Erming).

Zhang Lei is a guided missile design engineer sent down to the countryside during the ten years of chaos. In 1977, she returns to work on the "Magic Arrow." Test flight team leader Liang Dapeng was her lover ten years ago, but he was tricked into betraying her. He is depressed by their estrangement. During a test the missile explodes prematurely. Vice-Head of the Science and Technology Department Gao Erming tries to put the blame on Liang. One day, Zhang comes across a page of notes at Gao Erming's and realizes Liang was innocent and the real troublemaker is Gao. Zhang and Liang are reunited.

9. *Set Sail* (*Yangfan*), 1981, Pearl River Film Studio, Color, 9 reels. Screenplay: Zhan Xiangchi. Directors: Zhan Xiangchi, Yu Shibin. Cinematography: Wei Duo. Cast: Wei Ke (as Hao Ping), Ding Tiebao (as Li Pingfan), Hu Weisan (as Lu Yaqing).

After the smashing of the Gang of Four, alto Li Pingfan performs impromptu at the end of a concert. The audience notices she is wearing a hearing aid, and a girl cries out "She's deaf!" Her name is Lu Yaqing, and she was orphaned when her parents were killed in political movements. Although she has survived, she cannot forgive her own mistake. Li is deaf because of a beating she received during the Cultural Revolution, which Lu took part in as a rebel. On her way home, Lu is almost raped, but is rescued by Li's son, Hao Ping. When he discovers she has a good voice, he encourages her to apply for a song and dance troupe. However, when she meets Hao's mother, Lu flees in shame at the realization that she injured Li. After some hesitation, Li forgives her and sets out to bring Lu back.

> 10. *Revival (Suxing)*, 1981, Xi'an Film Studio, Color, 10 reels. Screenplay: Xu Qingdong, Teng Wenji. Director: Teng Wenji. Cinematography: Zhu Dingyu. Cast: Gao Fei (as Tian Dan), Chen Chong (as Su Xiaomei).

Beijing in 1980: businessman Tian Dan bumps into his old girlfriend, Su Xiaomei. They tell each other about their experiences since they split up, their beliefs, life, and their careers. Tian's father is angry, because he hopes his son will marry the vice section-head's daughter. To escape the pressure, Tian resigns and leaves for a new job in the South. Su rushes to the airport, stops Tian, points out he is behaving weakly, and tells him, "If you want to be ambitious, you must pay the price. If you want success, you have to suffer." Later, she goes to Beijing for her examinations and he sees her off. In their eyes, one can see a gaze towards tomorrow.

> 11. *Whirlpool Song (Xuanwo li de ge)*, 1981, E'mei Film Studio, Color, 9 reels. Screenplay: Liu Zinong, Liao Yun, Mi Jiashan, Yu Yang. Direction: Liu Zinong, Wu Lan. Cinematography: Li Zhenhuan. Cast: Zhao Erkang (as Gang Lisheng), Yang Yaqin (as Xin Yiwen), Pan Hong (as Lin Juan).

Folk singer Gang Lisheng is jailed on false charges during the Cultural Revolution. His wife Xin Yiwen is forced to divorce him. After his release Gang returns to the Yangtse and raises his infant son alone. Young doctor Lin Juan falls in love with him. One day, Gang bumps into Xin again. She is overcome with guilt, but when she tries to visit, her father-in-law chases her out. Gang is unwilling to draw Lin into his difficult life and rejects her love. A foreign musician friend of Gang's comes to China and the authorities prepare to rehabilitate him. Overjoyed, Lin Juan rushes to tell him, but he is on the river, taking part in a salvage battle. Worried, she seeks him out, but she is willing to wait forever.

12. *Spirit of the Foil* (*Jian gui*), 1981, Emei Film Studio, Color, 10 reels. Screenplay: Li You, Fu Xing, Gong Jia. Director: Zeng Mozhi. Cinematography: Zhang Jiwu. Cast: Xin Guiqiu (as Nan Fang), Chen Tianlu (as Fang Jiayuan), Shi Zhanju (as Qiao Fang), Yuan Mei (as Su Chunxiu), Xin Guiping (as Xiaojuan).

Basketball player Nan Fang and boxer Fang Jiayuan are lovers. They meet Qiao Fang and Su Chunxiu, an overseas Chinese couple who have returned to coach China's first fencing teams, which Fang and Nan join. Qiao gives Fang the foil that has been passed down from his ancestors. Fang is slandered as a spy during of the ten years of chaos, Qiao dies in a cadre school on the coast, and Nan is sent down to a cadre School. After the smashing of the Gang of Four, Nan goes back to her old profession as a researcher. Fang coaches a fencing team. Coached by Su, Qiao's daughter Xiaojuan has become a talented athlete. Eventually, she makes it into the fencing team and gains access to international competition. Fang passes Qiao's foil on to Xiaojuan just before she leaves. Despite injury, she is runner-up, and the older generation happily watches on television as the Chinese flag flies on the international fencing stage for the first time.

13. *Dance Love* (*Wu lian*), 1981, Emei Film Studio and Youth Film Studio, Color, 10 reels. Screenplay: Jia Mu. Direction: Gang Shixiong, Wen Lun. Cinematography: Cao Zuobing, Zhang Wenying. Cast: Zhang Jizhong (as Xiang Feng), Cheng Xiaoying (as Qumuahzhi).

Twenty years ago choreographer and director Xiang Feng met the Yi nationality dancer Qumuahzhi and won her love. But Qumuahzhi was killed by the Gang of Four and he did not stand by her in her time of need. Back in the Liangshan Mountains, Xiang is surprised to discover that Qumuahzhi is still alive. But she cannot forgive him until she discovers he has not lost his love for dance. With their difficult experiences, Xiang Feng and Qumuahzhi are reunited.

14. *The Corner Forgotten by Love* (*Bei aiqing yiwang de jiaoluo*), 1981, Emei Film Studio, Color, 10 reels. Screenplay: Zhang Xian. Direction: Zhang Yi, Li Yalin. Cinematography: Mai Shuhuan. Cast: Yang Hailian (as Shen Cunni), Zhang Chao (as Little Panther), Shen Danping (as Shen Huangmei), Zhang Shihui (as Xu Rongshu), Yang Qiufu (as Ying Di), Xia Feng (as Erhuai), Jin Di (as Ying Di's Mother).

The Gang of Four reduced Shen Cunni's village to poverty. Feudal thinking and the ultra-leftist line made her affair with Little Panther forbidden. She was driven to suicide and he was accused of rape and manslaughter. Her fate has made younger sister Huangmei avoid men. After the smashing of the Gang, Huangmei's childhood friend Xu Rongshu returns from the army determined to modernize the village. This wins her heart, but she is still nervous. Ying Di's mother and Brigade and Party Branch Head Bin destroy the love between Ying and Erhuai, and Ying is married to a man she does not even know. Huangmei's mother prepares to receive betrothal gifts, but Huangmei resists. The spring wind of the Third Plenum of the Central Committee finally reaches this remote corner, and people see a prosperous village before them. Cunni and Ying Di's misfortunes will not be passed on to Huangmei and she runs to Rongshu and a new life.

> 15. *The Rose that Should not Wither and Die* (*Bu gai diaoxie de meigui*), 1981, Guangxi Film Studio, Color, 10 reels. Screenplay: Li Yi. Director: Zeng Xueqiang. Cinematography: Meng Xiongqiang. Cast: Tong Ruimin (as Wei Li), Zhang Liwei (as Ruan Zhen), Shi Xian (as Li Wenxiong).

In 1972, Wei Li is injured when a mine explodes in a Vietnamese port he is clearing. The Vietnamese woman army doctor Ruan Zhen saves him. It turns out they were childhood friends on the border. Ruan's classmate Li Wenxiong also pursues her, but she gives Wei a rose when he returns to China. Her father takes her across the river border, and she and Wei marry and have a daughter. But Li leads Vietnamese border disturbances, shoots Ruan's brother, and arrests her. Her daughter stumbles on a landmine planted by the Vietnamese troops. Ruan flees. Trying to cross the river to China, she is shot. Li Wei jumps in after her, and he is shot, too.

> 16. *Xiaoyan and Dayan* (*Xiaoyan he Dayan*), 1981, Jiangsu Film Studio, Color, 10 reels, Liuqin Opera. Screenplay: Li Daren. Director: Jin Shuqi. Cinematography: Qiao Zhichang. Cast: Sun Yuxia (as Granny Wan), Wu Aiping (as Qin Dahai), Shen Qiuyun (as Dayan), Wang Xinghai (as Zhang Jinlai), Wang Zhihua (as Xiaoyan).

In fall 1976, Granny Wan has two daughters, Dayan and Xiaoyan. Dayan is engaged to Qin Dahai. Granny Wan and Dayan declare that if the betrothal gifts are not satisfactory, the marriage will not be registered. Cadre Zhang Jinlai, promoted during the Cultural Revolution, persuades Dayan to marry him instead. Xiaoyan objects to her sister's behavior, asks Qin to marry her, and he agrees. After the smashing of the Gang of Four, Zhang is criticized. He has to return all the money he has embezzled. Dayan and Zhang Jinlai divorce.

17. *The Side Road* (*Xiao lu*), 1981, Jiangsu Film Studio, Color, 10 reels. Screenplay: Ge Xiaoying, Jin Jiwu, Feng Ji. Direction: Jin Jiwu, Feng Ji. Cinematography: Luo Yong. Cast: Yang Xiaodan (as Ye Hao), Shen Zhimei (as Teacher Lin), Zhang Yi (as Teacher Zhou), Zhang Hui (as Teacher Yu).

When he was a child, Teacher Lin opened Ye Hao's mind. During the ten years of chaos, under the guidance of Teacher Zhou, he discovered a direction in life. As a young man, at his time of greatest suffering, it is Teacher Yu who helps him.

18. *The Crystal Heart* (*Shuijing xin*), 1981, Liaoning Film Studio, Color, 10 reels. Screenplay: Chen Zheng'an, Zheng Huili. Direction: Zhang Jianyou, Zheng Huili. Cinematography: Chen Chang'an, Zhou Yu. Cast: Liu Wenzhi (as Lai Zhiqing), Zhou Lan (as Yuan Wenping and Chen Ying), Su Jinbang (as Tang Ming), Sun Haidi (as Little Crystal).

Yuan Wenping and Lai Zhiqing are lovers. Lai's friend Tang Ming is investigated for writing praise on a copy of *The Biography of Einstein*. Lai takes the blame and is jailed. Tang gets involved with Yuan, who is alone and bereft, but then drops her. Despondent, she moves to a mountain village. After the smashing of the Gang of Four, Lai unexpectedly meets Tang again, and also a girl who looks like Yuan; the factory director's daughter, Chen Ying, who comes to admire him. Tang becomes jealous. They fight, and Lai tells Tang that Yuan died in that village and he has been looking after Yuan's daughter since. Tang realizes Little Crystal is in fact his own daughter. Lai, Chen, and Little Crystal form a new family.

Index